To Per
in dee
for you
to IAM Partner
for these many years.

Ray Register
12/1/1?
Escondido CA

Ray G. Register, Jr.

GALILEE WANDERINGS

39 years assigned to
the Holy Land

GlobalEdAdvance
Press

What readers are saying:

Anyone even casually interested in the biblical geography of the "Holy Land," the modern history of Israel and the continuing conflict between Arabs and Jews will find _Galilee Wanderings_ a fascinating read. Overlooked by most observers of the Middle East is the fact that God has been at work in this hotbed of ethnic, religious and historical conflict. Ray Register takes us along on a biographical journey that covers almost 40 years of evangelism and church planting in the cities, mountains and valleys where Jesus walked. Based initially in Nazareth, Register worked with the Arabs of Israel, but saw the power of the gospel result in a harvest of messianic Jews and later a movement among Muslim background believers. Readers will be exhausted by the pace of ministry and demanding responsibilities of this cross-cultural missionary and be touched by the powerful movement of God's Spirit.

— Jerry Rankin, President Emeritus
International Mission Board, SBC

Ray Register is unique among Southern Baptist missionaries. Talented, intelligent and persistent, Ray's memoirs take you on a fast moving, incredible journey. Refusing to accept failure or danger, Ray and family kept pressing on to an exciting conclusion to 38 plus years of extremely fruitful ministry in Israel.

This is a book not to miss.

— Phil Parshall
SIM, Sebring, Florida

Ray Register's journey in the Holy Land captures the raw reality of life in the Middle East. His heart for the people is unrelenting, and his devotion to the LORD is inspiring. *Galilee Wanderings* is a beautiful and fascinating book.

Blessings,

— Mark Siljander
www.BridgesNow.com

Ray Register is one of a kind storyteller! In a true Middle Eastern style of communication, he recalls his journey to Palestine in the 60s with such a vivid clarity that makes the reader feel as if he/she is sitting next to him in an apartment, or a government's office talking to a Muslim Palestinian leader or an Israeli official. I highly recommend this book to all of those who are interested in understanding Islam, Palestinian/Israeli situation, or planning to work among Muslims.

— Shahrokh (Shah) Afshar
Shahzamfactor.com

Ray Register is a man with rich and long experience as a missionary to both Arabs and Jews in Israel. His memoir is a swiftly-moving, chronological account in which he tells everything: victories, spiritual experiences, achievements, fun, failures, mistakes, conflicts, doubts, dangers. If it happened to him he is ready to tell it, and this makes his book not only an honest personal story but a historical document of the Southern Baptist mission work in Israel. While recording significant events in the development of churches and other institutions, he also introduces us to many interesting people and places, so that the reader gets a sense of the personalities, the cultures, the history, and politics of the whole area.

— Frances Fuller, Author of *In Borrowed Houses, a true story of love and faith amidst war in Lebanon*   inborrowedhouseslebanon.com

Dr. Ray Register was chosen to fulfill God's calling in Nazareth, in the Holy Land, following the tracks of Jesus Christ in the Galilee where Jesus walked on water on the Lake Kinneret; where He preached words of wisdom and preformed healing miracles. Pastor Ray's unique commitment to serve the Christian Arabic Community in Galilee for over 30 years, challenged him to adjust to cultural and mental differences, and relate to his audience using their customs and tradition. His vocation in the Holy Land made him feel the vibration of Jesus' teachings beyond the literal meaning of the Scriptures. When he shares the words of the Master, I (a Jewish Israeli woman) feel engaged in the spiritual experience far beyond beliefs. This book is timely and important in understanding the complex reality of the Holy Land, realizing the importance of spiritual vocation to bridge the gap beyond belief, and enhancing the authentic message of "love your fellow man."

— Ronit Gabay, Author of *Walking in the Footsteps of The Master*

Ever wondered how a man comes to be called to minister the Gospel to Muslims? *Galilee Wanderings* peers into the journey of Ray Register who spent nearly 40 years doing just that. Register is an insightful narrator with an unusual depth of knowledge of Islam. The result is a life well lived, and a story well told.

— Nadia Deen
Author of **A Demand of Blood**, *The Cherokee War of 1776*

I dedicate these memoirs,

First to the Lord

Who privileged me to live in His Land

And

To the memory of
Five senior IMB mentors and encouragers
Who passed over Jordan before me:

Robert L. Lindsey

Avery Willis

James W. Smith

Roberta K. Dorr

Chandler Lanier

And

To My Lord's kinsman, and our late son-in-law

Ilan Nissim Zamir

And

To his Arab brothers in faith

Saleh Abu Rakiyk

George Kazoura

Barnabas

Ibrahim Siman

GALILEE WANDERINGS
39 years assigned to the Holy Land

Copyright © 2016 by Ray G. Resgister, Jr.

Library of Congress Control Number: 2016958396

Register, Ray G. Jr. 1935 —

ISBN 978-1-935434-84-9

Subject Codes and Description: 1: Biography & Autobiography: Personal Memoirs BIO 026000 2:Religion: Christian Ministry - Missions REL 045000 3: Social Science: Sociology of Religion SOC 039000

Cover design by Global Graphics

Printed in Australia, Brazil, France, Germany, Italy, Poland, Spain, UK, and USA
Also available on Espresso Book Machine and anywhere good books are sold.

Order books from: www.gea-books.com/authors/ray_register.htm
or the author at IAMpartners@cs.com or any place good books are sold.

Published by
GlobalEdAdvancePRESS

a division of
Global Educational Advance, Inc.

TABLE OF CONTENTS

FOREWORD

In my thirty-five years as a missionary with the International Mission Board, I traveled to over 100 countries and met with over 500 missionaries. Many were working hard and had some success but I do not feel that any were as effective as was Ray Register in Israel. True, he did not have the numbers like those in Africa and other countries, but all know how difficult it is to work for Christ in Israel and especially with the Muslims in that country. Using all ways of measuring, Ray had been one of the most effective ambassadors for Christ in the Middle East over the past fifty years.

Galilee Wanderings is very interesting in that he relates real stories of new Christians and their difficulties in living for Christ under very difficult conditions. Dr. Register has not tried to sugarcoat the work of the missionary but rather has informed the reader of both the good and the bad that all missionaries must experience in their work for the Lord.

Of course, many Christians want to visit the Holy Land so that they can walk where Jesus walked. *Galilee Wanderings* takes the reader on a tour of all of Israel, especially the northern part of Galilee close to Nazareth. It was there that Ray and his lovely wife Rose Mary and their three children poured out their hearts for those he was called to serve. He lived the life of one committed to his people. He not only learned the language but also the customs of the peoples. He truly became one of them. The reader can very easily glean this from the many stories in the book.

To be a bystander and watch others work is one thing, but to get down where the average person lives and work with them on a personal level is something else. Ray has taken the reader down with him to show them the real needs of those living in Israel in a very tumultuous time. It was not easy, but of course, the Lord never did call missionaries to an easy life.

Dr. Register, who is now retired from active ministry in Israel, remains very active in evangelism and service to his Lord. In missionary circles we use the expression of "looking for ones footprints" in order to see if they have been active in a particular area. Even today, when one goes to Israel, the footprints of Ray and Rose Mary Register are easily seen in that country. This proves that he truly has a missionary heart. His book is worth reading by both the young and the old.

— Dr. William "Bill" Wagner

Director of Olivet Institute for Global Strategic Studies
Olivet University

PREFACE

Galilee Wanderings

Galilee Wanderings is a personal story of contrasts; North and South, East, and West, good and evil, war and peace, success and failure, beauty and ugliness, conservatism and liberalism, blessings and curses, monotheism and Trinity. Above all, it is experiences of mystery and revelation, of how God took a boy conceived out of wedlock and made him a man in the Holy Land. Had he been born in this postmodern age, would his life have been snuffed out by a convenient abortion? Instead, God chose to shelter him in the womb of a loving Yankee mother of rich ancestry and raise him by a macho southern father who was a Scout Master and problem drinker all at the same time! As Rick Warren explains in *"What on Earth am I Here For?"* "You are not an accident. There are accidental parents, but there are no accidental births. There are illegitimate parents but there are no illegitimate children. There are unplanned pregnancies, but there are no unpurposed people." *Galilee Wanderings* tells of one of those purposed people!

Again, it is a personal story of contrasts. It is a story of many bumps over the rocky roads of Galilee dodging potholes made by weather, or shells and bombs from periodic wars. So, hang on! This is a story that may jerk you around and startle you awake with an angel's nudge as it did me on that Galilee road as I sleepily rounded a curve at unsafe speed. It is my story, the story of God's discipline and grace during my Galilee wanderings.

I am indebted to my wonderful family, my lovely and patient wife, Rose Mary, my amazing children, Chuck, James and Cheryl, and the family of God, some Arabs, some Jews, some Russians, and to friends and colleagues in the church and business world who continue to affirm the contrasts in me.

Carolina Beginnings

A petite former Yankee fell in love with the handsome freshman class president at Newberry College in South Carolina, they married and I was born Ray Gustava Register, Jr. at the Richland County Memorial Hospital in Columbia, South Carolina at 12:30 PM on April 26, 1935. Ray G. Register, my father, grew up in Hartsville, South Carolina, the son of Ben (Benjamin Hampton) Register and "Tumpy" (Charlotte Cassidy) Register. Ben's father, Silas Register, helped Mr. Hart settle Hartsville in the late 1800's. His grandfather, James Calvin Register, a Civil War veteran, was probably a descendant of an earlier Silas Register, one of early settlers of South Carolina in the 1700's. Ben was a supervisor at Sunoco Mills in Hartsville and invented a special spool for the cotton weaving machines. My grandmother, Charlotte Cassidy Register, was from Sugar Loaf Mountain in Chesterfield County, and now thought to be a relative of President Bill Clinton's mother. I give this history, because until I was about 50, I did not believe my father's family had a genealogy! I later found most of my Register ancestors buried in the historic Wesley Chapel United Methodist Church graveyard in Oates, South Carolina, while most of the ones in Hartsville are buried at the historic First Baptist Church graveyard. This played significantly into my life since I spent summers in Hartsville with my cousin, William Calvin "Billy" Register Jr. and his sister Katherine Register (Serra) at my grandmother's house and attended church with them.

My father, "Ray Senior" was the first person in his family ever to attend college and was only 16 when he started. He chaffed under the strict discipline of his older sister Suzie, who expected him to be a preacher. The first holiday he returned to Hartsville from the University of South Carolina in Columbia, my Grandmother saw him stumbling down the path. She cried out to my Grandad, "Ray is sick!" Grandad Ben shouted from the back porch, "Aw Tumpy, he is drunk!" Daddy's propensity to get liquored up at an early age followed him the rest of his life. One drink, and it was as if a ferocious demon entered into him. To his credit, he told me to only call him "Daddy" since only God was our Father. He never drank at work, but saved it for the weekends when the family was around.

Ray, Grandad Ben Register and Cousin Bill, c 1938

Mother's people had a bit of a pedigree! She was born "Bette" Elizabeth Street Brough in Cook County, Chicago, Illinois, in 1916 to Agnes Kendrick Brough and William Brough. Agnes or "Nana" as we knew her was related to the Stevens family who were part owners of the Stevens Hotel, which they lost during the depression in 1929. It was renamed the Conrad Hilton Hotel. The Great Depression left them with only a city home, a glove factory, and a summer home on the shores of Lake Michigan, which I remember visiting several times. One of my mother's relatives is retired Supreme Court Justice John Paul Stevens. "Bill" Brough (pronounced like "rough"), my paternal grandfather, worked as an electronics engineer for the New York Telephone Company. He worked on the development of television in the late 1930's. The US military used this secret technology as "radar" in World War II. His ancestors were Brewsters and Capons who came over on the Mayflower. My late brother Hamp and his then wife Suzie, who was a legal secretary, later found their gravestones near Boston, Massachusetts. Nana graduated from the University of Chicago and the Parsons School of Design in New York. Nana and Bill divorced in New York when my mother was 12. Mother and Nana moved to Columbia, SC where Nana taught in a school for the blind. Mother developed a southern accent, which obviously impressed Daddy when they met as students at Newberry College. Years later, I discovered a clipping in a family Bible inherited by my adopted cousin, Bob Kendrick, about a Dr. Nathanael Kendrick, a Baptist minister who established the first Christian college in the Ohio River valley. This heritage influenced my life dramatically in later years.

My earliest recollection of life was growing up near Lake Murray, South Carolina. My father worked for the South Carolina Electric and Gas Company at their Saluda hydroelectric plant. My mother's uncle and adopted cousin's father, William "Bill"

Kendrick was vice president of the company. We lived in one of the white-framed power company houses near Lake Murray. We raised chickens and had a rooster who was as big as I was! The first picture of me was with my mother and me with a big clock around my neck! I remember one time going with my sister Betsy and Daddy to the lake, where Betsy proceeded to fall into the inlet to the spillway at the dam. Daddy had to pull her out by her hair! We had a big German shepherd dog that was killed in front of my eyes by a big Buick driven by a woman that hit him when I threw a wooden block into the road for him to fetch. She turned out to be the wife of Daddy's boss. Also, I remember being thrown and kicked by a pony. My father whipped him but it did not make my head feel any better! My first recollection of guilt was when I stole my neighbor friend's little red wagon. I was pulling it home when our next-door neighbor leaned out her back door and asked me, "Is that your wagon?" I recall also the time my father took the maid home and ran off the side of a bridge on a narrow road, breaking the axle on our new 1940 Mercury. He evidently was drunk, a sign of problems coming in the future.

Mother took me to Sunday school at the Lexington Baptist Church. My class met in a little closet under the steps. One day as she was driving down the street in Lexington. I became curious as to what would happen if I hit her with a large monkey wrench laying on the back floorboard. When I did she said, "Don't ever do that again!"

We moved to Spartanburg, South Carolina in 1940 just before World War II started. My father worked in the dispatching office at Duke Power Company. We lived in a beautiful gabled home on Lakeview Drive in Duncan Park. I used to walk to Pine Street Primary School where I kissed my first girl, Delaine Turner, and later became infatuated with the Episcopal preacher's daughter,

Mary Saterlee, who was taller than I was! My next-door neighbor's father, Bob Talbert, operated the movie theatres in town so Bobby and I always got into the movies free. I first began attending church in Spartanburg. My father was Cub Scout Master at the First Baptist Church. I remember Pastor Davis wore a coat with tails. We attended as a family. Mother and Daddy used to have late night arguments, which left a negative imprint on my psyche. I remember her telling him, "Ray Jr. is the only one who loves me."

Duke Power Company transferred Daddy to the Charlotte, North Carolina main office in 1946 where I attended the Dilworth Primary School for the sixth grade. We lived at 709 E. Worthington Ave. My parents became members of the Pritchard Memorial Baptist Church where I attended Sunday school and heard the sermons of William Harrison Williams. The thing I remember most was his horse illustrations. I attended one day at summer vacation Bible school. I thought it was "sissy." I made enough trouble they sent me home. When I was 14, my sister Betsy made a profession of faith and decided to be baptized. I was jealous since I was older and had not made a profession of faith. Therefore, I invited my Aunt Susie, Daddy's older sister from Florence, SC and all the family to attend church and watch me "walk down the aisle." I remember having one pre-baptism class where they explained the Gospel before I was baptized. My sister Charlotte was born around this time and later my brother Hamp. I attended Alexander Graham Junior High School where I learned typesetting and printing, a skill that influenced my later life. My parents encouraged me to continue in Scouting and this made the greatest impact on my moral conscience. I will never forget summer scout camp on the Catawba River and the mysteries of Indian lore I learned while achieving various ranks in the Boy Scouts and Explorer Scouts. I credit my desire to achieve in life mostly to Scouting. I came home from camp one summer and my parents found me a job delivering the Charlotte Observer newspaper at 5:00 AM in the mornings, a time I would not have chosen! I also mowed lawns and opened a savings account. I think I may have been the only person in the family to save money.

We moved to the country shortly afterwards. We lived in a hundred year old log cabin in "Possum Walk Valley" off Pleasant Grove Road in Oakdale past the Charlotte waterworks on Highway 16. I slept on the back porch through several winters and hauled water from our spring in the valley. I participated in 4- H Club at the West Mecklenburg High School and helped Daddy roof and remodel our home. We won the Future Farmers of America, F.F.A. award for home improvement that year.

Oakdale Cabin-before improvement

Oakdale Cabin 1952 (after Home Improvement)

My biology teacher at Paw Creek Junior High School made a lasting impact on my life. I learned from her that the same blood flowed through the black man's veins, as in the white man's veins. I stopped discriminating between the races because of this knowledge and not due to anything I learned in church.

I bought a horse named "Nell" with my savings from the paper route. Daddy and I farmed with Nell. I planted a special hybrid corn that yielded over 100 bushels per acre one planting season. I also commuted by rural bus to town and worked in the Mazingo Service Station gassing and parking cars at age 14. Later I got a job at Sears Roebuck in their automotive department and Daddy gave me the old family 1940 Mercury to drive to work. Mother pushed me to achieve the Eagle Scout Award. I went on to get the Gold Palm, The God and Country award and joined the Order of The Arrow thanks to her encouragement. **The greatest contribution my parents made to my life was keeping me in Scouting, taking me to church and staying married despite their constant fighting and drinking.**

I began attending the Pleasant Grove Methodist Church Youth Fellowship in the evenings because many of my high school friends went there. The Lord was beginning to convict me of my sins and showing me the big difference in how my family and I lived in our private times and the way the Lord wanted us to live. My moral life was far beneath my public profession in church and scouting. One Sunday evening in 1951, when I was 16, while sitting on the back row in the Methodist church, I heard Reverend Jack Cook preach about Jesus on the cross, being crucified for our sins. It was as if he was preaching right at me! I imagined I saw Jesus hanging on the cross because of my personal sins and hypocrisy. I privately confessed my sins to Christ that night and asked him to forgive me. I did not go forward in church, but I remember walking out into the night and seeing the stars sparkling in the sky. It was as if all creation had come alive, when in fact, I was spiritually reborn that night! I later talked to Daddy and explained that I thought I should become a Methodist. He told me,

"Read the Bible and decide which church is closer to the Bible."

I did, and decided to remain a Baptist, but I will be eternally grateful to the Methodists for my salvation! Later, in college and seminary studies, John Wesley became one of my models. Only years later would I discover that many of my paternal ancestors were Methodists. Two of my best friends in High School, Larry Wilkerson and Vaudry Williams became Methodist ministers. Larry became a leader in the Western Carolina Methodist Conference. I began taking an active part in leading the Methodist Youth Fellowship and attending Baptist Training Union at Pritchard Memorial. This experience helped me in public speaking, teaching and witnessing in the years to come.

My West Mecklenburg High School annual listed me as a "Shy but nice guy." I graduated in 1953 and did not have enough money to go to a major college, so I decided to spend my life savings of $400 on a cross-country trip with the Explorer Scouts.

I travelled by train to the World Scout Jamboree at Irvine Ranch, California. The trip, which led to Victoria, British Columbia and ended in Chicago, left a lasting impression on me. I am grateful to my senior Scout Master who insisted that I enjoy the beautiful scenery from the train, since I paid for it! My church experience gave me my salvation and Scouting helped me to develop my character and leadership ability.

My parents met me in Chicago and we brought my Grandfather, William, "Bill," Brough, back with us to Oakdale. He was now an invalid with multiple sclerosis. His second wife, a nurse, had died. His mind was sound and he pointed out the telephone company buildings as we went through each town. He paid to build a room onto our house and my parents kept him until he died years later when I was in the Navy. When he met my grandmother Agnes who was also living next door he asked, "Why did we get divorced?" They could not remember why! Agnes or "Nana" as we called her used to read to me from her Unity devotions. She recorded in her mother, Lucy Kendrick Street's Bible,

> "I see my grandson as God's perfect child. Manifesting God's perfection throughout his being. God's life cannot be impaired and therefore no illness, disease or harm can come to him."

I found a letter waiting on me when I returned from the trip out west from a distant cousin of my mother who was married to Ernest Gilbert in Reading, Pennsylvania. He offered to pay for my college education. I could choose the college, but he and my parents encouraged me to study engineering. "Uncle Ernest," as we called him, owned one of the largest earth-filled dam construction companies in the world and was a Presbyterian deacon. He was a friend of the inventor, Thomas Edison. He did not have any sons of his own but he put 12 young men through college. I was one of them! We later named our first-born son's middle name after him, Charles Gilbert Register.

Virginia Upbringings

I chose the University of Virginia, because of its tradition, beauty, and because it had an engineering school, along with liberal arts subjects. Daddy gave me a Revised Standard Version of the Bible, which I read the first year that I was in college. This book answered all the questions I had about God and life in general. At UVA, I was active in the Baptist Student Union under the leadership of Reverend Nathan Byrd. It was there I learned Bible study, practiced a devotional life, and met the love of my life, Rose Mary.

My first day at UVA in September 1953 I attended a first year student reception at the YMCA. I met a short, Arab Muslim from Damascus, Syria named Mahmoud Makki. He was the first Arab I ever met. He invited me up to his room. On the wall was a beautiful rug, which reminded me of a tapestry of King Tut my mother hung on our living room wall.

He said, "This is my prayer rug. I take it down and pray on it five times a day."

I began the daily practice of prayer and Bible study because of that Muslim!

Years later, while serving as an officer in the US Navy, a Jewish midshipman walked into my stateroom and said, "Mr. Register, do you believe the Bible?

I answered, as a good Baptist should, "Of course!"

He continued, "Do you believe every word of the Bible?"

"Yes," I replied, somewhat apprehensive.

"Do you tithe?"

"I do now!"

Therefore, I started praying and reading the Bible because of a Muslim and tithing because of a Jew!

Engineering school at UVA was a challenge for me. Aptitude tests I took in my senior year of high school showed that math would be a struggle. My family encouraged me toward engineering anyway. One day in first year engineering English class the professor remarked, "If Ray Register, who is an average student can get this, the rest of you should be able to understand it!" At least half the class dropped out the first year! Toward the end of the second year, I struggled with a course in statics, which was all about levers and triangles. I made a 70, which was short of the 75 needed to pass the course. For the first time, I had to go to Daddy and ask him for help to pay for summer school. God had been working in my heart about my life's calling and I was not sure that being an engineer was it! I took the first statics test in summer school and failed it. One redeeming quality was that the head of the Engineering School, Dr. Quarles, was also the teacher of our college Bible class at University Baptist Church in Charlottesville.

At the beginning of the summer of 1954, I attended Student Week at Ridgecrest Baptist Conference Center near Ashville, North Carolina. Great speakers like Chester Swarr and others challenged us to give our all to Christ. I felt certain that God was calling me into the ministry. My parents were not at all happy and kept encouraging me to stick it out in engineering. I was encouraged by Rev. Harry Thomas in Charlotte to preach my first sermon on Ephesians 6:10-20 on the "Whole Armor of God." That passage about spiritual warfare took on special meaning later in my career.

The next summer of 1955, the emphasis at Student Week at Ridgecrest was on world missions. I believe the keynote speaker was Dr. Baker James Cauthen. The wilting, challenging words of the hymn, by B.B. McKinney, "Wherever He Leads I'll Go" expressed my hearts longings. (See page 45) Someone got the idea of illustrating the proportion of lost people to the number of missionaries in various countries by stretching a colored paper mache ribbon around the Spillman auditorium. When they came to the Middle East, the ribbon stretched round and round that large auditorium! It was then that I told the Lord I would go to the Middle East where His own people need to know Him. I went forward on the challenge to commit my life to overseas service. One of the persons who counseled me in my decision was Virginia Wingo, who worked in an orphanage in Italy for the Foreign Mission Board. She gave me a verse from Isaiah 30:21, which said,

"And your ears shall hear a word behind you saying, "This is the way, walk you in it" when you turn to the right or when you turn to the left." These words kept me going in the years ahead.

When I got back home to Oakdale, I told Mother about my decision.

She replied, "I would rather you die as a soldier on a foreign field than to throw your life away as a missionary! We have dreams of your being an engineer."

I took her reaction seriously. As time went by, she knew I was not going to change my mind.

She said, "Alright, if you are determined to go through with this, we have a family tradition. You must study for your doctorate."

Only years later did I understand what she meant.

On returning to UVA, I went over to the summer registration at the School of Education to change my major to Commerce. Before I registered, I went downstairs to the bathroom, closed myself in a stall, and asked the Lord to lead me. I really felt Commerce would better prepare me for the mission field than engineering. When I got back to my dormitory room there was a letter awaiting me from Uncle Ernest. I began reading,

"I am so disappointed you are not continuing in engineering," he wrote.

I tore the letter in half. Out of the two sides fell a check for $500 I had torn in half! I read the rest of the letter,

"But I know that you are following the call of God and I want to continue to support you in the rest of your education."

I wonder what his reaction was when he got the cancelled check that I scotch-taped back together?!

My third year at UVA was filled with studies at the McIntire School of Commerce, trying to catch up on credits I needed to graduate. I was in the Naval ROTC and found Naval Science a real struggle. At the same time, I was active in the Baptist Student Union, the Delta Sigma Pi Commerce Fraternity and pledged to the Phi Sigma Kappa social fraternity. Another fraternity black-balled me for riding a bicycle to class. I also suspected it was because I was active in church and did not drink. My college roommates immediately introduced me to the Phi Sigs and we were a match. They tolerated the BSUers, Virginia players and other similar mavericks on the Grounds. I learned that fraternities were a bit like girlfriends who "Dear John" you. You only needed to cry for one night until another came along!

Speaking of girlfriends; the Lord graced me with some wonderful girlfriends through my high school and college years. They were all deeply spiritual persons. Two of them broke my heart and I broke another one's heart, one Presbyterian, one Methodist and one Baptist. On returning from my third year NROTC Midshipman cruise to Panama, and enduring the second "Dear John" from the Methodist girlfriend, I swore off women, that is, until I met Rose Mary.

In my fourth year at UVA, the BSU decided some of us would move back into the first year dormitories in order to recruit students for the church activities. The training session was the day before school at a 4-H Camp on a mosquito-infested river outside Charlottesville. I was late for breakfast. As I climbed the steps to the dining hall, I was startled to hear someone say,

"Where have you been all my life?"

I nearly fell back down the stairs! It was Rose Mary. She was upset I was late and holding everyone up from breakfast. She meant to say, "Where have you been all morning?"

She got my attention and never lost it after that. I dated her roommate from the UVA Nursing School who was a Baptist. But she finally told me, "I think you should date Rose Mary."

Rose Mary's dad was a Navy lawyer and she had lived in the four corners of the USA. He was now stationed at Anacostia near Washington, DC. UVA was Rose Mary's second choice. She applied too late to enter Duke University. Duke's loss was my gain!

I call our relationship a "mud pie romance" since we just oozed together. I started taking her with me to play the piano when I preached at Preddy's Creek Baptist Church on Sunday mornings. I was not ready to give her my heart because of past failures, so I tried to play it cool. She rode with me to Newport News for the fall BSU Convention in my 1949 Mercury my dad traded for the old 1940 Mercury when the windshield fogged over. I had made a previous date with a Baptist preacher's daughter from Washington, DC that night. After the meeting was over Rose Mary came up to me and asked me in front of the other girl,

"Are you taking ME home or not?"

I looked sheepishly at the other girl who told me, "I guess you had better take **her** home!"

When I got her to the home where she was spending the night, I kissed her at the doorstep for the first time.

She said, "I did not know I meant that much to you!"

I did not either! I kept dating other girls and took my former Presbyterian girlfriend to the homecoming game. Rose Mary's parents came down from Washington for the game so I slipped away and met them. Later I drove up to Anacostia and spent an evening with her family. I remember they argued in whispers, a vast contrast from my family who fought loudly at every meal.

My spiritual counselor during all the years at UVA was Nathan Byrd, the BSU Director. His example and counsel would lead at least 10 young men into the ministry and to the mission field. I was sharing with him one day that I was concerned about who I would marry when I finished UVA. I could not marry while in college because I was an NROTC student. Just as we were talking, Rose Mary came into the BSU Center, stuck her head around the office door, and said, "Hello!"

Nathan told me, "Ray that is the kind of girl you should marry!"

I replied, "No, she is too quiet."

Nathan said, "Ray, you do not need a party girl. You need someone to calm you down!"

I began to consider his advice. It was not always easy going.

One night on the way to the movies, we started talking about the future. Rose Mary told me,

"You need to marry some Southern belle!"

I said, "Fine!"

I turned the car around and took her back to McKim Hall where the nursing students lived. That weekend she went back to Anacostia to visit her family. We had a date set previously, but it was up in the air since we were mad. When I went to pick her up, she had gone out with another boy! I left a message that if she wanted to see me again she had better call me when she got back.

She did. She told me she thought it was over, so why should she wait around on me?

Christmas came and the BSU held a student missions convention in Nashville, Tennessee. I went alone while Rose Mary studied and visited her family. While there, I signed a commitment card on December 29, 1956, which I keep in my Bible:

MY RESOLVE

Having accepted Christ as my Saviour and earnestly desiring to grow into greater usefulness and spiritual power as a Christian and church member, I solemnly and joyfully engage myself in this holy covenant with my Lord--

I *resolve* to witness daily on my campus and in my community to the redemptive love and universal Lordship of Jesus Christ.

I *resolve* to become an informed Christian through a study of the Bible, world conditions, and opportunities for missionary service.

I *resolve* to support world missions with my life, vocation, prayers, and my gifts and to lead others to do the same.

I *resolve* to unite with other Christians throughout the world in carrying out the commission of Christ.

I *resolve* to prepare myself through serious study and dedicated professional training for a vocation in keeping with the will of God for my life.

I made my commitment to service in the Middle East at Ridgecrest Student Week in June 1955. The Nashville Resolve firmed up the decision. An incident took place that same day which was to influence my future. I was standing at the entrance of the convention hall when all of a sudden a young man from the Middle East burst through the door, walked past me, marched down to the front and took the microphone. He brought greetings from the Middle East! His name was Anis Shurrosh.

Two other extraordinary men with ties to the Middle East influenced my devotional life during the UVA years. The first, Oswald Chambers, served as a YMCA chaplain in Zeitoun, Cairo, Egypt in 1915. He died there of appendicitis in 1917. His wife

compiled his short devotionals to the British troops in the famous devotional book, *My Utmost for His Highest*. The other
that had a profound influence on my spiritual life was "Borden
of Yale," William Whiting Borden, who gave up the riches of his
family fortune in Chicago to go as a missionary to Muslims in
China. He died of cerebral meningitis in Cairo during his language studies in 1913. The famous missionary, Samuel Zwemer,
conducted his funeral. The theme of his life was "No Reserve, No
Retreat, and No Regrets." (*Wikipedia*) Their steadfastness and
sacrifice inspired me throughout our later career in the Middle
East.

The new year of 1957 brought serious challenges. I had to
finish all my courses to graduate and earn a commission into the
Navy. I had been through enough romances that I knew that if I
continued my relationship with Rose Mary into the spring that
it would get serious. Therefore, I had to check things out. One
afternoon I picked her up from McKim Hall and we sat in the car
on the hill next to the University grounds. I told her that I was
called to the ministry and asked her if she thought she could be a
minister's wife. She replied, "I think I can."

Then I told her I was also called to be a missionary and we
would probably live overseas. Would she be willing to do that?

She said, "I think I can do that."

Little did I know, in my feelings of spiritual superiority, that
God called her to be a missionary before he did me! I learned
this many years later long after we were married. Rose Mary
had more maturity at age 18 than any of the other girls I knew.
Perhaps it came from being a "Navy brat" and living in the four
corners of the USA. She also inherited the wisdom of her father
and mother's ancestors, going back to the early Quaker settlers
and the Adams presidential families. Whatever the reason, I
felt as comfortable around her as I did with my own sisters. In

addition, she was also very pleasing to the eyes and had a sweet voice!

During Spring break, I drove Rose Mary down to our home in Charlotte and introduced her to my family.

My mother told me, "She is the best one you have ever brought home!"

I fondly remember the powder blue dress she wore on that trip.

Later, back in Charlottesville, I had to turn my mind to studies to be sure I passed my courses at the McIntire School of Commerce and graduated. This led to an interesting twist. I had been taking Rose Mary home early on Sunday nights after our BSU "singspiration" so I could finish my class assignments. I learned that a medical student had been picking her up afterwards and taking her out. In fact, he used the telephone on my dormitory hall to call her!

I shared with Nathan Byrd that I had competition and did not know how to handle it.

He said, "Ray, if you think that med student can make her a better husband than you, just let her go!" So, the next Sunday evening I did not take her straight back to McKim Hall. I drove her up to the Observatory above the University.

She asked nervously, "Aren't you going to take me back?"

I said, "So you can date that medical student?"

I told her, "It's either me or him!"

She said, "It will always be you."

I drove her back and let her out as I waved at the med student who had been waiting for her the whole time! It was downhill after that. I studied hard, secure in her devotion and finally passed all my courses for graduation from the McIntire School of Commerce at UVA. I was to ship out with the Navy from Norfolk after graduation for a two-month South American cruise. I was not about to take a chance in Rose Mary not being there when I got back! We had a dilemma. We prayed much, knowing it was God that brought us together. In those days, for people of faith, there was no question of divorce. Such a thought did not factor into our decision to marry. The Lord called us both into his service. Our calling was irrevocable and so was our marriage. We knew from the Bible and the wise teaching of Nathan Byrd that a God-ordained marriage brings wholeness. There is no guilt. There is freedom to enjoy and to bless each other.

We decided to get married on my graduation day, since my family would all be driving up from the Carolinas. We called her family, explained, and invited them to our wedding! As a result, **I graduated from UVA, was commissioned in the Navy, and married all on the same day, June 10, 1957.** We held our wedding at 6:00 PM in the historic grey stone University Chapel and Rose Mary's dad arranged for our wedding party at the Charlottesville Country Club. We used his Navy officer's sword to cut the wedding cake. We spent the first night of our honeymoon in a little motel on Skyline Drive. I had to drive Rose Mary back to nurse's duty at 10:00 AM the next morning. John Hall, my roommate and fraternity brother let us use his apartment for the rest of the week. On Saturday, Rose Mary drove me down to Norfolk and I boarded the USS Bristol, DD 857 for a cruise to Chile. It was the first of a number of contrasting separations and reconnections in our early-married life, thanks to the U S Navy.

While in Chile, I visited the home of James and Fern Bitner, Southern Baptist missionaries in Valparaiso-Vina del Mar. I noticed that their refrigerator was almost bare. They toured me around Santiago and introduced me to a group of admiring female students in a Baptist school there. Chile, the Andes and the devotion of the Bitners and their missionary partners left a lasting impression on me throughout my missionary career.

The Navy was an experience I would not do without, nor would I want to repeat! I visited Bilbao, Spain, Bergen, Norway and Hamburg, Germany on my second cruise. We docked in

Ray and Rose Mary's Wedding Party, June 10. 1957

Dunoon, Scotland and London, England on my second. Finally, at the end of my second year of duty, we took a Caribbean cruise, which included St. Thomas, Virgin Islands, Kingston, Jamaica, and San Juan, Puerto Rica. We experienced storms at sea and a shipwreck. The vastness and majesty of the sea gave me a new appreciation for God's power. We lived in Newport and Providence, Rhode Island, and Boston, Massachusetts as I cruised the Atlantic and Caribbean and Rose Mary finished her nurse's training and affiliations.

Rose Mary was pregnant with our first child, Charles, "Chuck," Register when I finished my two-year tour of Navy duty. We moved back to my home in Oakdale near Charlotte, North Carolina and lived with my parents for the summer before entering Southeastern Baptist Theological Seminary in the fall of 1959. Rose Mary had to take Chuck with her back to Newport to finish two months of nurses training and lived with Navy friends Bob and Vera Thomas. She graduated at the top of her class and both UVA Nursing School and Newport Nursing School fought over who would get her grades to elevate their grade point average.

The Navy experience was character building. I was one of the few believers on our ship. The Squadron Chaplain designated me as the Protestant Lay Leader on my ship and I conducted worship services every Sunday on the mess deck in addition to my repair officer duties. One sailor who attended made the mistake of winning $1,000 at cards one night and disappeared in the middle of the Atlantic! We had a memorial service at sea for him. I had to visit his pregnant girlfriend to offer condolences when we got to port. Being a teetotaler, I did not use my whiskey ration when we came back in to port. The captain at that time was an alcoholic. He asked to use my ration, which I refused. The Executive Office called me to his stateroom and told me to give it to the Captain. I told him I could not, based on conscience. He asked me, "Do you want to see your wife when you get to shore?" I told him I was getting out of the Navy in a few months and I could wait! I noticed the picture of Bob Thomas' family on his desk. He also was a Baptist and the only other believing officer on board at that time. I found out later the Captain also threatened him if he did not give him his whiskey ration. Later, a new Captain, who was a believer from the CMA Church, replaced this Captain. He called me to his stateroom and said,

"Mr. Register, I understand you and the former Captain did not agree on the matter of drinking. I want to let you know, I agree with your position and any officer who comes aboard my ship drunk will get a green table." i.e. Court Marshall.

Ray as Ensign in US Navy, 1957

Studies at Southeastern Seminary quenched my thirst for the Bible. I was able to sit under the teachings of great men of character and Bible knowledge like Drs. Jessie Weatherspoon, Leo Green, Olin Binkley, Thomas Bland, Luther Copeland, John Eddins, Garland Hendricks, Marc Lovelace, Ed McDowell, Stewart Newman, Elmo Scoggins, George Shriver, John Binkley, Bill Strickland, James Tull, John Wayland, Truman Smith, Dick Young and Sydnor Stealy. The library became my second home and it was there I discovered books on Islam planted by the Ahmadis. Dr. Shriver allowed me to write my Church History term paper on "The Doctrine of the Afterlife in the Quran." Dr. Strickland made the Book of Revelation come alive as he unlocked the coded writings to a persecuted church. Dr. Lovelace taught that the Bible sites are called by Arabic names today. Dr. Scoggins filled my mind with stories of Israel and solidified my

calling to the Arabs there. Dr. Hendricks advised me in facing
the challenges in my pastorate in Whitakers. Dr. Green made the
Old Testament come alive. Southeastern was an excellent incu-
bator for our years in the Middle East.

Our first summer of 1960 we packed our 1949 Mercury, put
Chuck on the top of our belongings in the back seat and made
our way out west to Washington state. We stayed in the basement of Rose Mary's parent's home in Seattle. She practiced
nursing and I was interim pastor at Brooklyn Avenue Baptist
Church while their pastor, Dr. Harvey Roys attended the Baptist
World Alliance in Brazil. I sold Kirby vacuum cleaners out of
their office in Renton, Washington. We got back to Wake Forest
at the end of August just in time to rescue our furniture that was
being moved out of our seminary apartment. We relocated into a
larger apartment. During the year, Rose Mary became pregnant
with our second son, James Adams Register. Our seminary colleagues jokingly named our apartments, "The Fertile Crescent."
I contemplated what direction to take next year since my Navy
savings were running out. Looking back, we see that God was
preparing us for our Galilee Wanderings.

Section 1

Preparation and Initiation

Ray (on right) with Whitakers Baptist Church leaders, c. 1963

Chapter 1

CAN PREACHERS GROW CORN?

What more unlikely place to train for service in the Middle East than Eastern North Carolina? Never in a lifetime would I chose the corn and tobacco fields of 1960's Nash and Edgecombe counties and the little town of Whitakers, population 1,000; 600 whites and 400 blacks. They drew the town limits so that the whites would be a majority. The outhouses lining Highway 301 coming up from Rocky Mount were my first impression of the 4-year journey with the people of Eastern North Carolina. As I look back, I can realize how gracious they were to accept me, a young, inexperienced pastor with a wife and two kids. My fieldwork supervisor from Southeastern Seminary, Dr. Garland Hendricks, recommended me to the Whitakers Baptist Church so I could get pastoral experience before I went overseas with the Foreign Mission Board. He was a native of the area. His wise counsel was to keep me there. Having been raised in the Piedmont and the more sophisticated environs of Charlotte, Whitakers offered me a taste of the culture shock I would face in overseas service.

Whitakers shared the danger of other towns on Highway 301. The railroad ran through the center of town. Almost every year the train killed someone who got their car stuck on the tracks. Our little frame church sat right beside the highway and shook every time a truck roared by! The town had one caution light. A cop in a pickup truck used to arrest New Yorkers on the way to

Florida for speeding. Our aging congregation numbered about 100 souls. It is not surprising that in my four years in Whitakers I had probably a dozen funerals and only three or four weddings.

Three leaders in the church, along with their wives and families, influenced us; the Dixons, the Reids and the Rossers. Mr. Dixon was senior deacon. He acted as wise counselor and disciplinarian for seminary students like myself who were trying their wings in their first pastorate. Bob Reid was a young businessman who acted the part of a friend and occasional rescuer. Bill Rosser was a lawyer and son of one of the former pastors. He carried a large roll of dollar bills stuffed in his pocket. His and his beautiful wife Lillian were social leaders of the community and his daughter Claire played the organ. Her younger sister Janet was blooming into a challenging teenage beauty. His mother 'Miz Rosser', a former pastor's wife, was my encourager and critic, and had the world on her heart. They were a family about whom you could write a book. The Rossers entertained us for Sunday lunch every few months and our boys enjoyed playing with their son, Billy.

Some in Whitakers viewed spirituality from the perspective of practicality. I remember in my rounds of visits I often stopped at a service station out on the highway run by one of our more infrequent churchgoers. He asked me,

"Can preachers grow corn?"

That is to say, "Can a city boy like you do any good in Eastern North Carolina farm country?"

My reply was,

"I did grow corn! I grew up on a 40-acre farm outside of Charlotte. We grew hybrid corn and pigs, but no tobacco!"

Several incidences stand out in my memory of Whitakers. The first had to do with a church split in town, and outside of town. When we moved to Whitakers Baptist Church, I was their first 'full-time' pastor. Formerly the pastor filled two or three pulpits in rotation in churches in the outlying farming area. Now each church decided they would go out on their own. To complicate the situation, one of the country churches had its parsonage right next door to our church, in between the church and the Sunday school building! Therefore, the country church pastor lived right next to our church in town. I lived out on the edge of town in a house whose back yard bordered on a Fundamental Baptist Church that split from our church some years back. The upshot of the matter was, as I settled into the pastorate and the people got to know me better, I found that our deacons were going next door to our church to the other pastor for consultation. One day I happened in and there sat the Associational missionary.

He said to me,

"Ray, they are going to run you off. You had better leave before they do!"

The next day at Seminary, I told Dr. Hendricks.

He laughed and said,

"Ray, now you are getting used to the situation. You just go back there and keep on working."

I went back to Whitakers and visited deacon Bob Reid. I asked him to tell me the truth of what is going on. He said things did not look good for me staying. I asked him what I could do to change, and if I changed, did he think I could stay. He said he was not sure, but I could try! I did stay. The next year we brought in Reverend Bewey Shaver for a revival and baptized 15 young people! One was Bob's son Kent. The Lord used this testing and discipline to show me He could help me overcome seemingly impossible circumstances.

I was in Whitakers at the height of the race riots in the early 60's. Little did I realize I would be caught in the middle of the conflict. One Sunday morning I felt led to preach a sermon on the

Good Samaritan and how we should overlook racial differences. I did not know they brought out the fire hoses to scatter blacks trying to integrate the movie theatre in the neighboring town of Enfield that Saturday night! After I got home from church, the phone was ringing off the hook. It was Bill Rosser. He wanted me over to his office right away. When I got there, he did not ask me to sit down. He stood in the middle of the office.

He told me, "I have to put up with working with the blacks all week as a lawyer. I do not want to go to church on Sunday to hear about it. I go to church to forget about it. We know how you feel about this and you know how we feel. If you insist on pushing this issue, you will not make it to the mission field. Do we understand each other?"

I told him, "I do."

I backed off reluctantly. I learned years later that when the Whitaker's church called a new pastor they told him about this matter and explained that they were sorry for the way they reacted to me. They said that if blacks came to the church now they would be seated like any other person.

Concerning the other church that had split from our church and built on the other side of town just behind our parsonage, I will never forget the day our two boys, Chuck and James, then only three and one years old, got into the drainage ditch between our properties and could not find their way out. My family stayed home sick that Sunday. The screams of the boys interrupted their Sunday worship service. Rose Mary, who was home sick with a cold, had to run out in her bathrobe in full view of the other congregation to rescue them!

My boys kept our lives interesting in Whitakers, like the time they went out and chased a bull pastured by Mr. Dixon behind this church. Mr. Dixon had the bull removed from the pasture since he felt it was easier to reform the bull than our boys! Chuck used to get my attention by coming into my office when I was studying for my sermon and pull books out of my bookshelves and opening them and reading to get my attention. One of the dear ladies of the church kept insisting we bring our family to visit her. I threw caution to the wind and took them with me. The boys promptly started grabbing her antique ceramic dolls, breakable knickknacks and everything within reach. She never invited us back again! We never had any concerns about protecting the boys since they had a dog that guarded them fiercely. We had to make special arrangements to keep that loyal pooch from biting the garbage men.

I give special credit to our surviving in Whitakers for over 4 years to the prayers of Mrs. Strickland, a gracious homebound saint whom I visited every week or two. She was probably one of the most cultured and educated ladies in town. She had a wisdom and compassion she shared with me generously during our time there. She knew about our call to the mission field and she kept Heaven informed about our needs both physically and spiritually. Her name remains with me since one of my favorite professors at Southeastern Seminary was Dr. Bill Strickland who taught New Testament. He was the first person who helped me understand the Book of Revelation. Mrs. Strickland, though possibly no kin to him, helped me understand God's purposes in this time of preparation for all that was to come.

Rose Mary felt for the first few years in Whitakers that the congregation did not notice her even though she directed the choir, taught Vacation Bible School and sat in the nursery. She was always busy with the children at home since I was often gone several days a week to seminary. She gave birth to our son James Adams and our daughter Cheryl Marie Register at the Rocky Mount Hospital during our time there. It was not until the last two years when she worked as a nurse, studied at Carolina

Wesleyan College in Rocky Mount and got her name in the papers for making dean's list that the church members started affirming her.

The church showed their appreciation for our service when I graduated from seminary in May 1962 by giving me a $40 raise. $40 a year! I went to the deacons and told them I could not survive on the $200 a month salary. Either I had to receive more salary or go to work.

Mr. Dixon, in his usual candid manner said, "Then, go to work!"

I did. I sold World Book Encyclopedias and measured croplands for the Agriculture Department. When I got proficient at it they allowed me to do crop allotments, which meant having farmers plow up excess tobacco acreage. One day I discovered that I had calculated the allotment overage incorrectly. The farmer was already furiously speeding down the row on his tractor plowing under his tobacco. I chased him down the row to stop him, and finally caught up with him as he turned around!

Rose Mary helped with the finances by working as a nurse at the Tarboro Regional Hospital, or I might have destroyed the rest of the tobacco crop of Eastern North Carolina!

I can testify that when we left Whitakers we had paid all our bills and our freezer was full of fresh corn, beans, and other vegetables the congregation donated from their gardens. We took that freezer to Israel with us and ended up selling it to a local grocer near Mary's Well. We could get vegetables and meat fresh from the market every day in Nazareth and never used it. Similarly, all the seminary books went almost untouched, except for the Bible, because we were living in the Land of the Bible. No need for commentaries!

Whitakers And The FMB

The process of applying for mission service with the Foreign Mission Board of the Southern Baptist Convention was not without its challenges. As I mentioned earlier, **I felt called to missions in the Middle East ever since Student Week at Ridgecrest in June 1955. The Lord spoke to me through a graphic presentation of the needs of the area. Someone came up the idea of streaming a paper mache ribbon around the Spillman Auditorium to represent the thousands of people in each area of the world who were not Christians. When the paper came to the Middle East, it stretched round and round the huge auditorium. I knew then that if I was going to invest my life it should be in the same area that Jesus preached his Gospel.**

While at Southeastern Seminary, the stories that Dr. Elmo Scoggins told about his time as a missionary in Israel impressed me. I would come home and tell Rose Mary.

She remarked, "I will never go to a place with so much conflict!"

Later when we were going through the appointment process, she finally conceded. The Women's Missionary Union (WMU) had a mission study on Israel. She said,

"You can go to Israel and work with the Arabs. I will go and work with the Jews!" She remembered her concern for her Jewish friends from High School days in Waukegan, Illinois, and the Jewish merchant next door to her grandfather Adam's clothing store in Goshen, Indiana and felt an affinity toward them.

They called us to Richmond, Virginia to the FMB headquarters for interviews and psychological testing. Our psychological testing took place in another professional building. My nervousness increased when one of the pretty secretaries made a pass at me in the elevator. My psychologist told me that my response to the Rorschach test indicated I had a problem with my father and authority. Right on the nose! I loved my Dad but at the same time did not respect him when he was drinking.

The FMB requested at least 20 personal references from people who knew me from my childhood. They asked for two more references from each of these, so they had a good idea of what others thought about me. Just a few weeks before appointment Dr. Jesse Fletcher, the personnel secretary of the FMB called me into his office. He stood behind his desk, not even asking me to sit down, and told me,

"Ray, we have picked up on your references that you are a bit stubborn and have a tendency to lose your temper. I am not sure I can recommend you for the Middle East."

I replied, "I understand that the Middle Easterners are stubborn and have bad tempers, so I believe I will fit right in with them!"

"Alright," he said, "I will need some good references on you to offset the negative ones!" I had been holding back a few, just in case. Therefore, I told him I would give him the name of a church member who had come from the other church that split off from our church in Whitakers. She was a fundamentalist with a critical attitude toward people who did not share her views. When I got home, I visited Mrs. Blackman and told her I needed a good recommendation.

"Do you smoke, drink, and play around with women?" she asked me.

"No!" I said.

"Give me the recommendation and I will sign it.," she said."

So, it was because of Mrs. Blackmon and a few other kind souls that I was finally appointed as a missionary to the Arabs of Israel.

Our missionary orientation was a week at the University of Richmond with about 50 others headed around the world. I was particularly envious of Wayne and Frances Fuller who studied Arabic at Georgetown University for a year and were headed for Lebanon. Eighteen years later, we were to cross paths in Bet

Ray and Rose Mary Register,
Appointment 1964

Mari in the mountains of Beirut and even later after retirement celebrated their 50th anniversary in northern California. In addition, we met Mavis Pate, a missionary nurse appointee from Louisiana who was destined to leave a lasting impact on all of us in the years ahead. Dr. J.D. Hughey, former president of the Baptist Seminary in Ruschlikon, Switzerland, and now Area Secretary for the Middle East and Europe for the FMB was reluctant to send us to Israel.

"Ray, if you are going to study Arabic, you need to go to an Arab country, where we need you more," he said. He suggested Morocco, Libya, Jordan, or Yemen.

"I feel called to the Arab minority of Israel." I told him.

He thumbed through his notebook and said, "Jim Smith needs help as treasurer of the Israel mission. You have a business degree, so you are going to Israel!"

Strange how God uses the little things to get you where you should be. The Israel Mission, The Baptist Convention in Israel or "BCI," was having a hard time convincing Dr. Hughey that we should get some Arabic studies before going to the Middle East. He was of the opinion that if we were going to Israel and not to an Arab country that we should go straight over. A twist of fate, or God's unique plan worked it out. Dr. Hughey had just assumed his new position with the FMB and was taking a field trip to the Middle East. Dr. Goerner, his predecessor, was handling things back in the Richmond office in his absence. The BCI convinced Goerner that I needed the training.

He called and asked me, "Ray, do you need some Arabic training before you get to the Middle East?

"I really did not feel ready to go the Middle East without some basic language and cultural study." I told him.

He told me he would call Hartford Seminary and see if they had room in the fall class. He called me back just as the movers were taking our sofa out of the front door of the Whitakers parsonage and said, "Ray, you are going to Hartford Seminary to study Arabic and Islam. Tell the movers to pack your furniture for storage."

Therefore, we found ourselves at the Hartford Seminary Foundation for the fall and spring of 1964-1965. The adjustment for our family was almost as challenging as our move to Israel. Our children could not understand the Connecticut accents of our neighbors! One of the neighbors thought our son Chuck was making fun of her with his southern drawl. However, Hartford Seminary was just what we needed to quench our appetite for the language and culture of the Middle East. I enrolled in the former Kennedy School of Missions, now named the Duncan Black MacDowell Center of Islamic Studies. D. B. MacDowell wrote the classic *Development of Muslim Theology, Jurisprudence and*

Constitutional Theory (DMTJ). The school of Islamic studies published the prestigious *Muslim World Quarterly* (MWQ). The library had one of the largest collections of books on the Middle East in the USA. I read every book in the library on both sides of the Arab-Israeli conflict in the Middle East, which renewed my conviction that **Christ was the only answer to their differences**.

Dr. Dwight Baker of the BCI preceded us to Hartford and received his PhD for his thesis on *Religious Liberty in the Middle East*. The contacts he made there eased our adjustment. Rose Mary and I studied Arabic and Islamics with Dr. Elmer Douglas, veteran Methodist missionary to Singapore and Malaysia. His deeply spiritual and authentic teaching about the life of Muhammad, the history of the Muslim expansion, and the dilemma of the Muslim background believer set the tone for our ministry to Muslims for the years to come. We also were privileged to study the history of missions to Muslims with Marston Speight, then a PhD candidate and former Southern Baptist who went as a Methodist missionary to North Africa. We studied linguistics with one of the leading experts in the field. Rose Mary surpassed me in academic prowess. I managed to pass linguistics simply because I recognized some of the words as Arabic phrases we were studying. I guessed at the word 'fii' that it meant 'there is' in the colloquial language instead of the classical meaning 'in'. Therefore, I passed that course simply by chance, or as they say in Arabic, "God's will." Little did we apprehend how much the privilege of studying at Hartford Seminary would influence us in the years to come.

Wherever He Leads I'll Go 361

1. "Take up thy cross and fol-low me," I heard my Mas-ter say;
2. He drew me clos-er to his side, I sought his will to know,
3. It may be thro' the shad-ows dim, Or o'er the storm-y sea,
4. My heart, my life, my all I bring To Christ who loves me so;

"I gave my life to ran-som thee, Sur-ren-der your all to-day."
And in that will I now a-bide, Wher-ev-er he leads I'll go.
I take my cross and fol-low him, Wher-ev-er he lead-eth me.
He is my Mas-ter, Lord, and King, Wher-ev-er he leads I'll go.

Wher-ev-er he leads I'll go, Wher-ev-er he leads I'll go,

I'll fol-low my Christ who loves me so, Wher-ev-er he leads I'll go.

Chapter 2

THE QUEEN ANNA MARIA AND MT. CARMEL

Having served two years aboard a US Navy destroyer after graduating from UVA in 1957, the trip to Israel aboard the Queen Anna Maria was like being on a floating paradise! It was still cheaper to sail than to fly in 1965. In addition, it gave us ten days to wind down after the studying and packing. Our greatest concern on board was our children somehow slipping under the rails into the sea. I could remember my days on the 'tin can' in the Navy and envying the passenger ships that sped along on automatic pilot, stabilized by gyroscopes, while my little destroyer dove up and down with the waves like a roller coaster! In between eating, sleeping and swimming we took a short course in spoken Hebrew with a former leader of the radical Jewish Etzel group. We also were acquainted with our new Southern Baptist mission colleagues Dale and Anita Thorne from Tulsa, Oklahoma. We were impressed that both Dale and Anita claimed partial Native American heritage, as did many folks from Oklahoma. They were to expand our understanding of the variety of people that comprised the Southern Baptist family. Our exposure up until then was with plain old southerners. We laughed with Dale about an experience on the Queen Anna Maria. One day as he was climbing up the ladder to the swimming pool deck a girl in a bikini was coming down the ladder. Dale embarrassingly found himself with his nose in her navel!

We had a port call in Lisbon, Portugal, which was beautiful compared to some of the other ports I visited in the Navy. Then we stopped in Piraeus, Italy, which is the port for Rome. I remember a very harrowing taxi drive. The driver simply floored the pedal and drove down the middle of the road. I do not remember the sites, but was happy to be back safely on the ship.

Approaching Haifa by sea is nothing spectacular. Not like flying over the distinct shoreline of the Mediterranean, seeing the expanse of Tel Aviv and circling over the tiled roofs of the outlying suburbs. On that July morning in 1965, we watched patiently as the grey mountain range slowly grew in size as the Queen Anna Maria pulled up alongside the unpretentious dock. The long warehouse facing us was less than impressive. Standing on the dock was our missionary group of over 40 people waiting for us. A whole lot more than saw us off in New York harbor! Later I learned that the shortest was Marty Murphy, an exuberant choir leader from Goshen College in Indiana, who now led an international choir at Baptist Village. The tallest was Bob Fields, a lanky Kentuckian who reminded me through the years of what Abraham Lincoln must have been like. Then there was his vivacious, blond wife, Eddie who gushed compassion all over you. Next was Dwight Baker, who was short in stature, but long in experience among the Arabic-speaking people, standing beside his tall and candid wife Emma. I realize now what contrasts all these people were and what impressions they would have on my life in the years ahead.

The customs official had already checked our passports on the ship. We came to appreciate, through the almost 40 years we spent in Israel, the value of the A-3 clergy visa we had as a member of the BCI. BCI stands for "Baptist Convention in Israel." It gave us the status to stay in the country for a year or two without the hassle of having to come and go to renew a tourist visa every

3 months. Aside from our US citizenship, it was one of the most coveted possessions in Israel. We soon learned the value of belonging to a denomination that had been in the country prior to the formation of the State of Israel in 1948.

The next few days were a blur interrupted by the clang of the bell at Baptist Village. "BV," as we soon came to call it, was a former orphanage that later became an industrial school and eventually the camps and conference center for much of the Evangelical community in Israel. We slept in a guest bunkroom that was formerly a dormitory room for the orphanage. What I remember best is a group of American teenage volunteers running around outside our door and clanging the dinner bell that was supposed to signal mealtime only. Every time one of them came by our door, they would reach up and ring that bell. I endured one sleepless night. Then I went out discreetly, unhooked the clapper, and hid it in my room! I came to Israel to work with the locals and not a bunch of screaming (and clanging) American teenagers. It turns out they were summer camp counselors sent out from college Baptist Student Unions in the USA. They did make a valuable contribution to the camp, but not my sleep!

We could hardly wait until Dwight Baker drove us up to our little apartment at 6 Hator Street on Mount Carmel in Haifa. It was so great to be able to sleep through the night without that bell! He introduced us to Mrs. Belahuski, a vociferous, friendly Russian Jewess who clanked around the apartment above us in wooden shoes. Her upstairs neighbor was Mr. and Mrs. Feglan, astute but polite Israelis the likes of whom were the backbone of that little country.

Dwight and Emma Baker acquired a Christian Arab maid and babysitter for us from the little suburban village of Kababir less than a mile from us. Kababir was an Ahmadiyya Muslim settlement perched on a promontory jutting out from Mount Carmel.

Kababir served as a city of refuge for Arabs who had married outside the family or clan. Our maid was one of those who eloped with a husband who did not meet her family's approval. Kababir was to play a key role in our future.

Dwight chose as our Arabic language teacher Mr. Isam Abbasi, a poet and a Communist. He was from a leading Muslim family in Haifa. His father was the late Nurideen Abbasi, the former Inspector of Education in Nablus in Samaria. His mother was Turkish. We studied Arabic three full mornings a week with Mr. Abbasi, first in his apartment, and then at the newly opened Christian Service Training Center (CSTC) on Haganim Street in Haifa. We learned that the 1948 War of Independence interrupted Mr. Abbasi's education. Most of the affluent Arabs of Haifa fled to Beirut during the fighting between the Jews and the Arabs. Isam stayed back to care for his aging mother. He never finished college. Instead he became a poet and eventually the proofreader of the Communist weekly newspaper, *al-itihad*. He eventually fell out with the newspaper over a salary dispute. He told us that the Israeli FBI, known as the *shin bet* was displeased that he left the Communists. They told him that while he was a Communist they knew everything he was doing. Now they knew nothing!

Isam Abbasi was the ideal Arabic teacher for us. He was knowledgeable in the Quran and in politics. He would give us short lessons on current events and situations we would typically experience in town such as in the market, in the restaurant, at school, in the post office and at church. He helped me to prepare sermons in Arabic. He recorded them on the tape recorder and I literally memorized them. He had a beautiful Arabic script that became my pattern for writing Arabic. It was through him I was able to read the Quran and the Bible in Arabic and to quote sections of each in classical Arabic. We went through every Arabic language book and manual written up until that time. Many of the methods later developed in Arabic language learning were standard with Isam Abbasi. He would give each lesson in the Modern Standard Arabic (MSA), and then in the colloquial Arabic used in daily speech. Learning was not without its humor. I complained about his smoking in class. He told me, "I will quit smoking when you quit picking your nose!" We both stopped, at least in class.

The bond with Isam Abbasi lasted for his lifetime. His wife Selwa was an accomplished teacher and politician from Jaffa. They adopted a Bedouin girl who used to play with our daughter when we studied in his apartment. The girls remained friends for years. When our daughter later married a Jewish messianic leader, Mr. Abbasi took a taxi all the way from Jerusalem to Baptist Village to attend the wedding. Mr. Abbasi taught us Arabic from 1965 until we went on furlough in 1969.

Another person left an impact in our lives during our year in Haifa. Ibrahim Siman, a Baptist, was Dr. Baker's secretary at the CSTC. He would travel with me every Friday afternoon to translate for me in the worship services at the Rama Baptist Church, high in the mountains of northern Galilee. Ibrahim was active with the Mapam political party that promoted peace between Arabs and Jews. We attended several of their activities in the coming years. Ibrahim eventually moved back to his father's home in Nazareth and became the chaplain at the Edinburg Medical Missionary Society (EMMS), or Nazareth Hospital. Our families were to share many joys and sorrows through the years. Ibrahim felt called to move to Kababir and start home meetings for the Christians living there. He opened many doors to the Christian Arabs and Ahmadi Muslims for us.

One very important door was with Fareed Wajdi Tabari, a friend of Dwight Baker's and a former teacher at the Nazareth

Baptist School. Wajdi was the son of a prominent Muslim leader from Tiberias. He studied at the University of Beirut, and worked for the British Consulate in Jerusalem. He had an open mind toward Christians and discerning heart. He married an Arab Christian believer from the Plymouth Brethren Church. Brother Nofal and other Brethren used to come to his home in Kababir and have Bible studies for his wife. Wajdi played a decisive role in my academic progress in the study of Islam in the years ahead. I could say he and Isam Abbasi were my two native mentors and gave me a new understanding of how true Muslims can act and live and were lifelong friends.

I told the Lord when I went to Israel, "Please do not send me to a country with beautiful women. You know my weakness."

He did not answer that prayer in the way I expected. The women on Mount Carmel were beautiful! Rose Mary assured me that they were not any prettier than other women were. They just dressed to show it off more! One day at the post office, I noticed an attractive lady who was asking the postal clerk about a Messianic Jewish pastor who was being persecuted. I motioned for her to step aside, since the person she was looking for was written up in the daily papers because of his evangelistic activities among the Jews. Janet Cardwell studied Hebrew in the *ulpan* (Hebrew language school) in Kibbutz Miyan Zvi. Janet invited Rose Mary and me to the kibbutz where we met one of the kibbutz leaders. He was intrigued as to why we, as evangelical Christians would come to Israel. We explained about God's call for us to minister to the Arab minority.

He told us, "I cannot believe in God because of what the Nazis did to my family. I wish I could believe as you do!"

Janet babysat our children while we were in Haifa and later joined the Haifa Symphony Orchestra as a French horn player.

Life on Mount Carmel was an ideal introduction to Israel. The beauty of the ride up and down the Carmel is breathtaking! The expanse of the Mediterranean and the shoreline visible to the north up to Rosh Hanikora is unsurpassed around the world. The luxurious golden dome of the Bahai Shrine where the Bahuallah is buried is the centerpiece of the landscape. The ornamental gardens point down the mountain to distant Acre where the Bab is entombed in a beautiful garden. The British exiled both these Bahai leaders to Palestine from Persia before the State of Israel was established. The Bahais later built their world Hall of Justice beside the shrine on the mountainside in Haifa.

The Bahai Shrine in Haifa, Israel

The Central Carmel where we lived sported one of the only bowling alleys in the country. I frequented it on every occasion I could squeeze in. The local restaurants and parks were great for outings with Rose Mary and the kids. Occasionally we would ride the Carmelite, a subway with a 45% slant that rode down through the Hadar, or Central Carmel, to the Port area of Haifa. Rose Mary loved the shops in Central Carmel and we met many German Jews who fled Germany when Hitler was gaining power in the 1930's. Rose Mary had to learn German terms for numbers when ordering meat and paying at the cash register. She often said she did not know if she was dealing in German or Hebrew, and we were trying to learn Arabic! One such Jew was Dr. Gottesman who literally saved Rose Mary's life when she suffered from severe intestinal cramps and diarrhea. I thought we might lose her that first year in Haifa. We went to Dr. Gottesman and told him her symptoms.

He told her, "Smack your lips and tell me what your tongue tastes like. Is it sweet or bitter?"

Rose Mary said, "Sweet."

"Ah ha!" he exclaimed. "You do not have enough acid in your stomach to kill our local germs!"

He prescribed acid pills and the diarrhea and cramps went away almost immediately.

Dwight Baker encouraged us not to get involved in mission business during our first year of language study. It was good advice. Still, I occasionally accompanied him to special meetings at Baptist Village. I remember one time, on the long drive back to Haifa, he turned on the BBC Arabic broadcast.

I asked him, "How long did it take you to understand this language?"

He said, "It will come. Just keep massaging your ears."

Later we got the book and the tapes for Daud Abdo's, *A Course in Modern Standard Arabic* (Khayats, 1964) which helped us to learn the political Arabic of the radio and newspaper.

His advice not to be involved in the business of the BCI was short lived. I found myself in court against the leading Communist lawyer, Hannah Nakara, within the first few weeks in the country. The BCI had purchased land for a future church building in Rama from an Arab Communist family, the Ghattas brothers. They refused to pay the mandatory improvement tax on the land. I sat there in mild shock as the prominent Nakara lumbered into the courtroom. It all ended when they settled out of court to pay half the tax and the BCI the other half.

Another breach of his advice came when the BCI asked us to put a new VW station wagon on our passports. In those days, a new immigrant could avoid paying the 100% customs on a new car by having a special customs stamp in their foreign passport. My A-4 clergy visa gave me the same rights. The car was supposed to go to a senior BCIer, but the group met and assigned the car to us to avoid possible complications with the customs department. We ended up driving that beautiful little car our entire first term in Israel. I remember on one vacation trip to Eilat coming up on a shiny patch of highway in the Negev desert at about 100 kilometers an hour (60+ mph). Unknowing to me, it was rainwater that had washed down from the hills going across a long rain-wash dip in the road. I must have hydroplaned for several hundred feet!

Our neighbor across the cul-de-sac in Haifa was an Egyptian Jew, Mr. Mizrachi. He lost his driver's license when he immigrated to Israel. He took many frustrating drivers lessons and tests to no avail. I was glad to give him an occasional ride to Barclays Bank where he was the manager and we had an account.

Our children were our best ambassadors in Haifa that first year. One day Chuck, who was six, came in and said, "There is a neighbor who wants to meet you. I play with his son." It turns out the neighbor was an Orthodox Jew. We visited him one afternoon.

He asked us, "Why do your children always talk to my boy about Jesus? Don't you know we are Jews?"

I told him, "That's strange; I thought Jesus was a Jew."

I was secretly proud of my children that they were talking about Jesus!

He then said, "We Orthodox Jews dress in a particular way, and we pray in a particular way. How can I tell what you Baptists believe by the way you dress and pray?" It was a challenging question. I tried to explain that our faith was a personal experience, and we showed our faith in our daily actions of loving our neighbors. I later learned that this man regularly beat his wife and the neighbors could hear her screams.

One night near the end of our year in Haifa, we were sound asleep in our downstairs apartment. I felt a strange presence in the room and then heard a thump off the back balcony. We quickly realized that we had been robbed! The robber evidently came in from the office window in the front of the house and jumped off the balcony outside the children's bedroom. Later, one morning on my way to Arabic lessons, as I walked out our front door, I looked up at the roof of the apartment house next to us and noticed a man looking down. When he saw me, he ran. I called the police, but he had fled. He had been repairing the roof. Later we read in the newspaper that he robbed the third floor apartment of a woman. She woke up and started screaming. He went out her window and grabbed a drainpipe. It broke and he plunged to his death. He was from one of the Arab villages where I later worked.

Being new in the country I was naive in how to relate to the other believers we encountered. One day a Jewish Messianic believer visited us. He was a likable chap. However, I learned later that he had left his wife and married a younger woman. It was a scandal in the believing community. When I told Dwight about him his comment was, "Ray, you love all the rats!"

Another experience that went sour was when the new Child Evangelism (CEF) couple visited us and asked us to write them a letter recommending their services to the churches. They needed it to keep their visa. I complied since I knew it was a worthy organization. Dwight reprimanded me since such a letter needed BCI approval and could jeopardize our standing with the Christian Affairs office of the Ministry of Religion. The couple brought the letter back and later became one of our favorite ministry partners in Galilee.

One final experience before we moved from Haifa to Nazareth in 1966. Jim Smith called and wanted to introduce me to the leaders of the work in Galilee. I did not have a car at the time, so he told me to take the Arab bus from Haifa to Nazareth. My year at Hartford had not prepared me to understand colloquial Arabic and to anticipate the cultural shock of getting on a bus in a strange land and not knowing where to get off! Finally after riding through the Valley of Israel and up the mountain to Nazareth, which I had never seen before, the bus turned around at Mary's Well. I decide to get off, and by God's grace, found my way to the Baptist School where I met Jim. It was not long before I realized that there is a world of difference between Haifa and Nazareth.

AUG • 66

Rama Church members 1966. Abu Walid and Abu Omir to the right.

Chapter 3

BARK AND BRAY!

Within just a few days after arriving in Haifa Jim Smith or Dwight Baker, I cannot remember which one, drove me up to Rama village. They evidently installed me as pastor in Rama before I even got to Israel! A group of disgruntled Greek Orthodox and Greek Catholics approached Jim and the Baptists in Nazareth in 1963 requesting baptism. One of their conditions was that they would have a pastor provided, along with land and a building. Rev. Sakhnini of the Nazareth Baptist Church cautioned against accepting their offer, but it was decided to go ahead anyway, and I was part of the offer! Ibrahim Siman accompanied me that first year in 1965 as translator, since I was still studying Arabic.

Rama was an ancient village, traditionally one of the home-towns of Joseph of Aramathea, which translated from Arabic means, Joseph of Rama. Rama lay at the base of the highest mountain range in Israel, about 15 miles south of the Lebanese border and halfway between Acre and Safad. Rama's population at the time was about 5000 Arabs, made up of Orthodox, Catholic, and Latin Christians, Druze and Muslim refugees from the 1948 War of Independence (or *Naqba*, 'Disaster' for the Arabs).

The little Rama Baptist Church rented a room for meetings from Joseph, a carpenter married to Mary! The BCI purchased strategic property from the Ghattas family for a future building. The Ghattas' were Communists and refused, as many Arabs do, to pay the improvement tax levied on their land by the Israeli

government. The land had been a swap for land confiscated by
the Israelis after 1948. As mentioned above I had to be in court
against the famous Communist lawyer, Hana Nakara my first
weeks in the country The BCI decided to settle out of court and
share the payment of the improvement taxes with the Ghattas
family. I stayed on good terms with their family after that.
Ironically, the land confiscated from another Christian Arab
family in the village was given to them. I made a point of telling
the other family that our land was their land and our church,
their church.

Three families banded together to form the Rama Baptist
Church. First, the Hannah family led by the fearless and persistent "Abu Omir," or the father of Omir. Omir worked as the
treasurer of the Baptist School in Nazareth. He may have played
a part in getting his father to approach the Baptists. They were
dissatisfied with the powerful Orthodox Priest in the town. The
Shahouk family, led by "Abu Walid," or the father of Walid, was
not happy with the politics of the Greek Catholic Bishop of Galilee.
Building permits for the new land were delayed since a shepherd
had grazing rights on the land for a few years. Therefore, they
proposed buying the old Barclay's Bank building up in town. The
Derwish family lived in the basement of the property so they began attending meetings and became members.

One day after I had been pastor for several years, Abu Omir
was riding up into the village with me to the new meeting place
at the bank.

He told me, "Bark here. We bray there!"

When we got into the building, he said, "Get into the bulbit
and breach!"

The Arabic language does not have a 'p' so they use the 'b' instead! Over thirty years later when I lived in Kefr Yasif, Josephus
the Jewish historian's hometown, the neighbors told me the tale

of an American pastor who was told by his deacon to 'Bark here and bray there!" That is how traditions start in the Holy Land.

I wish that all my experiences with Abu Omir had been that humorous. His energy and strong personality were known throughout the region, in contrast to the steady, calm personality of his wife and his sons. As I gained more facility in the Arabic language, I began to understand what he was saying to me and about me. A conflict developed between him and the other family in the church. I tried to be neutral, which was not to his liking.

He told me in Arabic, "You are like a little boy!"

I told him back in Arabic, "I am not your little boy!"

He threw me out of his house. I very much regretted what happened. The upshot was, he threatened to sue the church for the tithes he had given. I had to tell Omir in Nazareth, "Your father is suing the church."

He went home and convinced his father to settle the matter. We gave him back his offerings to the church. He bought two calves with the money and they both got sick and died! Despite the break, I stayed in touch with Abu Omir and his family until he died, and still have contact with his children and grandchildren. Years later in the 1970's we finally completed the Rama Church Building. The struggle to accomplish this goal influenced a cataclysmic change in my life.

The Road To Rama And The Sea Of Olives

The road to Rama is a trip through history. Every Friday and sometimes during the week I traveled that road, for twelve years, beginning in July of 1966. General Montgomery built the road in World War II to supply his troops in their battle against the German General Rommel in North Africa. This particular section from the Golani Junction on the road from Nazareth to Tiberias to Rama village in Upper Galilee was a tank road. He used the rocks from the hillsides generously supplied by the Creator. It was one lane wide and very curvy, which meant either you or the other driver coming in the opposite direction had to give way and go off the road into the ditch, field, or embankment. I was in constant anticipation of playing "chicken," or who was going off the road first. You had to plan your strategy, if you had the time to see ahead, so you could make it to the next wide place mercifully provided on the few straightaways to provide relief for slower traffic. Therefore, if you could make it to the wide place in time to let the approaching driver get past, it was a win-win situation. If not, you held tight to the steering until you could see the white of his eyes and then one or both of you jerked the wheel and pulled off into the ditch to avoid a head-on collision. This particular day I had the road to myself and I was on the straightaway section of the road overlooking the beautiful Natofa Valley. This valley changed colors through the seasons of the year as different crops were planted and cultivated. The Natofa, or "Betof" as the Arabs called it did not need irrigation. It flooded in the winter season from the rains and the water "percolated" up through the soil the rest of the year. I had the "pedal to the metal" in the VW double-cabin truck the BCI provided for our work. That meant I could top out on a decline at about 90 to 100 KPH or about 60 miles an hour. I had been weary from a long week, staying up late drinking thick, black Arab coffee. Anyway, the nearly mile long decline and the monotony of the straightaway caused me to doze off momentarily. All I remember is I felt a nudge on my right shoulder and woke up just as I entered a 45 degree turn to the left. It was then that I realized I had a guardian angel riding with me! Otherwise, I could have ended up wrecked on an ancient Canaanite altar some archaeologist had uncovered beside the road. My Galilee wanderings could have ended before they had hardly gotten started.

One particular week I had to drive from Nazareth to Rama almost every day for business, weddings and a funeral. The jogging on the rocky road caused a severe pain in my neck. Remembering Dr. Churcher's clinic in Haifa, I decided to ask their help. The English nurse came at me with a huge needle, which she stuck, into my backside. That Vitamin B shot promptly moved the pain from my neck to my buttocks!

The drive from Nazareth to Rama is one of the most spectacular in the world. In the 1960's and 1970's when I made the weekly Friday run there were no super highways, just the standard two lane and one lane roads. First, you circle up the hill above Nazareth where you had a view of the entire city nestled in a cove in the mountains above the Valley of Israel, or Megiddo, ancient Armageddon. Then you wind down the mountain through Cana of Galilee after passing Meshed, ancient Japh Hefer, and the birthplace of Jonah. Then you pass Turan village whose fields are white unto harvest in the fall, and as tradition has it, where Jesus' disciples plucked grain on the Sabbath.

Fields white unto harvest, Turan

A mile down the road, at the Golani Junction, famous for the decisive battle for Galilee during the 1948 war, you turn north. Coming up on a rise, you take a sharp right down the decline above the Natofa Valley, which changes color according to the planting season. You wind through the village of Ailaboon and then down the mountain and up again through the village of Maghar, named after caves found there. Around the mountain on the other side you come upon a scene I called "Shangri-La," a beautiful valley that became the scene for James Michener's book, *The Source*. It is breathtaking. The locals call it the "Sea of Olives." Olive trees cover the valley and the mountainsides as far as the eye can see. Every prominent family in Rama cultivates a plot of trees in the Sea of Olives.

Ancient Olive Tree on Road to Rama

Years later when a modern highway was cut from Acre to Safad, the Israel Highway Department diverted the route to preserve two ancient olive trees that date back at least 2000 years. Their trunks are mammoth, at least 15-20 feet in diameter. The insides were hollow because of their age, showing that the trees lived by their skin and bark. The only other trees in the Holy Land that old are in the Garden of Gethsemane in Jerusalem. I often pondered, as I passed those trees; "What history they have seen!"

As soon as word got around in Rama that I had parted ways with Abu Omir, I received a message from the mayor of the town, Hana Moess, asking me to visit him.

When I went to his house, he told me, "I could not associate with you as long as you were partners with him. Now that you are not, I am ready to assist you in any way I can to accomplish your mission in my town. I know you are here to do the work of God."

He instructed the town clerk to assist me. Mr. Moess was invaluable in helping to receive the necessary permits to build our church. He was a valued and honored friend until the day of his death many years later.

Ray and Mayor Hana Moess in Rama, c. 1966

Rama is a very proud village. It has one of the highest percentages of college graduates of any Arab town in Galilee. Many are doctors, lawyers, and scientists. They pride themselves on their independence and heritage. The father of Abu Walid, "Abu Bishara" used to tell me Canaanite tales he learned from his ancestors. He was a *jabber* or a bonesetter. He could set broken bones better than most trained doctors could. His handlebar mustaches and Arab skirt and headdress made you feel you had stepped back into history. He was a kind and faithful advisor for this young foreign preacher.

Bible study in Rama. Abu Bishara seated to my left. c.1972

After the purchase of the bank building, we came on the idea of opening a kindergarten day care center. Im Walid, Abu Walid's wife and her daughters became the directors. Im Walid was from Nazareth and always had a humorous word about understanding the peculiar ways of the Rama people. Many of the children of

Rama got their head start through that little kindergarten. It set a pattern we used in several other villages like Turan and Yafa of Nazareth. It was a low cost project that added value to the Arab community and gave the Baptists a positive reputation.

One night my family accompanied me to Rama. We were sitting around talking in Im Walid's living room after supper. My daughter Cheryl, by that time, had become fluent in colloquial Arabic. Im Walid started teasing her to see how much Arabic she really knew.

She asked Cheryl in Arabic, "Aren't I pretty?"

Cheryl shot back, *"inti kharbani!"* Arabic for "You are a broken down woman!"

Im Walid and the other ladies got the laugh of their lives.

Im Walid in Rama cooking bread

One of the families who lived near the bank building were refugees from the village of Ikrit near the Lebanese border. Birim or Baram in Hebrew and Ikrit were two Arab Christian towns that the Israeli Army evacuated after the fighting in 1948. The Army claimed they were too close to the border and could be used for infiltration into Israel. The Israeli Supreme court ruled in favor of the villagers moving back to their homes. However, before them could return the Army destroyed their homes. A few families ended up in Rama. This particular family finally saved up enough money to buy a small piece of land below the village near the new bypass highway. They finally finished a larger house for their growing family. They lived previously as our neighbors to the bank building. One day I received word that a demolition order was issued to destroy the house since it was built before the proper permits could be issued. I immediately went to the office of the District Commissioner in Nazareth, Mr. Israel Koenig. Significantly, Koenig meant 'King" in German. Mr. Koenig was noted for his hardline against the Arab citizens of Galilee. His office was in a building overlooking Nazareth. He was like the modern day king of Galilee! I made his acquaintance while dealing with land registration for a number of our churches in Galilee. He greeted me cheerfully.

I told him, "I have a problem."

He asked, "What is it?"

I told him, "I am returning to the USA in a few weeks. I will be speaking in hundreds of Baptist Churches about Israel. I do not know how I am going to explain why this refugee's house is being destroyed."

His face paled.

He said,

"He has built without a permit. He has broken the law!"

I said, "Yes he has, and the Druze soldier who lives next door to him has done the same and his house is not being destroyed!" The Druze were favored since they served in the Israeli Army and Border Police.

Mr. Koenig replied harshly, "Then you have to bring me some real good reasons not to destroy his house!"

Within a few days, I was back in his office with letters from the Mayor and Social Welfare Department pleading the case of this refugee family from Ikrit. Their house remains standing to this very day! I learned that many times, more could be done person to person than can be done by demonstrations and protests made in public.

One of the young men from the Rama Church married a lady from Jordan. She came from a very distinguished family. Her uncle, a prominent businessman, attended the wedding. The young groom had a poor upbringing and his father was an alcoholic. For some reason he took to beating his wife. She was ready to leave him and return to Jordan. I took a chance. I enlisted the help of Monsour Inseir, the director of the Cana Baptist Center, to take the young man for a ride. Along the way, we told him what an embarrassment he was to our church.

"We married you to this lady from a prominent family. If you beat her again, you will answer to us. And her uncle will send someone from Jordan to beat you too!"

He said, "Pastor Ray, thank you for talking to me like that. My Dad was an alcoholic and he never disciplined me. I needed to hear that!"

He did not beat her again and they lived happily ever after. I learned that in the Middle East, the fear of corporal punishment could be a deterrent!

Section II

Nazareth-I Early Rains

Chapter 4

THE BEAUTIFUL HOUSE ON THE HILL

The modern city of Nazareth sits in a cove nestled at the top of the mountain range overlooking the Valley of Israel. In Bible times, this fertile plain was called the Valley of Megiddo, or Armageddon. In Jesus time Nazareth was a small village of stone houses built over underground caves, which gave all-weather protection from the heat and cold. A fresh water spring flowed constantly outside the village and was the main water source. Today the spring site is preserved by the Greek Orthodox Church of the Annunciation at "Mary's Well." Local tradition has it that the Angel Gabriel appeared to Mary while she was drawing water at the spring and announced to her the coming birth of Jesus. An ancient icon or painting inside the Byzantine chapel over the spring shows the baby Jesus in her womb. The spring still flows and yields some of the sweetest water in the world.

Down the street, in the center of town, the Roman Catholics, or "Latins" have built the huge Basilica of the Annunciation over the cave home of Mary and Joseph. Elaborate mosaics in the Basilica and courtyard depict various nation's interpretation of the Virgin Mary. Many are gloriously beautiful, but the bas-reliefs of Canada and the USA are the most hideous and grotesque! The modern basilica preserves the cave home of the Holy Family. A space capsule shaped dome covers the open altar where mass is said repeatedly for visiting pilgrims from around the world.

Before the construction of the Basilica of the Annunciation, our beautiful Jerusalem stone house in Nazareth dominated the hill above Mary's Spring.

The Basilica of the Annunciation in Nazareth

The "Baker House," as it was called, was the first house in Nazareth to have built-in electricity. Dr. Dwight Baker, who pioneered the revival of Baptist work in Galilee after the 1948 war, built the house as a mission center. He copied the curved arches of the veranda from those of Druze homes in neighboring Shefrarm, a seat of the Sanhedrin in New Testament time. The house was enormous but built practically without cost due to sale of land around it to select neighbors.

You approach it from the driveway up a winding stone stairway to the second floor, which was the living quarters. To the left of the entrance was a large meeting-dining room with a picture window overlooking a rose garden and a panoramic view of the city of Nazareth in the distance. To the right was the master bedroom with a private bath and shower, with an entrance onto the veranda. Straight in was the living room, which originally had a window into the kitchen for catering. The kitchen, to the left of the house, was large. It had a doublewide window looking out upon the back yard with a patio and trees lining the property. When we moved in there was a small patch of grass we called the "Betty Smith" memorial grass. Betty and Jim Smith, who preceded us in the house, kept the grass and the rose garden meticulous and won numerous Rotary Club gardening awards. An ancient stone ballistic ball, probably from Crusader times, sat beside the stone bench in the grassy area, offering an ideal spot for contemplation or intimate conversation with a friend. A basketball backboard stood at the center of a large play area for the kids. There were three bedrooms at the back of the house. One had a sink used by a live-in maid. Each of our children had their own dedicated bedroom with a secret closet space for hiding out. Downstairs through a long stairway in the kitchen was a large meeting hall with an office and a bedroom for guests. A shower bath and storeroom made the area livable, and served as a bomb shelter during several wars. The house was a unique structure, built of solid, reinforced concrete and covered with yellow limestone. A tunnel inside the downstairs wall drained off most of the water from the mountainside during the winter and served as a secret place for the children to hide in the summertime. The high ceilings, tile floors and stone structure kept the house cool in the summer, but made it a virtual freezer in the winter. The first few winters we rolled kerosene heaters around from room to room, but later added propane gas, which meant we had to be careful to vent the rooms. We bundled up in long underwear and wore two pairs of socks. Nazareth was 1000 feet in elevation. The weather could be chilly and occasionally snow!

The reason I dwell on the house is the total contrast to what I expected when I went overseas to serve as a missionary! I grew up in modest homes in the USA and even slept on the back porch of a log cabin in "Possum Walk Valley" outside of Charlotte during my high school years. When you think about living in the Middle East you think of sand dunes and tents, but here I was living in a mansion overlooking the city of Nazareth on a beautiful pine-forested mountainside. The Lord fulfilled one of my life's longings by giving me a home in the mountains! That house, though pretentious to some, served as a safe haven for me to return to after many Galilee wanderings. It was the scene of some of the most dramatic experiences in my life during the 26 years we were honored to live in Nazareth.

The beautiful house on the hill in Nazareth

Our coming to Nazareth was by design, not by accident. The Bakers had moved to Haifa where he opened the Christian Service Training Center (CSTC). We studied our first year of Arabic with Mr. Abbasi at the CSTC building when we lived in Haifa in 1965. The Thornes, who came over on the Queen Anna Maria with us, were studying Hebrew at Ulpan Akiva in Netanya. We were both uncomfortable working alone in Nazareth. Neither of us felt we could carry on all the work the Bakers and Smiths had started in Nazareth and the Galilee villages. The Smiths scheduled furlough in the USA in 1966-67. The Lytles and the Fields were also only a year in the country. We all decided to meet in Netanya one evening in the spring of 1966 and seek the Lord's will for our future placement. You might think that the big decision in mission work is when you 'receive the call.' It does not end there. It only begins. The bigger decisions often come when you are on the field.

After a time of discussion and fellowship, someone stuffed a pillow in my face to stop me from talking and we started to pray to seek God's will for our futures. In the end, the Thornes felt led to live in Nazareth and take over the school ministry on one condition; that the Registers would live in the 'big house!' We would take the village work. We moved into the big house in the summer and the Thornes moved into a rented home near Mary's Well and supervised the construction of a new home designed by the Smiths next door to our home. We used to say in jest that the house was the 'cross-eyed bear' and that we 'were suffering for Jesus.' We agreed with the locals to accept the house graciously as part of God's bounty. It served us well, and played a strategic role in the future of Baptist and Evangelical work in Galilee.

Ears Opened-Picking Up Fruit

We began our Arabic studies at Hartford Seminary in 1964. Dr. Douglas taught us the classical grammar from a book whose print was so small it made our eyes bug out! I determined from that experience that if I ever designed an Arabic language book, it would have large print. At least our introduction to classical Arabic got us used to the sounds and structure of the language. My introduction to Hebrew grammar from Southeastern seminary helped a bit, but the script is entirely different. We had a language laboratory at Hartford that gave us the opportunity to listen to tapes. George Khoury, a native Arabic speaker from Bethlehem, helped us practice our pronunciation. Combined with the study of the life of Muhammad, the History of Islam and linguistics, and Jewish life and forms, we had an excellent introduction to the language and culture before we ever landed in Haifa in July of 1965.

However, our ears were not tuned to the dialect of Arabic in Galilee. Colloquial Arabic is almost like a different language from Classical Arabic. Each town and section of the country has its own dialect. Therefore, we could read Arabic, since the script is the same, but it took some time to pronounce the words, and to understand what the people of Galilee were saying. As Dwight Baker told me, "Massage your ears!" I forced myself to listen to Arabic on the radio, and to sing hymns in Arabic in church. I could read the script, but could only understand a few words. I learned later that hymns are written in poetical classical Arabic and are a challenge. Some hymns are translated directly from English. It is the same with the Bible. The familiarity with the English text helps in guessing the meaning in Arabic. When we did try to speak Arabic, the local people knew we were using classical Arabic, rather than the normal colloquial or street Arabic of everyday life. They admired us for trying, but it did not help our self-image.

I began to dry up spiritually. For about a year and a half I restricted my input of the Bible and worship to what I could get in Arabic. Then one Thursday night, when the Lord knew I had about reached the breaking point, I was sitting in the Nazareth Baptist Church listening to Pastor Sakhnini hold forth from the Scriptures. My ears opened. He was teaching from Acts 1:8,

> "But you will receive power when the Holy Spirit has come upon you; and you will be witnesses to Me in Jerusalem, and in all Judea and Samaria, and to the end of the earth."

I was overwhelmed. For the first time in two and a half years, I understood God's word in Arabic. It was a Holy Spirit miracle! I ran out of church weeping. From that time on, I began feeding spiritually in the Arabic language. I learned later that this experience of the ears opening was a common one for missionaries like Hudson Taylor who learned Chinese. My life has not been the same since. Ahead of me was a vast harvest field in Galilee and the Arab world.

I determined after moving to Nazareth in the summer of 1966 not to involve myself in the politics and activities of the Nazareth Baptist Church and School. One very enterprising senior teacher at the school led a teacher's strike against Jim Smith when he was treasurer of the BCI. Jim was unable to raise the teacher's salaries. There was constant rivalry between the school leadership and the pastor of the Nazareth Baptist Church located on the same compound. I was already orientated toward village work since I grew up in the suburbs or country back in the Carolinas. I wanted to practice my Arabic and that was almost impossible in Nazareth where all the locals wanted to practice their English on me! Arabs are very impatient with foreigners who cannot pronounce Arabic well. Therefore, I set my eyes on strengthening the work in Cana, Turan, and Rama.

Cana of Galilee, or *Kefr Kana* in Arabic, is about 5 miles from Nazareth to the east on the road down to Tiberias and the Sea of Galilee. From our house, you wind up the hill past the Kashli or police headquarters. At the top, you get a panoramic view of northern Galilee and Mount Hermon on a clear day. Then you wind down through hairpin curves past the village of Rene, named after a Crusader general. Up another hill, you pass Meshed, biblical Japh Hepher, and hometown of the Prophet Jonah. You can stop on the downhill run to Cana at a wide place in the road and get a view of the picturesque village. It is probably not the site of the New Testament Cana of Galilee. It is said that the original site, Tel Kana is about 4 miles north in the Netofa Valley. It moved to the new site since the valley site is unreachable in the winter because of flooding.

Baptists had a small chapel with living quarters upstairs in Cana on the highway passing the village. Dr. Baker built the chapel with funds donated by a widow from the Bottom family in R.G. Lee's church in Memphis, Tennessee. Monsour Insair, a lay leader from Yaffa of Nazareth, directed the work in Cana with his family. Monsour assisted Kate Ellen Gruver, one of the pioneer woman missionaries who began the George W. Truett Orphanage in Nazareth for children abandoned in the fighting in 1948. Monsour, like Isam Abbasi, lost his opportunity for an education due to the war. He grew up in a village destroyed in the fighting near Majdal, west of Nazareth. Despite this difficult beginning, Monsour combined his building skills with a love for the young people of the villages of Galilee. He married Maryam from the village of Kefr Yasif, the hometown of Josephus, the Jewish historian. Monsour had little education, but he spoke Arabic a lot better than I did at that point. Over the objections of the more educated leaders in Nazareth, I gave Monsour the opportunity to preach in the worship services in Cana. The proud young people chided him for his poor grammar, but he overcame it with love and determination. We started weekly Bible studies and before long, a group of young men asked for baptism. To my surprise, the pastor and deacons of the Nazareth Baptist Church objected! I remember one rather steamy meeting at Pastor Sakhnini's home when they asked, "Under whose authority do you baptize these young men?"

I replied, "Pritchard Memorial Baptist Church of Charlotte, North Carolina!"

The impasse was resolved by the Nazareth church appointing Deacon George Laty to come to Cana to examine the candidates. George had an evangelist's heart and readily approved them. Looking back, I can see that the Nazareth church had nurtured the little chapel in Cana for several years before I arrived. However, strong Plymouth Brethren influence led to reluctance to baptize believers until they proved worthy. I found people all over Galilee wanting to follow the Lord in believer's baptism. It was like picking up fruit that had fallen from the tree.

Ray baptizing new believer in Sea of Galilee, c. 1966

Turan is the next village from Cana on the way down to the Sea of Galilee. Notice, I say 'down,' since Nazareth is 1000 feet above sea level and the Sea of Galilee is about 700 feet below sea level. Once you have been to the Holy Land these little topological facts jump out of the Scriptures and lend authenticity to the Bible. For instance, in John 2, after the wedding feast in Cana, Jesus went 'down' to Capernaum, which is at the northern end of the Sea of Galilee. One way you know that the so-called "Gospel of Barnabas" is a false gospel is that it has Jesus and his disciples taking a boat from the Sea of Galilee and getting out in Nazareth which is 1700 feet higher up! Whoever wrote this supposed gospel never took a tour of the Holy Land!

On the way, you pass the wheat fields of Turan, where according to tradition; Jesus' disciples plucked grain on the Sabbath and earned the criticism of the Pharisees. Earlier in the 1900's Shukri Musa Bishuti, the founding pastor of the Nazareth Baptist Church used to ride a horse or donkey to lead Bible studies in Turan. He and his predecessors found open ears and hearts among the Saad family who were members of the Greek Orthodox Church. Their elderly priest died and there was no replacement. Abu Fahim Saad wanted one his sons to fill that role. He opened his home for the Baptists to teach the Bible. Eventually he offered to sell them the land next door to build a Baptist Center. Monsour Insair, I, and occasionally a deacon from the Nazareth Baptist Church would drive to Turan every Saturday afternoon and hold Sunday school and worship services, or a Bible study at Abu Fahim's house. Abu Fahim was famous for his Arabic coffee which he served in little thimble sized cups from a brass coffee pot or *breek* after it had been boiled down in two other larger pots. One taste of Abu Fahim's *ahwey sada* (bitter coffee nectar) and you could stay awake through any sermon! It was the best coffee in Galilee.

Ray in Turan with Abu Fahim pouring his famous coffee (July, 1994)

One day in 1966, I was walking through Turan with Abu Fahim and his youngest son, Philip. Philip was a student at the Nazareth Baptist School. Abu Fahim mentioned again his dream of one of his sons becoming the village priest. Philip said to his father, "My dear father I respect your wish. I want to be baptized as a Baptist, like the Bible says!"

Though Abu Fahim was disappointed, he did not discourage his son in taking this step. He was the first person I baptized in my Galilee wanderings. He later studied at Mid America Baptist Seminary and became the pastor of the Haifa Baptist Church. His older brothers and sisters, though not all Baptists, were active supporters of the ministry in Turan village.

I kept practicing my Arabic under the patient tutoring of Mr. Abassi and finally felt it was time to preach in the local language. Mr. Abassi translated and taped the sermon. I memorized it. Pastor Sakhnini graciously allowed me to preach my first sermon in Arabic at the Nazareth Baptist Church. In it I challenged the local people to **live in the villages**. After the service, Suheil Ramadan, the chairman of deacons, visited me in my home.

He told me, "Though I appreciate your efforts in trying to learn Arabic and doing the work in the villages, I believe that we local people can do it better! I feel called to go out and live in a village and preach the Gospel. I only want one thing from you. Help me get seminary training."

The Lord convicted Suheil through a work accident when he nearly lost his arm after a plate of glass broke and cut him severely. Suheil asked his father's permission to leave the family business. He moved to Ruschlikon Baptist Seminary near Zurich, Switzerland and earned his Diploma in Theology. He and his wife, Fida, and their growing children returned to Nazareth after Seminary and moved to Turan to lead the work of the Baptist Center. He supported himself for many years from his work in the glass shop in the Nazareth market, becoming our second local 'tentmaker' missionary. It was quite a while before Pastor Sakhnini dared to let me preach again in his church! I had to get my Arabic sermon practice outside of Nazareth.

I got the idea of placing a bell in each village center to alert the people when we were holding meetings. Somehow, I found a company in the United States that still made farm bells. Therefore, I ordered several bells for the growing centers in Galilee.

Almost from the start of our Galilee wanderings, I served the Association of Baptist churches in Israel as their "Field Representative." The ABC formed shortly after we arrived in Israel in 1966 to encourage the growth of the Baptist centers and churches and to represent the national believers in the United Christian Council, the UCCI, before the Israeli government. Dr. Joseph Alkahe, a lawyer and the Jewish messianic pastor of the

Baptist Village Congregation was the ABC's first chairperson. Vera Stoehr, another Jewish messianic believer from the Narkis Street Congregation in Jerusalem, served as the Secretary. The Nazareth Baptist Church and its pastor, Rev. Fuad Sakhnini, along with deacons Fuad Haddad, George Laty and Suheil Ramadan played an important role in the ABC. Therefore, from the beginning, the ABC was a joint venture of both Jewish and Arab believers in the country. My senior BCI partners, Dr. Robert "Bob" Lindsey, Dr. Dwight Baker, Rev. James "Jim" Smith, and Rev. Milton Murphey played leading roles from the expatriate side. I was 'new man on the block' and all of these great men and their wives encouraged me during my formative years. As I made the rounds between the dozen small Baptist churches and centers of Galilee and the rest of the country, I had a chance to repeat the Arabic sermons that Mr. Abbasi helped me record and memorize. In later years, the ABC became more of a concentration of Arabic speaking churches and the Hebrew-speaking congregations merged into the growing Messianic Jewish movement.

Ray presenting bell to Monsour Nseir in Cana, c1969

While at Southeastern and Hartford Seminaries, the church growth teachings of Roland Allen attracted me. I read and absorbed his classic book, *Missionary Methods: St. Paul's or Ours?* (Eerdmans, 1927, 1960) and its sequel, *The Spontaneous Expansion of the Church*, (Eerdmans, 1962). Donald McGavran's, *Understanding Church Growth*, (Eerdmans, 1970) enthralled me. I bored the rest of the BCI by handing out a mimeographed summary of McGavran's book. It synchronized with the tribal and clan social structure of the Galilee Arab villages.

Through the years, I compiled the statistical report of the ABC to show the growth of the churches and their increased financial giving. There was always a tension between the financial support given to institutions and to church development. It all came to a head when the FMB, now the IMB, finally instituted the New Directions in the late 90's and left the development of churches solely to the responsibility of the local people. It resulted in most of the local pastors having to become bi-vocational to support their families. While I was in the position of Field Representative, I divided my tithe up between the churches and centers as a motivation for the local people to also give and share the responsibility. In addition, it lessened the financial impact when I went on stateside assignment and finally retired.

One of the real rewards is seeing young people we trained and partnered with now taking leadership in the churches and institutions around the country. In my heart, the desire was to see a church planted in every one of those hundreds of villages from the mountain border of Lebanon down to the Plains of the Jezreel Valley. *Galilee Wanderings* describes a partial fulfillment of that vision.

The site of many intimate encounters with the Lord took place in front of the picture window in the beautiful house on the hill. There, I looked out over the city of Nazareth and to the

Valley of Megiddo, or Armageddon. Periodically in those private times, the emotions of who I was and where I was, overwhelmed me. I simply poured out my heart to the Lord with profuse tears. The release and catharsis were healing. These experiences were only the prelude to a cathedral event to take place in the not too distant future.

Hamdy and Ray in the Netofa Valley

Chapter 5

My Friend Hamdy, "Woodwood" and the BCCI

Every Friday morning during my 26 years in Nazareth, my doorbell rang. It was Hamdy (name changed for security). Hamdy was a Muslim farmer from the Betof Valley, or *Netofa* in Hebrew. When I arrived in Nazareth in 1966, Bevin Woodhead, the engineer at the EMMS (Edinburg Medical Missionary Society) Hospital, or "Nazareth Hospital" drove me out to Hamdy's remote village for a visit. We went in the summer since the dirt path was impassable during the winter rains. The village of Rumaneh was a Roman outpost in biblical times that guarded the Netofa valley. Hamdy and his family and relatives visited the Nazareth Hospital for medical treatment, or to give birth to their children. Bevin, formerly of the Red Sea Team, befriended Hamdy and gave or sold him a Bible. Hamdy claimed that he dreamed about Jesus as a boy. He called Jesus "the Smiling One." He said that he heard angels singing in heaven, "Glory to God in the highest and peace and good will to men on earth." When he got the Bible, he found this verse in Luke 2:14. He knew then the dream was from the Lord. He consulted his father and he told him, "Listen to the missionaries. They are telling you the truth."

He went back to Bevin to inquire. Bevin told him, "When you want to poison a dog, you take a piece of juicy, red meat and put poison in it. The dog gobbles it up and dies. The religion you are following now is like that poison meat. You need the pure meat of the Word!" Hamdy showed up at my door every Friday morning for years to get that pure meat.

Bevin Woodhead, or "Woodwood" as Hamdy called him, felt the call to come to the Holy Land when he served with the Red Sea Team among the Donegal Tribe in Eritrea. He knew God was calling him to witness to the Jewish people. He found himself serving as engineer at the Nazareth Hospital working with the Arabs. As soon as I arrived in Nazareth, he took me under wing and introduced me to all his Arab friends in the Galilee villages. I remember one visit to Umm al-Fahim, a large Arab town just past Tel Megiddo. We were visiting a family who frequented the Nazareth Hospital. We read from Isaiah 53 and the grown Arab men started crying. They asked, "Who was this that was wounded for our transgressions and bruised for our iniquities?" We explained that it was Jesus. I long to see some of these men in eternity.

Bevin began to relinquish the work in the Arab villages to me. The Nazareth Hospital directors were concerned when he told them he felt led now to go the Jewish people. I believe they came to a gentlemen's agreement. They could not financially support such an endeavor, but they would not oppose it. Bevin went out and bought himself a Vespa motor scooter. He rode it to the surrounding Jewish towns and kibbutzim (collective farming communities) to give out literature and witness to the Jews. I remember he spent one night in the lockup in Migdal Ha-Emek for his endeavors. Bevin remained an inspiration to me all the years I knew him, and his home was always welcoming. He raised a son who became a genius engineer like himself and another who became an archeologist.

Hamdy became my door opener to multiple Arab Muslim villages all over Galilee, and into the West Bank of Jordan after the 1967 War. He had sisters and children married in several villages we visited regularly. He was related to the prominent Badran family in the northern West Bank of Jordan. One of their relatives was Mudir Badran, the late prime minister of Jordan. Though a klutzy, seemingly insignificant farm boy, Hamdy introduced me to Arab Muslims all the way from the Negev in the South to Metulla in the North. He used to coach me before visits and debrief me after visits about how people reacted to my presentations. We did not always agree on theology, but he and his family remain trusted friends until this day. It was as Jesus said, "Everyone who left houses or brothers or sisters or father or mother or wife or children or lands, for My name's sake, shall receive a hundredfold and inherit everlasting life." (Matthew 19:29 NKJV) I found through Hamdy and those like him, Muslims who became trusted friends for life.

Hamdy spent some of his winters with his father in a camp in the olive groves near the Sea of Galilee. Like many farmers from times past, they spent the winters in the sub-tropical weather of the Sea of Galilee 630 feet below sea level. They spent summers in the hills near Nazareth about 1000 feet above sea level. A drive down to the Sea is a trip through Bible history, down from Nazareth, through Cana of Galilee; past Turan with its wheat fields ripe unto harvest, then on down past an ancient site, which is a possible location of the Mount of Beatitudes, then to the panoramic overlook above the Sea of Galilee. You wind down through the streets of Tiberias with its black volcanic stone buildings and fortress, and level out at the shores of the Sea, now cluttered with fish restaurants, spas and hotels. Turning north, you pass the beautiful YMCA or "Dr. Hart" with its towering eucalyptus trees overlooking the water, then past the Church of Scotland cemetery on the mountainside. At Magdela, the traditional home of Mary Magdalene you pull off to an overlook of the northern portion of the Sea. Just past Magdela, there is a large ruins of an early Byzantine church. Then you turn left up the highway to northern central Galilee. Right there you take an immediate left into the Valley of the Doves, or *wadi hamaam* in Arabic. This hidden, off the path site, is the location of the disastrous battle where Saladin defeated the Crusaders in 1187 in the battle of Hattin. There in the shadow of the towering cliffs and under the olive trees I spent many an afternoon and evening sipping coffee, eating dates and talking with Hamdy, his father and their Bedouin friends from the nearby town of Wadi Hamam. What a place to start out my Galilee wanderings!

Just down the road from Magdala and around the northern shore of the Sea, you pass Kibbutz Ginnasor where they discovered the famous "Jesus boat" buried in the mud when a draught caused the Sea to recede. Then you come up on the traditional Mount of Beatitudes where Mussolini built a stylish chapel where Italian nuns still host guests. Down to the right, you run into *Kirya Deshe* the traditional site of the multiplication of the loaves and fishes. On past, you circle the little cove where Jesus pushed out in the boat to teach the multitudes. Then you come to Capernaum, a site restored by Catholic archaeologists. The ancient Synagogue, perhaps the one Jesus taught in, has been partially restored, as well as the house of Peter's mother-in-law. We had many a baptism and picnic under the shade of the trees beside the parking lot at Capernaum.

I learned from Hamdy that working with Muslims is a 'give and take' experience. He used me to get rides to the villages to see his relatives and I used him to make contacts all over Galilee.

Some of these I went back to on my own, or with another trusted friend. I knew also that he was very cautious person, who wanted to stay alive. His wife's family was very opposed to his traveling around with me, but we accepted that and always acted graciously to them. Her brother was the mayor or *mukhtar* of the village. Though I knew he did not love me, he did respect me. Years later, Campus Crusade produced the JESUS FILM and translated it into Arabic. We set up our 16-millimeter projector in the village square and showed the entire film on the side of the mayor's house. I remember women crying when they viewed Jesus scourged and crucified in the film. Hamdy's village became the laboratory for many of my experiments in sharing the Gospel with Muslims. (It was not my laboratory alone. Someone watched us.)

Years later, I befriended the Chief of Internal Security (*Shin Bet*) in Nazareth. He hung out at a little coffee shop in the town center. His daughter sent her children to our kindergarten at Baptist House in Jerusalem. He was a tall, redheaded Polish Jew who farmed in the Valley of Israel. We conversed in Arabic, he with a Polish accent and I with my Southern American English. I finally figured out that he was using Hamdy's village as a training ground for his new agents! I remembered seeing cars with young men leaving the village as I entered several times. He knew everything I was doing. When passing each other down town he would ask me, "How is business?"

I would answer, "Great!"

One day, years later in the early 1980's, I was visiting Hamdy in preparation for the visit of my cousin, Sarah Steagall, from Raleigh, NC. Sarah typed my Doctor of Ministry (DMin) report on an IBM Selectric typewriter with no mistakes! She knew Senator Jesse Helms in Raleigh. Hamdy told me he had a problem. Shin Bet trainees coaxed his younger, naïve brother into taking part in a tire burning protest on the road leading into the village. The police promptly locked him up for interrogation. He said, "How am I going to entertain your cousin and my brother is in jail?"

I went immediately to my Polish friend and told him, "We have a problem."

"What is it?" he asked.

I told him, "My cousin who is friend of Jesse Helms, leader of the House Foreign Appropriations Committee, is coming to visit tomorrow. You have locked up the brother of my friend Hamdy on false pretenses. How am I going to explain this to my cousin?"

Hamdy's brother was out of jail to greet my cousin the next day!

Hamdy's Friday visits continued year after year. I decided it was time to call a halt or see results. We started studying Fuad Accad's "*Seven Muslim Christian Principles*," which is now explained in his book, *Building Bridges* (BB). Fuad worked with the Navigators in Beirut. He put together the plan of salvation using verses from the Bible and from the Quran. We divided the seven in half and studied half a lesson every time for over fourteen weeks. Hamdy showed up at the door every Friday morning. We finally got to the last lesson where it said,

"I _____ hereby declare my faith in Jesus Christ as my Lord and Savior."

Hamdy read in Arabic, "I so and so hereby declare my faith in Jesus Christ as my Lord and Savior."

I told him, "You are supposed to say, 'I Hamdy hereby declare my faith in Jesus Christ as my Lord and Savior!"

Hamdy said, "I did that years ago!"

Duh! I was so dense I did not understand why this Muslim was coming to me on Friday morning rather than going to the mosque to pray! He was coming to me to study the Bible instead of the Quran. He was following the call of the "Smiling One" in heaven.

The same subtlety became apparent when two young men, Bedouin from the Negev desert, visited me years later in Nazareth. They were graduates of our Baptist Village industrial school where I spoke for their graduation. They came to ask my advice for a friend of theirs who wanted to become a believer in Jesus. We sat and talked for an hour or so, before they drank coffee and left. Later, I woke up to the fact that they were talking about themselves!

Interacting with Muslim friends in Arabic and other expatriates who had a similar calling enlivened me, and kept me on the growing edge intellectually, spiritually and emotionally. That is what I came to the Holy Land to do. It did test my faith from time to time, but nothing like having to cope with relations and politics in our local mission.

The Foreign Mission Board (now the IMB) of the Southern Baptist Convention (SBC) commissions missionaries with the blessing of the local churches to spread the Gospel around the world. They form local missions or conventions in the countries overseas to administer their work under the policies of the SBC. That means that you relate not just to the nationals of your host country but to your fellow missionaries who come from many of the 50 states of our great USA. You relate to two or more cultures overseas; your host culture and to the American culture of your mission. Woe to the young missionary who bonds too closely to the local culture, and forgets diplomatic relations with his own peers in the mission! My years at Southeastern Seminary and the year at Hartford Seminary prepared me to adapt to the Middle

East cultures and languages, but did little to prepare me for the challenges of cross-culture work with other missionaries from SC, NC, GA, TN, VA, TX, IN, OH, OK, NM, CA, and parts unknown. Do not get me wrong. They are all wonderful, highly motivated people, and when the crunch comes, they are the family of God who gather around you when a parent dies, a child goes astray, or there is a sudden war. I will go my grave in humble appreciation for all the wonderful co-workers who shared the burden of the lost with me in the Middle East.

But, and it is a big BUT, when it comes to deciding what each other should be doing in their work in a foreign country, it is another matter. Particularly when all decisions about goals, objectives, action plans, and budgeting require approval by all your fellow missionaries and their wives. I can remember counting votes on the way to annual meetings to determine if the BCI would fund my work for another year, or opening a new center. Bob Fields, from the hills of Kentucky, used to call it **"borrowing an axe!"** indicating the negative feelings one has going into an imagined battle. Our group, the BCI, used to meet at least once a month. Add all the committee meetings, and it could be once a week. Think about all the traveling, deliberations and emotional energy spent doing all this activity. One wondered what time was left to do the work you were called to do, as well as raise a family!

Nasrallah Benna, who replaced Abu George Shurrosh as facilities manager at the Nazareth Baptist Schools used to say, when we tried to tell him that there was no money for a project, "Ask the BCCI!"

I can remember us arguing in the "BCCI" about whether we should pay for curtains in the living room windows in our homes, or hot water tanks, and whether we should have air conditioners in our cars! The government solved the problem when they require all new cars to have air conditioning. They found it cut down on accidents in the stifling heat of the area.

The struggle over money and church planting policy was not all bad. No one stopped me from going out and sharing the Gospel or walking through open doors in opening new work as long as I did not ask for funds! Yaffa of Nazareth, just west of Nazareth, was one of those open doors. Yaffa, as I may have mentioned before, was a town settled by Christian and Muslim Arab refugees from the town of Majdal and other surrounding villages. The Iraqi army occupied the Majdal area in the 1948 war. When the Jewish army took the land back, new Jewish immigrants displaced the Arabs who gave the Iraqis shelter under duress. Monsour Insair's sister, Hanna and her mother invited us to start meetings in their home in Yaffa. Hanna was one of the first graduates of the Nazareth Baptist School and secretary of the Local Council in Yaffa, meaning she represented the Israeli government in the town. Knowing the difficulty I would have receiving any new funding from the BCI I agreed on one condition, that we would take up an offering starting from the second meeting! This was difficult since the Arab custom is to offer refreshments and coffee to all visitors. I explained to the family that if we met on a regular basis the meeting or "center" would need to pay for the refreshments, the rent, and open a building fund for the future. I mentioned this in our May 23, 1967 newsletter:

> "Also we have begun new meetings in Yaffa of Nazareth at the request of a Baptist family in this suburb of Nazareth. Many of those who attend are refugees from villages destroyed in the Arab-Jewish conflict of 1948. It is a thrill to see people reading the Bible and singing hymns for the first time. We have taken an offering since the second meeting to meet expenses. The people have responded generously despite a rather depressed economic situation. We know you will want to pray for this new work."

I remember going out in the garden of Stella Carmel Conference Center where we were holding our annual mission meeting in May of 1967 and weeping. Some pet project, probably in Rama, failed to win the necessary votes, and I had "had it" with the BCCI.

Marty Murphy came out, sat down beside me and motherly said, "Ray, I know this is hard on you now. The Lord is telling me this is not the end of the story. Something is about to happen that is going to change everything." June 10, 1967 was about to happen!

Chapter 6

THE 1967 WAR

(Changes on the Ground)

My Arabic improved by 1967 to the point I understood the Arabic radio broadcasts. Dwight Baker encouraged me to 'massage' my ears by listening only to Arabic and sing only in Arabic. One night we were riding back from a meeting at Baptist Village when he turned on the BBC in Arabic and I admired that he could understand it. The Arabic radio stations were beginning to play martial music. Jamal Abdul Nasser, president of Egypt and leader of the Arab world challenged Israel by closing the Straits of Tiran. I could hear the word, *harb*, Arabic for "war" often. The Israelis were saying *milhama* (Hebrew for 'war') and calling up the reserves. Our first hint that things were serious was when the police showed up at our door demanding the shotgun that Jim Smith gave us for safekeeping when he left on furlough. I hid it downstairs in the storeroom high on a shelf under double lock and key. The police officer had a list of everyone in town who had a weapon. He collected them all. I learned that this was a practice in the Middle East to prevent rebellion in time of war.

On that Monday morning in early June, we drove down from Nazareth to Baptist Village for our monthly BCI meeting. On the way, we noticed people doing weird things. They were running out in the highway stopping cars. We learned from a desperate woman who flagged us down that the government had ordered all the hospitals evacuated to make room for the anticipated wounded they were expecting. **When we got to BV, we discovered we were at war.** Israel attacked the air bases of the surrounding Arab countries at breakfast time and in a few minutes destroyed their combined air forces. Syria, Jordan and Egypt declared war. Syria started shelling Tiberias from the Golan Heights above the Sea of Galilee. Jordan shelled Jewish West Jerusalem, and Egypt attacked the Negev.

We Americans gathered upstairs in the Field's living room at Baptist Village and just started the meeting about 10:00 AM. Our children played together outside. All of a sudden, we heard a low flying jet and machine gun fire over our heads. Rata-tat-tat. Then a huge explosion! Boom!

Our children related that they looked up and all they could see was fire coming at them. A Jordanian Hunter jet slipped across the border and attacked a secret airbase next to Baptist Village. They blew up a transport plane with Israeli jets right behind them. (Some of the MK's and journeymen rescued the wounded pilot who parachuted into the BV orange grove). The BV staff recently dug a bomb shelter under the building. We ran so fast down to the steps that I left my shoes upstairs!

I thought, "Mama, why did I leave you and come to this crazy country?"

I went through two years of the Navy and never faced battle except for another Navy ship sideswiping us. We stayed in that dirt bomb shelter all day listening to the news broadcasts on the radio. We prayed for Frank and Marge Hooper who were pinned down by the shelling in West Jerusalem. The Home Kids, from the George W. Truett Orphanage, who were babysitting, played games with our children. Finally, as dark approached, we decided with Dale and Anita Thorne to try to get back to Nazareth.

We painted our headlights black leaving one slit for light, followed each other and decided to take the northern Yokneam pass through the mountains since the Megiddo pass road was too close to the border. When we turned into the pass, we were amazed at the hundreds of Israeli tanks lining the hills. Arriving back in Nazareth, we hurriedly cleaned out the basement storeroom we converted into a makeshift bomb shelter. The Arab forces were bombarding the Jordan and Israel valleys. We could feel the concussion of the shells as they hit. Then, as the night progressed, the shelling moved away into the hills and we knew the Israeli forces were pushing back.

Just before the war broke out a Jewish doctor at the Sharm Menashe Mental Hospital called us and asked if his wife could come and stay with us during the war. He feared for her safety so close to the border and knew she would be safe among the Christian Arabs of Nazareth. It turns out she was the daughter of a South African pastor. When she married her Jewish husband, she renounced the Lord. She explained to us that as the years passed she missed the faith of her childhood. One day she asked Jesus to prove he was alive by simply giving her five minutes of his presence. She explained that one night she awoke to a warm presence in her room. She saw Jesus standing at the foot of her bed. She basked in his love and warmth. Then he turned to walk out the door. She cried out, "Lord, don't leave me!"

He turned to her and said, "You only asked for five minutes. I either stay forever or not at all."

She said, "Lord, please stay forever!"

She started praying for her Jewish husband who began to open his heart to Jesus before they returned to South Africa.

In six days, it was all over and the situation on the ground changed. Israel now controlled all of the Golan Heights of Syria past Kuneitra, the entire West Bank of Jordan including East

Jerusalem, the Old City and the entire Sinai Peninsula of Egypt. The FMB asked Norman Lytle in Jerusalem to coordinate relief activities for the Arab churches now under Israeli control. He asked me to assist since I knew some Arabic by then. The streets of East Jerusalem had the smell of death, particularly across from the American Consulate where Jordanian soldiers had fallen in defense of the Old City. Their helmets were stacked in a make-shift memorial. We met with the members of the East Jerusalem Baptist Church who were then meeting downstairs next to the Baptist Bookstore on Rashid Street. I visited the bookstore only a few weeks before at Easter and met with Bill Hern, veteran SBC missionary to Jordan and Egypt. He later played a major role in my Doctor of Ministry degree. Bill purchased a property, which later became the location of the East Jerusalem Baptist Church and the BCI later assisted in getting legal title to it.

Traveling through the West Bank, we noticed army boots strewn next to burnt-out Jordanian tanks. We learned from the local residents that the tank crews fled when the Israeli planes flew over. They abandoned their tanks and took their shoes off. Then many went home and dressed in their pajamas, hoping they would not be discovered as soldiers. I met several such soldiers when visiting in Arab homes in the West Bank.

Rose Mary and I visited the Hooper's in West Jerusalem shortly after the war. They took us down to their basement they used as a bomb shelter. As they huddled together against one wall a shell burst in their yard. Shrapnel broke through the base-ment window and ricocheted around the room over their heads! God spared them from being our first casualties, but their lives were never the same afterwards.

When the Bakers left for furlough, I traveled with Ibrahim Siman who edited the Baptist sponsored *al-Jama'ah* Arabic magazine. We visited several West Bank biblical sites and towns to gather information for feature articles. One prominent person we met was Basam Shak'ah, the mayor of Ramallah. Basam met Baptists while studying in the States and was very friendly to us. He drove us around and showed us where he cleaned out refugee camps and settled the Palestinians in new homes. He despised the refugee camps. He said the Arab politicians used them as a political football. Later a Jewish terrorist group set a bomb in his car and blew his legs off. We also met the Mayor of Nablus from the Masri family. One of their relatives was later to play a role in my Doctor of Ministry project in the USA.

The 1967 War radically changed our Arabic speaking churches. Now, they were able to visit their kin and fellow believers in the Arab churches in the West Bank and Gaza. They imported the inspirational Arab music from Jordan. Our churches experienced revival through conferences at the Hope School in Bet Jala, next to Bethlehem. The church in Gaza could now attend conferences in the West Bank and Galilee. The leaders of the Galilee churches could now visit their brothers and sisters in Gaza. It was like a family reunion.

The war changed the lives of many of our colleagues who worked in the Middle East. Jim and Betty Smith were on furlough in the USA. They were returning to Israel with plans to move into the new house being built next to our house in Nazareth. When the war changed the situation on the ground, Dr. J.D Hughey, the Area Director of Europe and the Middle East toured to assess the situation. Ed Nicholas, the Chaplain at the Gaza Baptist Hospital needed to leave on furlough after the war. Dr. Hughey asked me if I would be willing to move to Gaza since I knew some Arabic. I told him that if I left Israel now I would never come back. I was having difficulty with the BCI and needed to stay and work through some issues. He said, "Then the Smiths have to move to Gaza!" Jim and Betty received the word in their hotel room in

New York as they were planning to return to Israel. They were in a state of shock. As it turned out, the BCI allowed them to rent a house in Ashkelon and commute across the border into Gaza on a daily basis. The Thornes moved from their rental into the new home next to ours on Baptist Hill in Nazareth. The Smiths recorded their many experiences in their biography, *In Their Midst*, Interfaith Fellowship in Israel 1955-1989 (ITM).

The opening of Gaza offered the wonderful opportunity to network and fellowship with our colleagues from the FMB. We made many trips down to Gaza to fellowship with the Dorr, McGlamery, Moore, Atkins, Peach, Hodge, and other families as well as the unique single female doctors and nurses. Roberta Dorr, who later moved to Yemen with her family where she authored, **David and Bathseba,** became a major encourager of my future writings. She always cheered me on when I got discouraged, saying, "Oh Ray, you can do it!"

Rev. Ed Nicholas and Ray
Gaza Reading Room, c. 1969

I had the privilege of encouraging the Gaza Baptist Reading Room in the years ahead through some small gifts from my book sales. Unfortunately, the reading room and computer lab became the target of radicals in the years after Israel withdrew from the area.

My opinion of the Arab world changed with the new reality. In Israel, we learned about how the Jews returned to the Holy Land and turned the dessert into blooming, fertile fields. I learned that the Arabs had done the same thing. Driving to Jenin in the West Bank I saw verdant experimental farms. The valleys of Samaria were green and productive. The Jordan valley had irrigation systems. Gaza was full of productive orange groves. Ramallah and areas north of Jerusalem were full of beautiful stone houses and garden restaurants.

Ray with West Bank Leader after 1967

I learned also that there were two main factions in the West Bank. One supported Jordanian rule and was loyal to the Hashemite Kingdom. The other was proud Palestinian nationalists who felt marginalized by the leaders in Amman. Villages and towns divided between these two loyalties. Some welcomed Israeli rule, since at first it appeared that Israel would exact less taxes than Amman! Slowly disenchantment settled in as assassins began taking out any leadership that might vie against future Palestinian rule of the area. There was a period before the return of Arafat when you could travel from Nazareth to Jerusalem and then down to Gaza without stopping for a roadblock. It was one country but it did not last long. I heard Menachem Begin say, "There is a Palestine. Its name is Israel. Any Arab who wants to live in peace with us, *ahlan wa sahlan!*" (Arabic for 'Welcome')

Chapter 7

SHOCK

(A good look at myself)

The contrast between the real world and the imaginary can be shocking. The best seminary preparation is only a distant peek into the reality of the Holy Land. What I could only imagine from the pages of the Bible now became real people and everyday events. Arabs and Jews in the Holy Land are just like Jesus' disciples. They quarrel. They compete for their place in the kingdom. They marry, eat, sleep, give birth, raise families and die. The greatest shock to me was how real it is! What my western worldview considered as fantasy in the Bible now became reality. Road signs in Hebrew and Arabic, the food, the hills and valleys mentioned in the Bible, all become daily experiences. It hits you; **The Bible is a record of real life in a real place, and you are living in it!** What is more shocking, it forces you to take a good look at yourself.

My second shock was being part of a mission or Baptist Convention that represents our church in the Holy Land. They came from all over the USA. Growing up in North Carolina I was member of churches that thought pretty much the same way about most subjects. I went to church partly to get away from conflict at home. Now, in Israel, I was part of a group who were from all over the USA, and each had a different way of doing things. The tensions in the country spilled over into mission meetings. I learned very quickly that the majority of our group who worked in Jewish Israeli areas and in institutions had a different view on budgets and church development than I did as a field evangelist working in the Arab villages of Galilee. We spent an inordinate amount of time and energy on planning strategies and budgets and enlisting support for projects I held dear.

Then, there was my inner conflict as I felt the spirit sucked out of me while adapting to the language and culture of the local people and to the other culture of our BCI group. I began seeing myself in a completely new light and realizing that the spiritual props and scaffolding that held me up in the USA were being removed one by one. I stood naked before myself. My soul was bare. I began to lose that personal feeling of closeness to God that I once had.

I remember telling Rose Mary late one night after a recurring bout of losing my temper, "I am not mad at you. I just do not know if God exists anymore!"

I made a new covenant with the God I no longer knew for certain, whether He existed or cared. I told him, "Lord, if you really exist, I have to start all over again with you from the beginning."

I got a copy of Bob Bratcher's *GOOD NEWS FOR MODERN MAN* and began reading it as if this is the first time I ever read the Bible. *GOOD NEWS* was a down to earth, newspaper style translation of the New Testament. Slowly the pieces began to fit together again. Here it was; the real Holy Land, the real disciples, the real Jesus, as well as the real me. Little did I realize the God I was not sure of was already planning a way of escape!

Tehran

In 1969, The Shah of Iran was progressive and repressive at the same time, another part of the contrasts in the Middle East.

He nationalized the vast mosque properties and exiled Ayatollah Khomeini eventually to France. He allowed USA citizens to come to Iran and open institutions to train his new Mullahs. He sent vast numbers of young people to the USA for university and military training. At the same time, he had a security service second to none in the Eastern world. There were good relations between Iran and Israel. You could fly from Tel Aviv up to Tehran in about three hours.

Southern Baptists, through the FMB placed representatives in Iran to take advantage of the new openness. My future doctoral advisor, George Braswell, was one of these. George taught English to the Shah's mullahs, or young Muslim clergy, at the prestigious Armaghan Institute in Tehran. George, along with others and myself working among the Muslim population in the region, participated in the first Southern Baptist conference on the Muslim culture in Tehran in the 1969. He later wrote, *To Ride a Magic Carpet*, (1977) documenting his experiences. George played a key role in our future work in the Middle East.

Our airliner took off from Tel Aviv and headed northwest out to sea, looped north over Cyrus and climbed east over southeastern Turkey and landed in the elevations of Tehran. The Alborz Mountain of Damavand loomed over 18,900 feet to the north. Tehran is a vast city of modern buildings. The building code requires an enclosed veranda of each home to allow privacy for the women of the house.

The meeting participants were the giants of Southern Baptist work in the Middle East; Bill Hern of Egypt, Paul Smith of Jordan, Dale Thorne of Israel, Jim Ragland of Lebanon and many others. The special feature was the impromptu visit of Virginia Cobb and Nancy Wingo from Beirut. Virginia suffered from terminal cancer and came by to say a final goodbye on her way to the USA. Her sacrifice deeply inspired me. I later had the privilege of meeting her family in Statesboro, Georgia while on furlough. Johnni Johnson, a participant in the conference later wrote the story of Virginia Cobb, *The Gift of Belonging*, (1975) which became a model for our work among the Muslims. Dehquani-Tafti, a former Muslim and bishop of the Episcopal Church in Iran was the keynote speaker of the conference. His memoirs, *The Design of My World*, (London, 1959) share his faith journey. In it he described the church as God's flower garden of indescribable beauty and diversity. His son was martyred in Iran several years later after the Shah was overthrown.

George was the consummate host, reflecting his southern Virginia upbringing. He brought in an Iranian friend who sold us a beautiful Persian rug we brought back in our suitcase. We enjoyed a tour of the University of Tehran, the Shah's palace and crown jewels, and the Tehran market. On our day off, we met Persian families picnicking in an historic park and found them exceptionally friendly.

After the conference, Rose Mary and I took a taxi over the Alborz Mountains to the sea resort of Babolsar. We booked into a local motel for the night. While Rose Mary was in the shower, a knock came on our door. I opened it to find a beautiful, neatly dressed woman standing there.

She said, "Mr. Smith, you called?"

I said, "Just a second, I will ask my wife!"

She said, "Oh, I am sorry; there must have been a mistake."

I watched out our window as she got in her car and drove away. I assume it was customary to provide company for traveling businessmen. Good thing Rose Mary was with me!

We flew down to Isfahan and booked into the Episcopal Church guesthouse. Isfahan is one of the most beautiful cities in the world. The Iranians call it in Farsi, *Isfahan, nisfi jihan* or "Isfahan, half the world." Isfahan's ornate blue tiled mosques defy description. One evening we dined in the Khan where the Persian poets used to recite their verses. We ordered a dish of caviar for only $5.00! We learned from the waiter that John D. Rockefeller used to fly in once a year just to dine there.

Our Persian guide took us through the beautiful mosques and the brass shops the next day. As we were walking along, he remarked, "Your wife is like a Persian rug!"

I acted offended and asked, "What do you mean, calling my wife a Persian rug?"

He said, "Because the older she gets the more beautiful she looks!"

I had to take that as a complement. We saw the women washing their Persian rugs and laying them out to dry on the rocks beside the river. We learned in a rug factory that the weavers always make a deliberate mistake in the pattern, because, "Only God is perfect!"

I reflected on the plane ride home, as we literally coasted down from Tehran to Tel Aviv, how the Lord used the Tehran Conference to revive my calling to the Middle East. I was not alone in the effort. Many others shared my vision of taking the Good News to the Muslim people. God was not through with me yet and he had more surprises in store!

Shortly after returning to Nazareth, word came that one of the BCI couples in Nazareth needed to return for furlough in the USA. Dr. Hughey did not think it would be good for both the Registers and Thornes to leave Nazareth for furlough at the same time. Someone needed to leave a year early. It did not take long for us to decide who would leave first. Four years was long enough for me. We needed a respite. We were packed and out of there so fast, the local Baptists wondered if we had been fired! It was God's timing.

On the way to the airport, we stopped at Sallie and Chandler Lanier's house in Kefar Shmaryahu. I told them I did not think I would be back.

Sallie said, "Ray, you go home and get yourself together and come back. We need you!"

She explained that the older guys in the BCI liked to beat up on the younger guys. They were like a bunch of chickens who ganged up on the wounded one. This was all part of the game. Her pep talk left me open to consider returning.

Chapter 8

PREMATURE FURLOUGH

When we went to Israel in 1965, the Foreign Mission Board expected us to stay on the field for five years. Some serving in the third world areas overseas could come home for a year's furlough after four years for rest, medical exams and deputation. We were blessed to be able to come home a year early due to the personnel situation in Nazareth. I was emotionally and spiritually burned out. Our year of orientation studies at Hartford Seminary in 1964 led smoothly into another year's study in 1969 to complete the Master of Arts degree in Phenomenology of Religion-Islamics. We used the want ads in my home town of Charlotte to buy a big red Ford station wagon. We packed all our stored belongings and our three children into it and drove north. When we arrived in Hartford, we used the want ads again to find a rental house in South Hartford, since it was too late to get campus housing.

Chuck, Jimmy and Cheryl enrolled in a primary school about a block away. The teachers were upset that they read their numbers backwards until we could explain that was the way they did it in Arabic, from right to left! The kids later told us frightening tales about ice-skating in the basement of the condemned Remington Typewriter factory across the street. They would bring their friends home for lunch. We later learned the other parents worked during the day, and one boy was from a single parent home. We particularly liked our Catholic babysitter who became a family friend for many years. Rose Mary attended a

Hebrew class in the mornings, so I bought a Sears dishwasher on payments, rather than wash the dishes!

I studied Intermediate Arabic under Dr. Isa Boulatta who formerly taught at the Saint George School in Jerusalem. The other students in class were peeved with me since I was ahead of them with my four years' experience in Galilee. I took an excellent course on the history of Vatican II, which gave me an overview of the positive changes in the Catholic Church. Dr. Willam Bijlefeld, former Dutch Reformed missionary to Indonesia supervised my MA project, "Kababir, an Ahmadiyya Community in Israel." Judge Wajdi Tabari, who lived in Kababir in Haifa, Israel, was my main source. I also took a seminar on the history of Christian missions to Muslims taught by Marston Speight who was then a PhD candidate at Hartford. Marston was from Southern Baptist background and served with the Methodists in North Africa. It was then I became acquainted with Lyle Vander Werff's, *Christian Mission to Muslims* (William Carey Library, 1977) which is the best summary of the history of Christian work among Muslims ever written, in my opinion. I had the treat of attending special seminars in the office of Daud Rahbar as he shared the experiences that led to his revolutionary book, *God of Justice* (GJ). I resonated with these excellent studies at Hartford since they confirmed the experiences I had in my first four years in the Middle East.

The capstone of my experience at Hartford Seminary was one evening when I attended a special meeting with Bob Bratcher, the author of *Good News for Modern Man.* I thanked him for producing the book that restored my faith during the spiritual wasteland of those first four years in Israel.

Attending Hartford Seminary was an experience in contrasts. Here I am, as a conservative, southern, Bible believing Christian, attending one of the most liberal northern seminaries in the USA! I learned that students and professors who could not stay in Claremont Seminary in CA, considered one of the most liberal in the country, ended up at Hartford. The contrast was; I found most the professors in the Hartford Seminary Islamics program to be conservative and evangelical. Most served as missionaries in the Muslim world.

Another plus for our family was to be able to visit New England and experience the beauty and heritage of the area. Our neighbor in Nazareth, Sami Geraisy was studying for his PhD in Social Studies at Boston-Brandies. We visited his family during this time. Our children and his got in a rock throwing fight with some of the Boston youth, just to keep up the Middle East tradition!

Still, I was in a state of shock over my four years in the Holy Land. Was I able to return to the same situation, now that I saw the harsh reality of the area? I saw myself as I really was but had no desire or ability to change. That too was about to change.

Chapter 9

C<small>HALK</small> T<small>ALK</small> R<small>EVIVAL</small>

Both times we lived in Hartford, we attended the East Hartford Baptist Church. The pastors, Walter Agnor and Charles Norwood were inspired men who encouraged us in our times of need. East Hartford was one of a number of Southern Baptist churches that began as missions to the northeastern USA. The traditional Congregational and Baptist churches were declining and some turned into museums in remote towns in New England. The Southern Baptists brought back a spirit of evangelical renewal to the local communities, while ministering to the military and businessmen who moved north from the south. They suffered from prejudice from some northerners who saw Southern Baptists as tent revivalists. They faced difficulties in getting permits for church buildings and persevered despite restrictive building codes. The center of the Southern Baptist work in New England was the restored home of Luther Rice in Northborough, Massachusetts. Rice supported the work of Adonirum Judson, the famous missionary to Burma.

I needed refreshing. When I came home from Israel in 1969, I never wanted to see another Southern Baptist missionary, and certainly did not want to be part of a mission! With the possible exception of Norm and Martha Lytle who always received us into their home in Jerusalem with cheer and practical jokes. We argued with the Lytles over whether the BCI should pay for hot water systems in our homes. Norman told me we were to sleep in their bedroom that night.

"There is a bathroom out that door." He said.

I stripped down to my underwear and went in to brush my teeth. To my surprise and embarrassment, I found myself standing on a balcony with all the Jewish neighbors staring at me! From that time on I determined to steal all the strawberries from any dessert he was served.

The pastor at East Hartford invited Wendell Bellew, Baptist Student Union director from Georgetown, Kentucky to preach a revival one weekend. Wendell used chalk talk to illustrate his sermons. Using incandescent chalk, he sketched beautiful scenes that took life when he shined lights on them. I was deeply impressed during one of these chalk talks illustrating God's call. I told the Lord,

> I will go back to Israel for you, Lord. I will not go back
> for the Southern Baptists, or for the Arabs. But I will
> go back for you!

I learned later that three other missionary couples in Israel and the Middle East entered into missionary service under Bellew's inspiration. It was the turn around that began a spiritual revolution in my life. The words of Ross Coggins, missionary to Indonesia, renewed my Ridgecrest vows, and inspired me to keep on keeping on for Jesus.

Send Me, O Lord, Send Me 293

1. O God of might, O Son of light, O Ho - ly Spir - it sweet,
2. With ho - ly fire my heart in - spire Thy Spir - it's sword to wield;
3. O that in me my Lord may see A bear - er of the name;

Thy church ex - pand till all shall stand At Je - sus' pierc - ed feet.
With bor - rowed might I'll take thy light, Till dark - ness' doom be sealed.
That men may see his love so free From age to age the same.

Let all who once thy Son disowned Re - joice to see him now enthroned;
If oth - ers stop to count the cost, For fear of earth - ly trea - sures lost,
Be this my ev - er - last - ing song, He took up - on him - self my wrong,

Yet while one stray - ing soul there be, Send me, O Lord, send me.
I'll count it gain to die for thee; Send me, O Lord, send me.
And cried while fac - ing Cal - va - ry, "Send me, O Lord, send me."

Words, Ross Coggins, 1956. Tune SURABAJA, E. A. Hoffman, 1891; arranged, James Bigelow, 1956. ©

Things were not going well at my home in Charlotte. Dad was nearing foreclosure on land in Blacksburg, South Carolina and our home outside Charlotte on Pleasant Grove Road. We moved there to the outskirts of Charlotte when I was in Junior High School. I used our log cabin in "Possum Walk" for a home improvement project for the 4-H Club. It burned down when I was in the Navy and the new house rebuilt around the garage apartment I slept in while in High School. When I came home in 1969, he asked me to take up payments on both places so he would not lose the house. I was ignorant about finances and wary of getting involved in a bad deal. He and my brother used my Gulf credit card to run up gasoline bills while I was overseas. I suspect my mother reported on them to the oil company and Gulf notified me overseas that unauthorized persons were using my card.

I decided I would go to court with my Dad in Spartanburg, SC and see if we could save the land in Blacksburg. He had a house half built on over 70 acres of land, with a river running beside it. The court was in the judge's office. I learned later that the prosecutor was the judge's son-in-law.

When the judge read the order, I said, "I did not know that you take away land in the USA like they do in Israel!"

The judge said, "Yes, we are going to take your Dad's land away."

The judge's son-in-law got the land! I was able to go back to Israel and tell the Arabs who whined about the Israelis taking their land, "I got my land taken away in America!"

My mother was increasingly apprehensive about her future. I thought she was imagining things. Both my parents had a drinking problem. Much later, I learned that the money they received from her relatives in the North ran out. In addition, the free telephone service expired when my Grandfather Brough died. He worked for the New York Telephone company and was involved in the development of radar in World War II. My brother Hamp was now in Viet Nam. She pitifully told me, while standing on the tarmac at the Charlotte airport, when we left to go back to Israel, "I will never see you again. I will pray for Hamp to get back from Vietnam, and then I will go. I cannot hold on any longer. I know the Lord will take care of you." Her words still haunt me.

Section III

Nazareth II Renewal

Chapter 10

RETURN TO GALILEE
AND DEMON POSSESSION!

The problem I faced during my first term of orientation to Israel was what I call, "remythologizing the scripture." I got the impression in Seminary that many of the events and sayings in the Bible were the figments of the Middle Eastern mind, or their way of saying and doing things. Some of the textbooks taught us to "demythologize" the Scripture. The problem is, when I got to the Holy Land, I found to my shock that the Scriptures were true! The dirt, rocks, Biblical places and all were real. In addition, the hardness of heart and competitive spirit of men was the same as in the Bible. Very little really changed. **In fact, it was so real that the romance was all gone.** There was an element missing from my seminary training that left me unprepared to deal with the spirit world. That is why reading Bob Bratcher's *GOOD NEWS FOR MODERN MAN*, helped to revive my faith during the first term. It was like reading today's newspaper and I could begin to understand how Jesus was dealing with real people and real problems. Little did I expect that my second term from 1970-1974 would cause me to "re-mythologize" the scriptures!

The first thing I encountered on returning to Israel in 1970 was a case of demon possession. The Arabic newspapers carried an article about a family pursued by a familiar spirit. The family moved from house to house in the Jenin area south of Nazareth but could not get away from this tormenting spirit. Dr.

Bob Lindsey and Rev. Fahid Karmout, pastors of our Hebrew and Arabic churches in Jerusalem and Bethlehem felt led by the Lord to investigate and pray for these poor people. They called me and asked me to drive south and meet them in Jenin. We drove out to the village of Zebabdi and met a man walking on the side of the road. We asked him to take us to the house of the people tormented by the spirit. He was a Christian schoolteacher and became a believer because of the experience! He led us way out into a field to a little stone house to meet the family. The wife's hair turned prematurely grey from fear. She told us about cupboards crashing to the floor, articles flying through the air and showed us aluminum pots pitted with holes like those from a welder's torch. We talked to the children and found a 13-year-old boy had been talking to this spirit out in the field. He described it as dressed like a girl with the head of a goat. Lindsey and Karmout prayed for the boy and the family and ordered the spirit to leave them and their house. The family stabilized because of their prayers. *Kaarlo Sevanto Pioneer* describes that as a result of this incident over 3000 copies of the *Gospel of John* were distributed in the area (pp. 231-232).

I returned home that night so scared I was afraid to turn off the lights! For the first time in my life, I realized there was a real devil and demon spirits. I began searching the New Testament and discovered that Jenin was the same area that Jesus healed the Ten Lepers in Luke 17. I began to see that the one-third of the ministry of Jesus that I had missed all these years was true. He cast out demons, healed the sick and raised the dead in the very area I was working. From that point on, the Lord began revealing things to me that would change my life and my ministry.

Chapter 11

JOE UNDERWOOD AND A SLEDGEHAMMER FROM HEAVEN

In April of 1971 Rev. Joe Underwood, evangelist from the FMB preached a revival at the Nazareth Baptist Church. Joe was always an encouragement. The local Arab people loved his Gospel preaching and overflowing friendship. He stayed in the guest apartment in the downstairs of our home, the Baptist House. On Thursday evening, we were on our way to church and Joe told me he was uncertain about what to preach that night.

I told him,

"Preach about baptism. These Orthodox and Catholics do not know the meaning of believer's baptism."

So, Joe preached about baptism. I sat in my usual place toward the back of the church. All of a sudden it hit me like a sledgehammer out of heaven; **"You are a hypocrite! You were not a believer when you were first baptized!"**

For many years it bothered me that I was baptized because my younger sister Betsy made a profession of faith and was about to be baptized. I invited my Aunt Susie and the rest of the family to come to church and see me make my "profession of faith" and be baptized with Betsy. I was 14. It was not until two years later when I was convicted of my sins one Sunday night at the Pleasant Grove Methodist Church in Oakdale, outside of Charlotte, that I received Jesus as my personal savior. I argued for years with my Methodist, Presbyterian and other Protestant and Catholic friends, trying to convince them that believer's baptism by immersion was the only Scriptural baptism. Now the Lord was telling me I was a hypocrite! I could now understand the reluctance of those who grew up in a covenant tradition to being re-baptized.

I sat there thinking,

"What am I going to do? Just sit here and keep it to myself, or obey the Lord? What are they going to think when an ordained pastor and missionary in his 40's asks to be re-baptized?"

At the end of the service, I worked up the courage to walk forward. Pastor Sakhnini did not want to tell Joe Underwood about my decision, so he shoved me off to the side.

Later when we got home that night I went down to the Pastor's house after Joe finished eating dinner and they were sitting in the parlor. Pastor Sakhnini asked Joe, "What are we going to do with a missionary that has not been scripturally baptized?"

Joe answered, "Baptize him!"

One of the local leaders later wrote the FMB in Richmond questioning my being re-baptized. The FMB backed me up and told him this was my first scriptural baptism since I was not a believer for the first one. I wrote a letter on April 23, 1971 explaining my decision:

Last night in the revival service, the sermon of Dr. Underwood pricked my conscience. He told us that baptism was a personal expression of our faith in the death and resurrection of Christ, and our commitment to die to sin and live for Christ. I remembered, as I have been on several occasions in the last few years that when I was baptized at the age of 14 that I had not had a personal experience of salvation. As best as I can remember it was for me a ceremony I endured in order to please myself, my parents and loved ones and my honored pastor. It was not until

I was 16 and my pride and self-righteousness had been shattered that I had the revelation of Jesus dying on the cross for my sins, and the experience of his forgiveness and new life. Therefore, I had been a fanatical Baptist for two years and yet had no personal knowledge of Christ. My mind converted but not my heart.

So now, 20 years later, I find myself a missionary preaching to people to trust Christ personally and be baptized, and I myself have not practiced what I preach. Therefore, in light of the clear teachings of the New Testament and the leadership of God's Spirit on my conscience I am asking to be re-baptized as a believer.

I hope my experience will help those of you who also want to follow Christ in believer's baptism, but for reasons of respect for parents and tradition, have as I have, refused until now to follow Christ in believer's baptism.

A few days later, we all went down to the Sea of Galilee for the baptism. My two sons, Chuck and James, renewed their faith in the Lord at a summer camp in Longview, Washington while on our furlough in 1970. I was going to baptize them. Pastor Sakhnini reminded me that I had not been properly baptized myself! Therefore, he baptized me first and I then baptized the boys. Little did I realize that this act of obedience to the Lord's clear message to me was to open the floodgates of spiritual blessings in the months and years ahead. It was the prelude to Jesus revealing himself as the **Baptizer in the Holy Spirit** as promised in John 1:33. My "Galilee Wanderings" took on new directions that day in the Sea of Galilee!

Growing up in Jesus' hometown and the Galilee he loved, gave our children unique opportunities to explore the countryside. One day they decided to take me on a hike to Mount Tabor, the traditional site of the Transfiguration. The Roman Catholics built a church on top of the sugarloaf mountain that sits about eight miles as the crow flies to the east of the city of Nazareth. Would you believe, there are three altars in the church, one to Moses, one to Elijah and one to Jesus! We knew an American priest there who was very friendly, but by his red face, you could tell he was an alcoholic! The church often exiled priests with drinking problems to remote locations. They became addicted by drinking the wine left over from the Mass, since according to their doctrine; it transforms to the very blood of Christ and cannot be thrown away. Anyway, back to the hike.

I must have been feeling vigorous or needing some bonding time with my boys. They invited several friends over to the house and told me to get my hiking shoes on, and a canteen of water. Then we headed down the hill from our house and up the hill on the way past the potter's house and the District Commissioner's office overlooking the city of lower Nazareth. Then we hiked through the industrial section of Upper Nazareth, past the Ammunitions Factory and out the road to the Arab village of Ein Mahil and around Mount Sartaba to the foot of Mount Tabor. So far, I was keeping up with them. Then we headed up the mountain. There are about 10 switchback curves for automobiles to get up the mountain. However, we went straight up! They reminded me of a bunch of jackrabbits. By the time we got to the top of the mountain and to the church, I was worn out. There was no way I could walk back home. I had to call Rose Mary to come get me. The boys hiked back on their own. I marveled at how strong Jesus must have been as a boy to hike those hills!

Chapter 12

DR. CRISWELL AND THE
BAPTIST FRIENDSHIP HOUSE

We were privileged not only to live in Nazareth, Jesus' hometown, but also to meet some very unusual people under equally unusual circumstances. While in the Navy in 1957-1959, we lived for three months in Boston, Massachusetts and attended a large Baptist Church that met in an old opera house, the Tremont Temple. One Sunday we heard the famous Dr. W.A. Criswell speak. Never would I dream that I would be the point man in one of Dr. Criswell's worldwide adventures. As pastor of First Baptist Church in Dallas, Texas, Dr. Criswell befriended a wealthy Jewish couple. The husband died and left his estate with his wife with instructions to honor Dr. Criswell for his friendship. When the Jewish National Fund, the *"Keren Kayemet"* heard that this money was available, they offered the widow to help in finding a location for a "Friendship House" to honor Dr. Criswell. There was a Keren Kayemet forest on Mount Sartaba between Nazareth and Mount Tabor, the traditional site of Jesus' transfiguration. They proposed that the widow use her funds to dedicate a section of the forest and a building on the mountain to Dr. Criswell. The Foreign Mission Board asked me to coordinate the dedication of the project on the Israeli side.

Dr. Criswell did not want so much commotion made over his simple friendship with this Jewish couple but he complied so as not to offend the widow. Finally, after many preliminary discussions Dr. Criswell agreed to accept a section of the forest to be dedicated to him, along with the Friendship House. Coincidentally, there was a Jewish-Arab friendship group meeting in Nazareth who needed a meeting place. On June 14, 1971, several busloads of members of Dr. Criswell's church in Dallas attended the service of dedication on the hillside of Mount Sartaba. Officials of the Association of Baptist Churches, local mayors, the Ministry of Tourism, The Jewish National Fund, and the Protestant Community Choir all took part. We had a "symbolic" groundbreaking for the Friendship House. Then all the little ladies from Dr. Criswell's church piled unto the buses for a trip up the mountain. The JNF forestry service had bulldozed a narrow road around the mountain overlooking the Valley of Israel. I will never forget the screams of those ladies from the flatlands of Texas as we rounded the curve up that mountain on that narrow road with a drop off into the valley below them! They scrambled from the right side of the bus overlooking the valley into the seats on the opposite landside. When we finally reached the top at an improvised turn-around, there was the proposed Friendship House. It was a little stone tool shed used by the forestry service! Now I understood why the groundbreaking was only symbolic. The years passed and the Friendship House never materialized, but the JNF got their contribution for the forest.

Chapter 13

SORE FEET AND DOWN PAYMENT (GLORY!)

(Praying Mennonites, Teaching Methodists, and Pentecostal Episcopalians)

During the 70's the Lord began sending people to Israel to teach about the Holy Spirit. Our good Mennonite friends, the Krieders and the Swarrs began praying for the Lord to keep all the kooks away and send only those people who would bless us. One of those blessings was Richard Beales from New England. Richard attended Asbury Seminary where the revival broke out. He taught about the ministry of the Holy Spirit in the life of Jesus. During his time in Nazareth Rose Mary experienced a fresh anointing of the Holy Spirit confirming her experience at baptism. She remembered coming up out of the water and the Holy Spirit filling her with joy at her baptism in the First Christian Church in San Diego, California. She could not understand why the people in the church were not as happy as she was.

I began getting the feeling people were praying for me. Deep down inside I knew there were things in my life, like uncontrolled anger, that were not the fruit of the Spirit, but I openly admitted that I did not have the power to control it. The Foreign Mission Board warned me before appointment that it could cause a problem in my ministry. Everywhere I went during this year of 1970-71, it seemed people were having prayer meetings. One evening I ended up at Baptist Village in the home of my adopted sister, South Carolina missionary Sarah Bivins. She and Lee invited Richard for a Bible study. He taught about the work of the Holy Spirit in the life of Jesus. A French-born Jewish girl sat listening and engulfed in a quite spirit of joy. She lifted her hands in quiet praise to the Lord. As I was observing I came under a severe conviction of sin. The Lord marched every vile act I had ever committed before my eyes. I told Richard what had happened and he said I needed to confess.

I said,

"Yes, but not to you!"

I went back to Nazareth and Rose Mary became my priest as I poured out my heart.

Her reaction was,

"All this happened before you met me, so you are forgiven."

My heart felt clean like a newborn baby. I was so tenderized I was shy to see Richard and tried to avoid him to tell him what had happened.

During this time Ibrahim Khazal, a teacher from the Nazareth Baptist School whose family lived in Rama, fell sick. Ibrahim used to travel with me from Nazareth to Rama on Friday evenings when I went to preach. He entered the Belinson Hospital near Baptist Village for an operation. I went with Sarah to visit him. We told him about Richard Beales and his willingness to pray for the sick.

Ibrahim said,

"Please bring him to me. I do not believe I will survive this operation."

I saw Richard that evening briefly, as I let Sarah out for a prayer meeting at the Swarr's apartment. However, I drove away quickly to avoid speaking to him. **The next day Ibrahim had the operation and died on the recovery table!**

The Lord told me,

"You cannot play around with me. It will cost you and others!"

He got my attention. .

A few days later, I was in Jerusalem and attended a meeting at the Anglican School led by the Hunters from Australia. The wife gave her testimony of growing up in an alcoholic home, which spoke to my heart. I went up later to speak to her but she told me she did not have time for me because I was "too intellectual." Later as the group was praying and singing, I felt as though the ceiling opened and love and warmth poured out on me from my head and came down through my body to my feet. I could remember a warm feeling in my chest during meetings at the Pleasant Grove Methodist Church, in Oakdale, but this was the first time I felt this wonderful sensation throughout my whole body. I guess this is what some would call the "baptism in the Holy Spirit" although there is much controversy in the use of this terminology among believers. This was all to prepare me for what was ahead.

I had just arrived home in Nazareth from visits in the villages one evening when the phone rang. Lee Bivins called to tell me that I had a call from the States. I should call my family immediately. I called home and my brother Hamp answered the phone. He said **Mother died in her sleep.** I was completely devastated. I remembered her telling me she would never see me again, but that she would pray for Hamp to get home from Vietnam. She died five days after his return. She was only 55. It was November 3, 1971. It was too late for me to arrange to fly to the States. I mourned in front of the picture window overlooking the city of Nazareth in our beautiful home on the hillside.

Later that week, I drove down to Emmanuel House in Jaffa of Tel Aviv to pick up Costa Deir to bring him back to Nazareth to speak the next day in the Nazareth Baptist Church. It was Saturday night. Costa was a jolly, barrel-chested Greek-Arab who grew up in Ramla-Lod (ancient Lydda) with Fahid Karmout. He was the director of missions for the Elim Bible College in Lima, New York. When we got to Nazareth, I sat down with Costa in the room with the picture window and began to describe my sorrow and pain over Mother's death. He said, **"Ray, the Lord revealed to me that you are a key to Galilee. He wants to bless you!"** He began praying for me. I felt a great swelling in my chest and told him to stop or I would burst!

He said,

"Do not be afraid. The Lord is a gentleman and He will not embarrass you."

I stood up, my hands went up and I started praising the Lord. It was as if the Lord and I were carrying on a two-way conversation. For the first time in my life, I knew God was a loving heavenly Father and he loved me. I lost track of time in the euphoria of this divine moment. Finally, Fuad Sakhnini, pastor of the Nazareth Baptist Church, arrived to get Costa to spend the night at his house. Rose Mary tried to meet him at the door and steer him to the living room so he would not see me. He walked past her, came in with us, raised his hands, and started praising the Lord with us! We were all caught up in the joy of the Lord.

By the time of the worship service, the next morning the word was all over Nazareth that Ray Register was a changed person. People whom I had offended met me and told me what I had done or said, because they were confident now I would not get angry with them. The joy I experienced was so real I did not want it to go away.

Monday morning I woke up, lifted up my hands and started praising the Lord to see if the joy would return. It was as if the Lord flew a bi-plane over me with a banner behind it saying,

"Be still and know that I am God!"

I said, "All right Lord. Please make me a witness to the Muslim people of Galilee. You know how hard they are to reach. If this is like it was in the Book of Acts, prove it to me by making me a witness to these people."

I drove down to the Post Office at the *Moscobia* (former Russian Compound) to get the mail. As I got out of the car, I saw a man running down the street to meet me. He was a school-teacher friend of mine who was crippled.

He told me, "Mr. Register, I have a Muslim friend who is a professor at the Haifa University. Go with me and tell him about Jesus!"

We went to see this man and told him about the Lord. He later fell out of the back of a truck in a procession to a wedding party, hit his head and died. I believe he knew the Lord. I later visited in the home of the local muezzin of the Mosque of Peace and saw a Bible in the Quran stand on the floor. He told me his wife liked for him to read the Bible to her. The wife, it turned out, was the sister of the professor!

That afternoon, I was down at Mary's Well and another friend, Najeeb, "Abu Lutuf" Khoury, came up to me. He was secretary of the large government high school in Nazareth and a member of the Greek Orthodox Church. He told me that he used to be the Communist youth leader in the villages around Nazareth. He used to go out and lead all the Muslim leaders astray. Now he wanted me to go with him, tell them about Jesus, and give them a Bible. He took me throughout the week to eight villages around Nazareth and introduced me to the Muslim leaders. We told them about Jesus and gave each a Bible.

One day the doorbell rang. Standing in front of me were two longhaired young men.

I said, "Lord, who have you brought me today?"

It was Joel Chernof, son of the pastor of a Messianic congregation in the USA with his friend Rick. They formed the Lamb music group. Rick had been on drugs. He was now clean and wanted to be baptized. They spent the night downstairs in our journeyman apartment, and our children enjoyed hearing them sing and play the guitar. They remember it especially because a scorpion ran across the room to attack them and my son James stepped on it and killed it! The next day we took them to the Jordan River and baptized Rick. A picture taken of the event showed the apparition of an arched light like a dove above our heads! I then took them up to a mountain near the village of Deir Hanna where they spent several days retreat in prayer with Father Wilderbrand, a Catholic monk.

The Lord sent someone to my door for spiritual ministry for one solid year, with the exception of one day! I began reading the Bible all over again and understood the ministry of Jesus as the baptizer in the Holy Spirit and the power he gave to believers for spiritual ministry.

I recorded the events of this dramatic time in a newsletter home on December 15, 1971.

> "The miracle acts of God in the past few months here in Nazareth have made the Christmas story take on a strange new relevance. They have convinced us anew that God's Spirit is still the comforter for the lost world, as He was when He visited the young devout Jewish maiden at the well, which still flows near here, and she brought forth a son, Jesus, the Savior of the world. These acts have been the literal re-creation of the New Testament stories in all their realness.

First and foremost was the healing of our sister missionary Anita Thorne, from Tulsa, Oklahoma. She was stricken by a severe case of peritonitis. When the efforts of local doctors and modern medicine appeared to be failing, we all gathered in prayer for her. Each of us was directed by the Spirit to go immediately to the hospital to pray for her and anoint her with oil as related in James 5:14. She related later that this was the turning point in her illness. She is referred to as "Lazarus" by the hospital staff who marveled at her sudden reversal and quick recovery.

The fires of revival were fanned by this obvious act of the Lord. Church attendance increased. The local population has been more open to the Gospel than ever before. Bible study attendance at the Nazareth Baptist Church increased five-fold. There have been professions of faith even among young men from prominent Muslim families. Deacons, pastor and missionaries have been meeting almost daily for prayer and God keeps bringing answers. Even the local mission has been revived and held a conference to study the work of the Holy Spirit.

Village work has been directly affected by the revival in Nazareth. Local leaders have responded with more flexibility and ingenuity in services and attendance has increased to the place most of our meetings are full. One young man responded to the Gospel message in Yaffa of Nazareth. His change was so obvious that he was baptized after only one month of instruction. He has already given a powerful testimony in the meetings and is requesting more opportunities to speak. Every week he is taking us from house to house to visit and witness to his friends who in turn are coming to meetings and accepting Christ.

On a recent visit to a Bedouin sheikh in the Negev desert, we related to him that the Holy Spirit was healing the sick, converting sinners and filling believers in the Galilee.

This devout Muslim reacted, "Why of course it is happening, for according to your scriptures Jesus was born of the Holy Spirit, and God answers the prayers of a pure heart!"

This man still in his prime at 75, read the Bible discreetly among the leaders of his tribe.

Perhaps the most real and personal work of God's Spirit is the comfort and encouragement He is bringing to us since we learned of the sudden death of Ray's Mother last month of pulmonary thrombosis at age 55. Only the direct ministry of the Spirit through the above events and the encouragement of many visits, letters and prayers have sustained us through this personal loss, at such a distance. On the day of her funeral, we had the privilege of baptizing the young man mentioned above in the Sea of Galilee. We have felt drawn into the company of a larger family that the Lord promised to those who leave home for the Kingdom's sake (Luke 18:29-30). It does not lessen the burden or the desire to be at the side of loved ones, but it does sustain us."

Movers in the 1972 Renewal: Revs. Sakhnini, Hammond, Deir, and Smith

Mavis Clothed in White

On January 16, 1972, the Lord took another of his choice servants home. Mavis Pate, operating room nurse on the Ship Hope, ended up in Gaza as a Southern Baptist missionary after working in East Pakistan (now Bangladesh). She trained Arab nurses in operating room procedure. We were in the same missionary orientation in Richmond in 1964 and I had seen her once with Sarah Bivins at Baptist Village for just a second. I remember the smile on her face. I learned later that she was on a search for the joy of the Holy Spirit.

That Sunday night she got into the mission vehicle after church to drive into Israel to pick up a new car the next day. As she, Rev. Ed Nichols and his two daughters were driving out of Gaza, they were attacked by a barrage of AK-47 machine gun fire from an orchard near the 7-Up Bottling plant. Mavis was hit in the head and died instantly. Ed and one of his daughters were wounded. He later transferred to Beirut and survived the war there before retiring. The PLO apologized for the shooting and said they did not intend to target them. Moshe Dayan's wife, Ruth shopped in Gaza that day and they hit the first car to leave town after dark. The group that attacked the car was later found hiding in a hidden room behind a large cupboard in the hospital.

The funeral of Mavis Pate was a time for all of us to count the cost. It was the first time one of our group had been killed. Our friend and IMB colleague, Jarrell Peach, physiotherapist at the hospital, coordinated the funeral service for Mavis. I was impressed by his composure in such a time of stress. Now the Lord was showing us the price that might have to be paid for serving him. Both Jews and Arabs attended her funeral. They could not get together in life, but they were together because of her death. After the funeral, she was buried in a little garden behind the Nursing Home on the Gaza Baptist Hospital compound. Her grave is still there as a reminder of her sacrifice. The Hospital was later turned back to the Anglicans and is now the Gaza "Ahli" Family Hospital. Her family held a memorial service for her at the Social Springs Baptist Church near Ringgold, Louisiana. I later wrote Mavis' life story. Broadman published it as "CLOTHED IN WHITE, The Story of Mavis Pate, ORN" in 1991 after the Gulf War.

Mavis' death caused a great deal of introspection among our missionary group especially for Sharon McPherson, who with her husband Jim served in Gaza and Ramallah. Sharon led a Bible study for the missionaries on martyrdom in which she concluded that martyrdom is a gift, not to be sought, but one the Lord prepared you for at the right time. Jim and Betty Smith, now in Ashkelon and Gaza, write about the tragic event in their memoirs, *In Their Midst*, pp 210-211:

> We don't understand why one who was so aptly described by an Israeli Journalist as "a nurse of mercy" had to die. We do know, however, that for the first time we saw Muslims, Jews and Christians sitting together in the Gaza Baptist Church.
>
> We do know that a Jewish friend wept when she heard of Mavis' death and said, "And to think she died in my place," perhaps because the shooters thought they were ambushing Jews...We do know that there was complete sincerity in the tight handclasps of Arab friends on the Gaza Baptist Hospital grounds who say, "Please don't blame us. We loved her. We would not have had such a thing to happen."

Mavis' martyrdom led a number of young women in the USA to come to Gaza as nurses. Years later the Women's Missionary Union contacted me for copies of *CLOTHED IN WHITE*, since they were honoring women who served the Lord. Later, in the 1990's, I picked up a Druze soldier hitchhiking in Galilee who used to drive Mavis out to the refugee camps in Gaza. He was very touched by her devotion and sacrifice.

We had one occasion that a group of nuns at the Sisters of Nazareth Hospice asked Rose Mary and me to talk to them about the Holy Spirit. I shared with them some of the things the Lord was doing and pointed out some Scriptures. That Sunday night they came dancing into the Nazareth Baptist Church exclaiming they had gone to the Sea of Galilee and baptized each other!

I told them, "I am a Baptist minister. Why didn't you have me baptize you?"

They said, "We read the Scriptures and it did not say anything about having to have a Baptist minister baptize us, so we baptized each other!"

The FMB became concerned that things were getting out of hand in Israel with the renewal among the missionaries so they sent some board members to check out the situation. On the way to a summer conference in the mountains of Cyprus, we were on a bus riding up to the hotel. A member of the Foreign Mission Board sat beside Rose Mary. He began asking her about the renewal in Israel.

He asked her, "Are the missionaries Spirit-filled or charismatic?"

She answered, "I do not know about the missionaries, but the nationals are! They just read the Scriptures and do what it says."

Rev. Joe Underwood, the FMB evangelist, came to lead another revival in at the Nazareth Baptist Church May 17-31, 1972. This time he rode the wave of spiritual renewal and the results were even more dramatic as I noted in a newsletter home on July 8, 1972;

Primarily was the wonderful revival services May 17-31 led by the Rev. Joseph Underwood of the Foreign Mission Board and the Homer Phillips, Musicians from Washington, D.C. As you know the local people have been praying daily for the whole year that God would bless these meetings. During this year, the Nazareth Baptist Church has been experiencing a spiritual renewal with growing attendance and response from the large group of young people from the Nazareth Baptist School. Prayers for power in witnessing and healing have been answered directly by the Lord. One visitor from England remarked recently that he felt the presence of the Holy Spirit the moment he walked through the gate of the church! The Spirit of the Lord was present from the first revival meeting on Sunday morning, May 21 when 22 young people responded to the invitation. They were under deep conviction and some were weeping. By the end of the week, 153 decisions for Christ were made and many others rededicated their lives. The combined results of the meetings in Nazareth, the villages, Ramallah, East Jerusalem and Gaza were 193 decisions for Christ. There were at least three Muslims who accepted Christ publicly. Adding those who made decisions in the weeks before the meetings there are over 200 persons who need follow-up for spiritual growth. This leaves the local believers and us with a heavy burden of visitation for which we ask you to pray. Already visits are being made and a new believer's course has been started.

Our daughter Cheryl was one of this group of school age children who was baptized along with her best friend and neighbor, Ruth Laty and our next-door neighbor, Riad Haddad, both children of deacons from the Nazareth Baptist Church. While the Lord was working dramatically in the lives of the people of Galilee, he was continuing his work on me.

Chapter 14

THE "BOB AND RAY SHOW"

The Scorpion's Den and Primal Scream

The BCI and the FMB struggled for years to find the proper role of our organizations in church planting and development overseas. Some felt that our foreign group should not be financially involved in the building of churches, especially of church buildings overseas. They felt the local people should put up all the funds for such projects. The problem was, we were deeply involved in the financial support of schools and hospitals. Why not in church projects? I for one, and my mentor, Dr. Finlay Graham, President of the Beirut Baptist Seminary and later advisor for church development, believed in the 'shared purse'. The locals and we should share in projects of mutual interest.

Our mission meetings were so consumed in discussions over church development policies that the BCI designated Bob Lindsey and me to settle the matter. They called us the "Bob and Ray Show!" Bob was concerned that the locals would not take ownership of church buildings if we put up most of the funds. He remembered his visit to Kefr Mishki in Lebanon and seeing the birds fly in and out of the church from broken windows the local people had not fixed. Bob was a formidable opponent to most of my proposals in the BCI meetings for the building project of the Rama Baptist Church. Recent events softened my heart. I yearned for compromise and reconciliation with Bob. He also had been sensitized by the acts of the Holy Spirit. The Lord gave him great ability in prayer and spiritual discernment through face-to-face encounters with people who had been physically and spiritually bound. Not only was he an intellectual giant, but he was now a spiritual mentor.

Bob was staying at a little place he owned in Poriya, a Jewish settlement above the Sea of Galilee, south of Upper Tiberius. It was there, at what we called the "Scorpion's Den" that he did his New Testament research. When he stayed away in Jerusalem, the spiders and scorpions took up residence. Bob asked me to come down and meet with him so we could settle the issue of church development in Rama and other villages. On the way down from Nazareth I asked the Lord to help me and Bob come to an agreement.

I told the Lord, "You know how stubborn both he and I are, so please help us!"

Within five minutes after arriving and sitting in his little living room, Bob and I came to an agreement. It was to be the foundation of a church development plan later agreed on by the BCI and the Association of Baptist Churches. I was overwhelmed. I recorded the results in a brief report home in July 8, 1972;

> After more than seven years of study, discussion, revisions, prayers and frustrations the Baptist Convention (mission organization) has agreed on a plan for church development and voted to begin construction of the Rama Baptist Church building. Much study and prayer are yet needed as the $10,000 allotted by the Foreign Mission Board from Lottie Moon Offerings and a $5,000 special gift added to local savings will not go too far at the present rate of inflation. But this will "work together for good" as it will place a needed responsibility on the local people in Rama, making the church building more their own project.

After our short and decisive agreement, Bob's wife Margaret fixed us a little supper in the kitchen. We sat down at the table and Bob broke bread and prayed. All of a sudden, I found myself on the floor on my back. The Lord started teaching me things. Some might say I was "slain in the Spirit."

I could hear Margaret exclaim, "What is happening to Ray? Should we call a doctor?"

Bob told her, "It's alright. The Lord is teaching him things."

I heard my Mother singing in heaven, "Safe in the arms of Jesus!"

Bob picked me up and carried me into the living room. I had the urge to write. I motioned for Bob to give me something to write with. He could only find a crayon. So, I started to scribble on a piece of paper. All of a sudden, I realized my nose was running, and I remember my Dad writing me and telling me that,

"A snotty nose boy was born in Columbia, SC and now that snotty nose boy is overseas as a missionary doing the most wonderful work in the world!"

Love for my father welled up in my heart. The Lord gave me stanzas of a hymn for him that I never remember hearing, **"Oh, for a Closer Walk"** by William Cowper, 1731-1800.

> Where is the blessedness I knew when first I saw the Lord?
> Where is the soul-refreshing view of Jesus and his Word?
> What peace-full hours I then enjoyed! How sweet their mem-'ry still!
> But they have left an aching void The world can never fill.
> Re-turn, O Holy Dove, re-turn, Sweet messenger of rest;
> I hate the sins that made Thee mourn, And drove Thee from my breast.

(Baptist Hymnal, Convention Press, Nashville, 1958, p. 365)

The Lord so overwhelmed me that Bob and Margaret wanted to drive me back to Nazareth. I told them I was all right and headed out. As I passed Turan village I could feel the demon spirits over that town rise up. I rebuked them in the name of Jesus! When I passed through the narrow curve of the road of Cana of Galilee the demon spirits rose up with a roar! They fled when I called on the name of Jesus. I learned that night about the power of the name of Jesus in contrast to the bondage of demon spirits that bound the hearts of men and women worldwide. It was a power I had not tapped until that night.

Richard Beales challenged me, in the beginning of this adventure with the Spirit, to study the Gospel of Luke to learn about the work of the Spirit in the life of Jesus. I learned that Jesus was born of the Spirit. The Spirit led him into the wilderness to be tempted. The Spirit came upon him at his baptism. He healed by the Spirit. He gave up the Spirit at his crucifixion, and the Spirit revived him from the dead. **God, the Holy Spirit, was the missing link in my understanding of the Trinity, the Virgin Birth and the resurrection**. I had been a Baptist who did not know the Spirit, similar to those believers in Acts 19:3. I realized that in the three years at Seminary I only had one-half of an hour's class on the doctrine of the Holy Spirit! Now I was actually experiencing the acts of the Holy Spirit in my life and seeing Him work in those around me. He had been there all along, convicting of sin, righteousness and judgment, but I had not recognized Him. At the same time, I came into a new understanding of God as Heavenly Father, divine Son and precious Holy Spirit. I realized that the Trinity is not just a doctrine to be understood, but a reality to be experienced! The Lord's Supper became a celebration of the real presence of Christ through the Spirit. Worship became a living encounter with the Lord. The words of hymns took on a new and fresh meaning. Marriage became an experience of the mystery of Christ and the Church. Later this understanding gave me new insights into witnessing with Muslims. The Book of Acts became the handbook for church planting as the Spirit spoke to new believers. The name of Jesus took on a new power as we saw him heal the sick, cast out demons, and raise the dead. It was no longer what happened 2000 years ago. It was happening today right here in Galilee!

Section IV

War and Renewal

Chapter 15

1973 War, Revival and The Hebrew University

One of the positive signs of renewal in Galilee was the new enthusiasm and willingness of local believers to support Arab evangelists. In the past any visiting evangelist, especially American was expected to provide his own travel and upkeep. As the Holy Spirit swept the country the manager of the Nazareth Hospital Bookshop in the market, Miss Eidie Khoury, began collecting money for the support of Evangelist Bajat Bartaseh of Jordan to speak in the churches. Eidie was a prolific women's evangelist in her own right and held Bible studies in her home in the "Arab Shikun" (Hebrew for "apartments") for years.

One Saturday in October 1973, I was on the way to Rama village with evangelist Bajat Bartaseh for a meeting at our church. Planes flew low over Nazareth and I heard the word, "harb", Arabic for war. Syria and Egypt attacked Israel by surprise on Yom Kippur, the Jewish Day of Atonement. By the time we got to Rama, the planes were flying low in the valley below the village. On the way home, the army stopped our cars and painted over the headlights. That night I was out in the garden with son Chuck and the hillside of Yaffa of Nazareth lit up with a huge explosion. I learned later that Syria was attacking with Frog missiles (similar to the V-2 Rockets in WWII). That night approaching explosions shook us out of bed. We ran downstairs and spent the rest of the night in a makeshift bomb shelter in an underground closet.

We continued meetings in the villages during that month of war sometimes under blackout conditions. One evening in Turan village, we could hear and feel the shelling in the Jordan valley. The Holy Spirit fell in the room and I saw the pastor and his sons and others fall on their faces. The pastor, Suheil Ramadan, experienced healing in a deaf ear. That night the Turan Baptist Church was born.

While the Lord was blessing us with revival in the churches, the Jewish people were suffering the loss of sons in almost every home. That month over 3000 Jewish men perished, and the country was in mourning despite having finally pushed the Arab armies back to the 1967 borders. The country lost the equivalent of all the American losses in the Vietnam War in just one month. I remember taking Thomas Horny, a messianic Jew from Czechoslovakia, to the cemetery in Upper Nazareth to grieve over the grave of one of his friends killed in the war.

Following the 1973 War, I entered the summer program at the Overseas School on Mount Scopus of the Hebrew University. I studied classical Arabic and Middle East subjects. One of my classmates, a brilliant redheaded Catholic from Harvard University, Valery Hoffman, later became a believer, partly as a result of having gone with us to a prayer meeting in Latrun, a possible location of Emmaus. I loaded our yellow VW van with students from our dorm one evening and drove down to Latrun. During the meeting, the prayers and praise rose up to the ceiling and Glory poured out. Someone spoke in an unknown tongue. Thoughts suddenly came to my mind, but I was shy to speak all of them. Someone else immediately spoke all the words.

"I the Lord love you and want you to turn to me with all your heart. If you do not turn I will cause you to despair so you will want to take your own life. Then you will turn!"

Valerie and I met years later at a Muslim evangelism conference at the Navigator's headquarters in Colorado Springs.

She exclaimed, "Ray Register what are you doing here?"

I replied, "Valerie Hoffman, what are you doing here?"

She was not a believer when I knew her in Jerusalem. She told me the story of her conversion.

She said, "Remember the meeting you took me to in Latrun. At the time I was running from the Lord. I ran all the way to Tunisia where I came to the point of wanting to take my own life. Then I turned to the Lord. That prayer message was for me."

She later became a professor at the University of Chicago and wrote her doctoral thesis on Sufi Muslim women in Egypt.

During the fall semester at the Overseas School on Mt. Scopus, I stayed in the room of Father Jacob Barclay on the Mount of Olives. He roomed in the home of the Arab Muslim family who holds the keys to the Church of the Holy Sepulcher in the Old City of Jerusalem. Barclay was on furlough in Canada. I rode a Vespa motor scooter across the Mount of Olives past the Augusta Victoria Hospital to Mount Scopus for classes in Hebrew, Arabic, Modern Middle East history, Arab culture and Quran. I used my GI Bill scholarship from the Navy. On the weekends, I traveled to Rama and Nazareth. This became the foundation for my doctoral studies at Southeastern Seminary. During the year, some of my fanatical Jewish classmates threw hand grenades on the Baptist House in West Jerusalem. It was quite a colorful year. One of my professor's husband was in Sharon's army in Egypt. I remember her telling us,

"We are saving Arafat in order to make peace with the Palestinians in the future."

I was sitting in the student lounge one day when a man walked in dressed in a flashy white 'zoot suit' and cowboy hat. Someone told me he was a CIA recruiter! One day I was listening to the Voice of Israel English news and heard a Christian chorus, "Seek ye first the Kingdom of God." They recorded a meeting held in the apartment of Shira Lindsey, daughter of Gordan Lindsey of Christ for the Nations in Texas. I used some of his writings on the Holy Spirit translated into Arabic for outreach. I attended Shira's meeting and other Messianic meetings in Jerusalem that year.

I got my supply of Arabic Bibles from Shlomo Hizik who had an office on the Mount of Olives. Shlomo in earlier years was a bodyguard for Ben Gurion. One day Shlomo told me that the Jerusalem police wanted to talk to me. I went down to the police station in the Russian compound and found an elderly plain clothed police officer seated at a desk in a room full of other police workers.

He politely asked me to take a seat.

I asked him, "Why am I here?

He said that they were trying to pre-empt troubles between religious groups. There were radical Jewish groups who might attack Christian groups and they wanted to protect us. I assumed he meant Rabbi Kahane and radicals who were causing problems in the country.

I asked him, "What can I do about it?"

He passed a pad of paper across the desk with a pen and told me to start writing.

I asked, "What do you want me to write?"

He said, "Write this statement; "I Ray Register hereby declare that I will not evangelize Jews!"

I looked at him and raised my voice, "I will never sign your statement! This is in violation of my human rights and contrary to the United Nations Declaration Israel signed when it became a state. You can put me in prison. I will never sign this!"

Heads were turning in the police station.

He sheepishly said, "No! No! Please be calm. All I am trying to do is to protect you."

I said again, "I will never sign your statement."

It appears they had called a single female missionary in and she had signed the statement under duress. They gave this assignment to this older police officer who was about to retire. **His warning was not without cause as the Narkis Street Baptist Church later burned to the ground.**

Chapter 16

DIALOGUE WITH MUSLIMS

The year at the Mount Scopus campus overseas school at the Hebrew University in 1973-74 was very satisfying. I studied conversational Arabic with Omar Uthman from Bet Safafa. I had an excellent course on modern Egypt and the Middle East. I became acquainted with the vibrant Messianic Jewish and Arab evangelical meetings in Jerusalem. Now I had to decide where and what I was going to study for my doctorate. I thought I might do a project with the Nazareth Hospital where I had been presenting Child Evangelism flannel graph parables in the outpatient clinic. That did not work out.

Southeastern Baptist Theological Seminary in Wake Forest, North Carolina admitted me to the Doctor of Ministry program for the fall of 1974. Dr. George Braswell, who we visited in Tehran, Iran, was now professor of missions. He agreed to be my doctoral supervisor. Whitakers Baptist Church, my former pastorate, invited me to preach for a week's revival service. On Thursday night the entire front row was packed with Arabs! Sitting among them was an American girl, Pat Hamad.

She said, "If you want to work with the Muslims, here we are!"

It turns out Pat's mother was a Register from Lamar, South Carolina. Pat grew up in the North Rocky Mount Baptist Church. When she was a young teenager, the church split. Their court case was in my Commercial Law book at UVA.

She said, "I could not understand what they were fighting about?"

She dropped out of church and eventually married Subhi Hamad, a Muslim from Beira-Ramallah, north of Jerusalem. They had five children and sent them all back to study at the Quaker school in Ramallah because of the perceived bad morals in American schools. Pat introduced me to Muslims all over the area. One day I visited them in Rocky Mount. We sat in their breakfast nook.

Pat said, "I remember a verse we learned in Sunday School. I want you to explain it to my husband in Arabic. It was John 3:16 and it went something like, "For God so loved the world,,."

She opened the door for me to share the Good News with her husband and many other Muslims in the area.

We were living at the missionary residence of the Hayes Barton Baptist Church in Raleigh. Dr. Fred Corbin, professor of plant science at N.C, State University was an active member. He knew Muslim students at N.C. State and was faculty advisor to them. Through him, I met Joseph Qubain who was president of the Arab Club. Joseph was the one Christian among 99 Muslims in the Club! He was related to Bishop Qubain in Jerusalem. The Muslim Student Association (MSA) was looking for a venue to celebrate the Prophet Muhammad's birthday. We arranged for the director of the Baptist Student Union to offer the facility. We had over 100 Muslims from around the world feasting and praying at the BSU! They were very surprised that we would be so open to them. The network that opened up became the ready fieldwork laboratory for me to test a guide to dialogue with Muslims that Judge Wajdi Tabari helped me to develop in the Holy Land. When I presented the idea to Dr. JD Hughey from the FMB, he called Kate Ellen Gruver at the Home Mission Board and they proposed to endorse the project. Kate Ellen worked in the orphanage in Nazareth in 1948, which helped to re-establish Baptist work in the country after the 1948 war. She had an MA from Harvard in Islamic studies and agreed to be my fieldwork advisor. Dr. Braswell would be my academic advisor. She and Dr. Hughey proposed that the FMB and the HMB support me for the two years it took to do the doctoral project!

Another of God's provisions for the D.Min project at Southeastern was missionary colleague, Bill Hern, who I knew from our short visit to East Jerusalem in 1967. Bill was on indefinite medical leave and retirement in Raleigh due to cancer. Of all the people that the Lord could provide to coach me during my work with Muslims, none could be better than Bill. Bill opened the work of the Foreign Mission Board in Egypt. He also started the Jerusalem Baptist Church. Along with Kate Ellen Gruver and George Braswell, he had the most first-hand experience in working with Muslims in the Middle East. In addition, Bill was a spiritual giant who loved the Lord deeply and the Muslim people also. He and I shared ideas and experiences while playing tennis in Raleigh. The Lord put together an exceptional team to mentor me during those two years in Raleigh.

Another of His provisions was housing for the second year. The Hayes Barton Church gave us their missionary residence for the first year. Deacon Roland Danielson provided a beautiful downstairs home for the second year. The Arab oil boycott bankrupted Roland the year before when he invested in a motel. Despite this, he gave his home to someone working with the Arabs!

The Doctor of Ministry program at Southeastern became the ideal approach to creating and testing my ideas with Muslims. I networked with Muslim students and professors at NC State and Shaw University. One student from Iran was married to the daughter of the Minister of Agriculture of Iran. They invited me to their small apartment in Raleigh while her father was visiting. I admired her beautiful tablecloth on the little table where we ate. Her father flew back to Iran and brought me a large one of Omar Khayam's poem;

"A jug of wine, a book of verse, and thou beside me in the wilderness."

Later I invited him to a special dinner at Hayes Barton Baptist Church. He was very curious about what we did with all the rooms in the educational building. As I toured him around the facility, we entered one room with a painting of the Lord's Supper on the wall.

He saw it and remarked, "I once saw that picture in the home of a Christian friend. I always wanted to know what it meant."

I bought him a similar picture of the Last Supper from the Sign of the Fish Book store.

Bette McKee, in Cary, invited me to meet other Muslims who attended a student meeting in her home. One young man from Iran was a devout Muslim. He was a follower of the Ayatollah Khomeini who later overthrew the Shaw and returned from exile. He was a nice young man but obviously wanted the other Muslim students to follow the strict rules of Islam.

One of the employees of the Sign of the Fish bookstore near the NC State campus was engaged to a Muslim student engineer from MIT. I met him. He was a very pleasant young man. Nevertheless, when she married him, had a son, and returned to Iran with him, she had to come under the domination of his mother and the practices of the Muslim renewal in the country. She later escaped with her son back to the USA, similar to the story in the book, "*Not Without My Daughter*."

While speaking in a conference in my native home, Columbia, South Carolina, I appeared on the local TV. I wore my Arab headdress. The station received several negative calls.

Then a lady asked to meet me later. I had the privilege to meet
Delores Shamsedeen, wife of Izadeen Shamsedeen who was then
a professor of economics at the University of South Carolina, my
father's alma mater. Delores was a Baptist from North Carolina
and had met "Deen" at Berea College in Kentucky. They are both
now with the Lord. Our families have kept up with each other
through the years and in many countries. Their daughter Nadia
Dean visited with us and assisted OM in Nazareth. Through her
Dad's contacts, she met government leaders in both Lebanon
and Jordan. Recently she used the intercultural experiences to
write, *A Demand of Blood, The Cherokee War of 1776*.

My friend, retired missionary in Bangladesh and classmate
in the D.Min. program at Southeastern, Dr. Charles Beckett, invited me to Petersburg, Virginia to meet a Muslim psychiatrist
married to a Baptist lady. I knew his family in Nablus in Samaria.
I was able to meet him again later at a reunion at the University
of Virginia. With these and many other contacts with Muslims
in North Carolina, South Carolina and Virginia I was able to
test a Guide to Dialogue and Interfaith Witness with Muslims
and determine its effectiveness in training Christians to understand Muslims. Judge Wajdi Tabari taught me the key questions
Muslims ask Christians. Tabari was family judge of the Sharia
Court in Joppa of Tel Aviv. Joppa is the port where Jonah sailed.
He told me that Muslims ask these questions to cause Christians
to doubt their faith and become Muslims! **The Lord gave me
verses from the Quran and the Bible, in Arabic, to answer these questions.** I incorporated them into the Guide.
The DMin program gave me a step-by-step approach to minister
to Muslims and to train Christians in witnessing to Muslims.
When I presented the final project report Dr. Braswell told me,

"I do not accept corrections or addendums to the final
report."

My late cousin, Sarah Steagall from Florence, South Carolina was then working for the North Carolina Agriculture Department in Raleigh. She generously typed the final report on an IBM Selectric typewriter without any mistakes!

I found the experience at Southeastern Seminary very affirming, especially the interest in some faculty members in the renewal in Israel. It was humbling to share God's blessings, especially with Dr. Leo Green, beloved professor of Old Testament. Sarah and Lee Bivins from Baptist Village in Israel studied at Southeastern earlier and knew he was open to the blessings of God. He was hungry to hear what the Lord was doing there. The excellent studies in Theology with Dr. John Eddins expanded my thinking on the doctrine of the Holy Spirit. I was also privileged to study with Dr. Theodore Adams, Dr. Bob Richardson, and Dr. Raymond Brown. Dr. Don Cook, a former pastor of Whitakers Baptist Church was academic dean and rescued me from being dismissed from the program because of a "C" I made on the course on Clinical Pastoral Education at Butner Mental Institution. The director of the course insisted on grading on a curve for a small class and refused the Seminary's request to give a pass-fail grade. He also thought I had been insensitive to another classmate who was a former charismatic and had bugged me during the class discussion sessions. The most encouraging part of the course was the long rides back and forth from Wake Forest to Butner with fellow classmate and pastor, Dr. Mike Moore. Dr. Randall Lolley, President of Southeastern Seminary, grasped my hand at graduation and reminded me the way had not been easy!

While I was out finding and talking with Muslims and attending classes at Southeastern, Rose Mary learned to play hand bells at Hayes Barton with Frances Corbin, wife of Fred Corbin, my faculty friend at NC State. Two of our children, James and Cheryl, took part in the bell choir with her. Frances and other friends raised the funds for Rose Mary to take three octaves of Schulmerich hand bells back to Israel with us when we returned in 1976 after my graduation.

Before returning to Israel, we attended mission's week at Ridgecrest where I presented a session on the Middle East. I met Dr. Baker James Cauthen, then Executive Director of the Foreign Mission Board, in the corridor and invited him to attend. He said with a concerned look on his face,

"Ray, you aren't going to talk about the Charismatic movement are you?"

I said, "Dr. Cauthen, I am only going to talk about what the Lord is doing to lead Arabs and Jews to Himself!"

He looked relieved and attended. His affirmation prepared us for what we faced ahead back in Galilee.

Chapter 17

LEBANESE RELIEF

During our two-year absence from 1974 to 1976, civil war broke out in Lebanon on the northern border of Israel. The Christian Lebanese in the south formed the South Lebanese Army. Israel opened its border to allow the wounded to be carried to the hospitals in Israel for treatment. In addition, Israeli businesses gave employment to the southern Lebanese cut off to the economy of their country in the north. My friend and first translator from Haifa, Rev. Ibrahim Siman, started a ministry of transporting wounded Lebanese to the hospitals and delivering food and clothing to the border. Ibrahim developed a strong social consciousness from his training as a youth with the socialistic Mapam Party at the Givat Havivah center in Kibbutz Barkai near Hadera. When we arrived back in Nazareth in the summer of 1976, Ibrahim called me and said,

"I need you. I have a very important assignment for you."

Knowing Arabic and loving the people I could not refuse him. Ibrahim previously helped me in 1969 with my Master's degree thesis by introducing me to Judge Wajdi and the Ahmadi leaders in Kababir on Mount Carmel in Haifa. For one whole year, we drove almost daily to the border "Good Fence." Israel opened crossings on its northern border at Rosh Hanikora, Hanita-Alma Shaab, Irmeish, and Metulla. Each border crossing left its memories. Rosh Hanikora is near a UN outpost and was located at the western-most point of Israel and the ancient crossing point for the army of Alexander the Great. Alma Shaab is a Christian village just across the border from the Israeli Kibbutz Hanita, high on the mountain range separating the two countries. Irmeish is at the halfway point and the hometown of the commander of the Southern Lebanese army, General Saad Haddad. Metulla is at the western, most northern portion of Israel and near a strategic castle, which dominates the landscape facing Mount Hermon.

Ibrahim received a request for us to hold a wedding in Alma Shaab. A couple wanted to get married and there was no priest or pastor left in the town to marry them because of the war. We got permission from the army to go over into Lebanon where we held the wedding in a Presbyterian church.

Traveling back and forth to the border at Irmeish was challenging. I always knew when I left the house in Nazareth in the morning I may not make it back in the evening. I am not sure Rose Mary realized that I might leave her a widow in those days. We approached the border on narrow roads that led through bushy canyons, which were natural traps for ambushes. I always imagined rounding a curve and coming face to face with a tank or a soldier with a RPG. My concerns were probably unfounded since the area was secured by the Israeli and Southern Lebanese armies. We became familiar with the officers and men of both armies during that year. They knew we were on a humanitarian mission and tried to facilitate our giving aid to the wounded and sick.

I will never forget the Lebanese who suffered at the hands of opposing factions in that country's civil war. I remember one father carrying a child whose limbs dangled like limp rags. The child was ravaged by polio, since the normal vaccines were not available due to the conflict. They brought another young Shiite woman to the border whose body was covered by sores.

She had been given improper medication and later died at the Safad Hospital. We were responsible to transport dead bodies of civilians back from the hospital morgues in Safad and Afula to the border in my VW truck. Ibrahim raised the money to pay for their coffins.

We experienced interesting encounters with the Israeli officers at the border. One young officer at the Metulla army post called us in one day to inquire about the Arabic Gospels we always included in our food and clothing packets. We thought he would prevent us from doing this in the future. Instead he asked for a copy in Hebrew for himself! One day I entered his field office. He shouted into his phone and banged it on the table.

I asked him, "How can you communicate like this during a war?"

He replied, "They always work during a war!"

Churches of all denominations gave us food and clothing to take to the border. I made several trips to Jerusalem to receive clothing from the Sisters of Zion on the Via Dolorosa. The nuns there nicknamed me, "John the Baptist!" Some Lebanese who could not return to Lebanon stayed in the country for work or marriage and became members of the churches. This contact with the Lebanese was an introduction to momentous events for our family in the years ahead.

1977 was an active year for our family as indicated on our newsletter home,

"Galilee Happenings"

Much has happened in Galilee since we last had a chance to write many of you:

The Rama Baptist Church building was dedicated on March 25, 1977. We were thrilled to greet 150 village leaders and missionary friends for the service, which highlighted over fifteen years of Baptist witness in that village. The spring which threatened to undermine the foundations of the building during construction was converted into a baptistery, and yes, we rang that bell donated by friends in the States. The church is located on one of the most beautiful sites in the Galilee

May was climaxed with revival meetings in Nazareth and the villages, featuring Rev. Joseph Underwood and Mr. & Mrs. Sid Reber of the Foreign Mission Board in Richmond, Virginia. It was a time of inspiration with twelve young men and women committing themselves to Christian service in the Galilee.

During the last part of June, Ray attended a Muslim-Christian dialogue conference at the Hartford Seminary Foundation in Connecticut. Chuck, now 18, returned to the States with him to enroll for his senior year of high school at the Harrison Chilhowee Baptist Academy near Knoxville, Tennessee. Ray got him settled there and was able to visit some of you during this hurried time.

In July, our son Jimmy, now 16, worked in "5-Day Clubs" or Vacation Bible classes in Rama and seven surrounding Arab villages. Over 500 Arab children attended and nearly half of these accepted Christ. Many of these were Muslims. In Rama, we showed a film on the life of Christ, which attracted 100 boys and girls. Many of these continued to attend Sunday School and worship services every Sunday afternoon.

August was spent finishing up the kindergarten in Rama for school opening. We now have twenty 3 and 4-year-old Arab Christian, Muslim and Druze children enrolled. Most of their parents are teachers in the primary school (public) next to the church.

Throughout the year the bell choir formed by Jimmy and Rose Mary has made performances in Nazareth, Baptist Village near Tel Aviv, Gaza, and Rama. They expect soon to perform in Ashkelon and are preparing for Christmas. Recently they finished bell tables made from packing crates. Rose Mary is starting the junior bell choir with some new members.

Cheryl, now 14, is an interesting example of the "MK" vitality and versatility as she bridges two cultures weekly from the MK Dorm near Tel Aviv to Nazareth, with an active social life in both. All the children are doing well in school, but of course we miss Chuck who is so far away.

Continue in prayer for us as we seek to be faithful to the Lord in his calling. Pray especially that He will keep things happening in Galilee.

Rama Baptist Church was our closest work to Lebanon along with the bookshop and Church in Acre. George Kazoura, who himself was a refugee from Maghar village near Rama, assisted me with the Rama church while I was helping in Southern Lebanon. We constructed the Rama Church building together and once got stuck in a pool of plaster! George took over the Rama Church in 1978. Dr. J.D. Hughey quipped that my experience in Rama was similar to the story of the field tick;

"A field tick can hide in the grass for 13 years before it has to attach itself to an animal to get blood to live."

I held onto the work in Rama for 13 years before turning it over to George. I told him I was giving him the church at zero, because I had so many problems there. He went on to build a foster home, the House of Love, to assist Muslim and Christian Arab children from problem families. He used the Yiddish and German he learned while studying in Bible college in Krishona, Switzerland to gain the proper permits from the Orthodox Jewish controllers of the Ministry of Education and Welfare. He was particularly gifted in summer activities for the village young people and enrolled hundreds in summer school. He struggled with the exclusiveness of the Rama town people since he came from another village. We learned from the experience of the responsiveness of children to the ministries there not to visit the parents of Druze students, since the exposure caused the parents to stop their children from coming to our church.

One of the sad reflections on our Galilee Wanderings was the failure of our church development program to turn over the Rama Church and House of Hope to local ownership. Continual delays due to wars and local rivalries prevented the ABC, BCI, and FMB (IMB) from ever accomplishing this. I remember on one occasion that George prevented the property from being confiscated by the local council by his tenacious determination to remain on the property. George passed away unexpectedly in 2015. His family still lives there. One of the facts of life in the Middle East is that someone has to physically live on church properties, especially in remote villages, to prevent vandalism.

Pastor George Kazoura (RIP) and Ray at the Rama Baptist Church
House of Love Foster Home, August 1995

Heaven will tell us how many Muslim, Druze and Christian Arab young people and adults came to know Jesus because of George's determination to remain in Rama.

While at the conference in Hartford Seminary, I had the privilege of rooming with Don McCurry who had worked in Pakistan. It was the beginning of a long friendship, which lasts until this day. Don is a senior missionary that I can always look up to for advice and prayer.

Leaving Chuck at Chilhowie Academy was one of the most difficult experiences of my Galilee wanderings, aside from the death of my mother. Reflecting back, I now realize that he sacrificed the most of any of our children since he was already 6 years old when we went to Israel. He had to adjust to the new culture and languages at a much older age than our other children did. He did well in conversational Arabic, but it was not until years later in 1976, after returning from two years in the USA, we realized he was struggling to study in Arabic in Nazareth. He finally told us, "I have to go to the American School."

After he studied a while at the AIS, we learned that he was two years behind in English comprehension. Enrolling him at Chilhowie Academy was an abrupt and painful solution. While there, the Holy Spirit zapped him after attending a meeting at a Four Square Church in Knoxville. Little did we know that the Lord was getting all of us ready for a terrifying event in the future.

The bell choir proved to be one of our best outreach activities in Nazareth. Jimmy and Rose Mary enrolled several students of the high school classes at the Nazareth Baptist School. Eventually they formed three groups which practiced several times a week in the large dining room in our beautiful home in Nazareth. I complained that they kept me awake during my naptime! The BCI bought a yellow VW minivan with an automatic transmission for the bell ministry. We cut the bell tables from packing crates to fit into the back along with the bells. I became "Rose Mary's chauffer" during this time in our lives. The pinnacle of the bell choir ministry was playing in Manger Square in Bethlehem on Christmas Eve. Israel Television recorded the bell choir and played reruns for years. It was a tremendous tool for interfaith witness to all the Christian denominations and Jewish groups who appreciated the music. Rose Mary planned yearly Bible retreats for the bell choirs at Baptist Village. A number of these young people trained to be camp counselors. Former members of the bell choir, now adults are the leaders of the Baptist school, churches, businesses and government agencies all over Galilee today.

The Nazareth Bellringers led by Rose Mary at the Nazareth Baptist School
(c. Christmas, 1978)

Child Evangelism Fellowship (CEF) was an extremely effective way to reach children and parents in Nazareth and the Arab villages. It was a simple, Christ centered and visual approach that was easy to learn and use. We knew Wayne and Carol King, directors of CEF from the first year we were in Israel. Jimmy and Cheryl were active in their outreach. Jimmy used to ride a Vespa motor scooter up to Rama and the villages high in the mountains near Lebanon to lead "5 Day Clubs."

One day he came home and told me, "Daddy, they are going to beat me up if I go back again." I told him to befriend one of the tough boys in the village gang and they would protect him. He took my advice and came home relieved! I later served on the CEF Council in Nazareth. I used the flannel graphs on the Parables of

Jesus to present the Gospel to the outpatients at the Nazareth Hospital. Walid Khlef, poet and teacher of Arabic who lived next to the Nazareth Baptist School, taught me the colloquial Arabic to tell these stories to Muslim Arab villagers who came to the hospital for treatment. Years later, my friend Hamdy and I were visiting the ancient site of Cana of Galilee in the Netofa valley. We ran across a Muslim shepherd who recognized me from one of those times at the hospital.

He told me, "I never understood how Jesus died until I heard you speak at the hospital!" This was another highlight of my Galilee wanderings.

A unique plus to raising your family in the Holy Land is taking family outings to the various sites around the country. In the first few years, we used to take camping trips to Ashkelon and Eilat. Swimming and picnicking at the Sea of Galilee was routine, as well as to the ice-cold waters of Ein Herod and the warm waters of Sakhni (Gan Haslosha) where King Herod built a spa in the Valley of Israel at the base of Mount Gilboa below Nazareth. After 1967, we took the family camping in the Sinai dessert. On one occasion, we were camping on the shores of the Gulf of Eilat with other BCI families. A pleasingly plump Journeyman girl was sunbathing on the shore when a camel driver came around the bend.

When he saw her he asked, "How many camels?"

I said, "Twelve."

He said, "Sold!"

The next morning, he came back around the bend and we started counting. **Sure enough, he had brought the twelve camels!** The journeyman girl started running, until we convinced her it was only a joke. Another time our son Jimmy was testing out miniature rockets. One fell on an Israeli army jeep as it rounded a bend in the road! Our last great adventure was a trip through Sinai with BCI friends. We climbed Mount Sinai early one morning to watch the sunrise. At the foot of the Mountain, I read a letter signed by the Prophet Muhammad protecting Saint Catherine's Monastery. On the way, I offered a Sheikh on a camel a copy of the Gospel of Luke in Arabic. He told me he already had one given to him by a monk at the monastery!

We chose a location every year to visit for our local vacation. One of our favorites was Kibbutz Ein Gedi near one of King David's famous cave hideouts above the Dead Sea. You pass Jericho, Qumran (where they found the Dead Sea Scrolls hidden in one of the caves) and Ein Feshkha on the way where fresh water pours out of the mountains on the shore of the salty Dead Sea. We enjoyed walks around the kibbutz cactus garden and swims in the salt mineral pools nearby. Just a few miles down the road is the mountain fortress of Masada with its heart-stopping views and electromagnetic wind currents. You can stick your hand up and feel the static! The Holy Land is inexhaustible in its contrast of beauty and harshness.

Our newsletter of January 10, 1979 showed the upbeat results of our life in that land of contrasts:

> We have had an exciting year and want to share highlights with you before leaving for a "short" furlough in the United States.

> Ray attended the Conference on Muslim Evangelization in Colorado Springs in October. It was a confirming experience after years of study and building of friendships with Muslims in Israel. He was given opportunity to share his experiences and to make and renew acquaintances with over 150 participants who minister among Muslims around the world. The conference highlighted the growing receptivity of Muslims to the Gospel when approached with sensitivity to their culture and felt needs. I believe it was here that I played tennis with the late Christy Wilson, Jr. who pioneered work in Afghanistan.

> After the conference, Ray had enjoyable visits with Jimmy at the University of Louisville, Chuck at Carson Newman College in Tennessee and with family and friends along the way. He was grateful to find his father completely recovered from open-heart surgery.

Rose Mary's junior bell choir was featured as part of the Israel Television's program on "Christmas in Nazareth" in December. The older bell choir and friends of Cheryl (35 active teenagers!) celebrated New Year's Eve with a party in our home and Ray gave a New Year's challenge in Arabic. We are seeing the Lord work in His unique way in the hearts of many of these Arab young people.

The church in Rama has had an active program this year under the leadership of George Kazoura. During the summer, he directed a vacation summer school lasting a whole month. At the end, 20 of the 45 children enrolled indicated that they had accepted Christ as personal Savior. There was good attendance at a special Christmas candlelight service and a children's party. He has begun a language course for young people with English, German, and French being taught. Offerings for the church have been high and the kindergarten has 27 preschoolers enrolled. George and his family need your prayers as he assumes full responsibility during Ray's furlough.

Turan Baptist Center will celebrate the dedication of its new building on January 27, providing expanded KG space, worship hall, and full basement for youth ministries. Suheil Ramadan, director of the center, supervised construction. Turan continues to be a very responsive ministry under the capable leadership of Suheil and his wife Fida. The kindergarten enrolls 60 children. Southern Baptists have contributed over $25,000 to this building project through the Lottie Christmas offering and the Cooperative Program.

The moving of the Norman Lytles to Haifa and the return of David Groseclose, former Journeyman, who will live in Cana of Galilee, have reinforced ministries in Galilee. Ruth Rexrode, formerly of Calloway Gardens, Georgia, is serving as secretary to Dale Thorne who is now the administrator of the Baptist Convention. We also look forward to the coming of the Ray Hicks, former Journeyman who are in Arabic studies. All of these along with the capable local leadership and your prayers and support give us new hope for the strengthening of ministries all over Galilee.

The Sullivan Baptist Association in Kingsport, Tennessee, is providing us with a furnished home for our furlough February through June 1979.

Ray, Chuck, Cheryl, James and Rose Mary in Louisville, Kentucky, 1979

Chapter 18

1979 MOODY PUBLISHING

The FMB instituted a more flexible plan for furloughs and stateside assignment so we were able to return to the States in the spring of 1979. Becky Lampley Leonard from my home church of Pritchard Memorial in Charlotte and her husband Jerry arranged a furlough home in Kingsport, Tennessee, which was Jerry's hometown. Becky and Jerry lived formerly in Viet Nam and Saudi Arabia working in construction and had a heart for worldwide missions. Kingsport was the home of Kingsport Press, one of the largest in the country. I arranged to have my D.Min. Project report, *Dialogue and Interfaith Witness with Muslims*, typeset on a large IBM machine in someone's basement. A local printer, Watson Lithograph, helped me arrange the book for publishing. I brought the films of the manuscript home to proofread during the day and they corrected them at night. Finally, Kingsport Press bound the book. Moody Book Store in town gave me their logo as a publisher and assisted in distribution. I used a beautiful picture of the Basilica of Annunciation and the Mosque of Peace in Nazareth on the cover. I learned in publishing that more mistakes are made on the cover of a book than inside the book. I later found three typos on the back cover! The book was finished in time for me to drive across the mountains to have the first book signing in the Baptist Bookstore at Ridgecrest Baptist Assembly during mission's week in July of 1979.

Book signing at Ridgecrest, July 1979

In the beginning, I hoped that Broadman Press, or the Home Mission Board and the Southern Baptists would help me publish the book, but God had other plans. Kate Ellen Gruver felt the book was "over the head" of the average Southern Baptist. There was apprehension among some Baptists about publishing a book with the theme of "dialogue" since it was considered a liberal term by some. I made it clear in the book that we started with Muslims as fellow human beings and communicated the Gospel in terms they could understand. **The Baptist reticence in publishing the book was a blessing in disguise** since it allowed me the freedom to reprint on demand and share it with many other different churches and groups. The book, to date, has been through 10 printings, two translations and sold over 10,000 copies, mainly when I teach or speak.

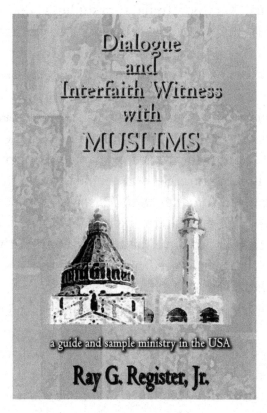

Dialogue... 10th printing

After returning to Galilee in June of 1979, I taught a short course at the Bethlehem Bible College using the book as a text. One of the students started translating it into Arabic on his own. In order to bring the translation under control I asked Yousif Qubti, teacher of Arabic History at the Nazareth Baptist School to do an official translation in Arabic. Later I contacted my FMB colleague, Francis Fuller, at the Baptist Publications in Beirut and they set the book up on film under the generic title in Arabic of *muhadatha beyn al-asdiqa* (Conversations Between

Friends). Some years later, Dr. Hawlngam Haokip, President of the Manipuri Baptist Convention came through Israel on his way back to Imphal, Manipur, India from studies at Southern Baptist Seminary. He took a copy of the book to be translated into Manipuri to train his people in outreach to Muslims. The translation manuscript was destroyed accidently when Dr. Hawlngam's children cleaned out his office and burned the translation, thinking it was trash. I finally made a trip to Manipur years later with Global Mission Fellowship, now e3, and finalized the publication. There are plans to print it in Mandarin, and hopefully Spanish and French in the future. Several people through the years have commented that *Dialogue,,,with Muslims* helped them to understand Muslims and share their faith easier. I believe that is the reason the Lord gave me the verses from the Bible and the Quran. His Spirit graced me during those years of Galilee Wanderings in order to teach and bless others.

Many unusual servants of the Lord influenced the development of my ministry to Muslims and future writings. One was Charles Marsh, a veteran missionary to North Africa, who I met in a conference in Cyprus. Charles emphasized the need for security in dealing with Muslims. He told about how his first 12 converts were martyred because he taught them to express their faith publically. He learned to teach his new Muslim believers in Jesus to be cautious and wise in sharing their faith until a large enough group gathered so they could protect each other.

Sami Odeh, a native of Nazareth who lived in Birmingham, England visited in the villages of Galilee with me after he was expelled from Yemen after leading a number of Muslims to the Lord there. Sami taught me to watch for response in the faces of individual Muslims among the families we visited. Then, follow up on the ones who show interest in order not to waste time on those who were unresponsive.

Roy Whitman, a veteran missionary to Jordan, visited Nazareth after the 1967 war. Part Jamaican with dark skin and fluent Arabic with a British accent, he served as chaplain to Christians in the Jordanian Army. The locals admired Roy for his integrity and love for the Arab people. He taught me the importance of ecclesiology and ethics in church planting. I asked him why a certain American mission could justify taking their pastors to court in several counties in the Middle East. He explained that they sent their American missionaries out as bishops, and never elevated the local Arab clergy to their level. They believed in "falling from grace," which justified them in taking the local leaders to court when they disagreed with the missionary leaders.

I mentioned Dr. Finlay Graham earlier. He always encouraged me to improve my Arabic, which could be a struggle in Israel due to Hebrew being the national language. On his last trip to the Galilee he brought me a thick copy of *A Dictionary of Modern Lebanese Proverbs*. (Freyha, Beirut, 1974) He told me if that did not improve my Arabic, I could simply memorize all the words in the Arabic dictionary, like he did! Finlay was as determined in Arabic as in other areas of his life. A former RAF pilot, he was noted for his fast driving. On retirement from the IMB, the BCI presented him with a busted piston from a VW mini-cab truck he accidently put in reverse going down the mountain from Jerusalem on one of his trips.

Reverend Walter Wasserman, long-time German missionary in the Middle East, held conferences in the West Bank to encourage Muslim believers and those who worked with them. The British interred Walter's family in Haifa during World War II. He maintained contact with thousands of Muslim inquirers around the Middle East through colorful Gospel literature and cassettes of the "Youth Center" in Switzerland. Whenever I complained about the Muslim believers I knew having difficulties and persecution, he remarked, "Ray, all the Muslims I know have the same problems all over the Middle East. They simply have to live through them, and they grow in their faith. It makes them stronger." When he learned through a professional market study that the majority of the population in the Middle East were functionally illiterate he changed to audio and visual mediums. I asked him one time "Where do you send a person to train in Islam and Arabic?" He replied, "Al Azhar University in Egypt."

Two encouragers from the IMB were Bill Marshall and Bill Wagner who served as Church Planting consultants for our area. Bill Marshall and his wife Alice lost two households of furniture in the civil unrest when Turkey took over parts of Cyprus. We enjoyed visits to their home in Kyrenia during conferences and vacations. Bill Wagner was instrumental in gathering workers and Muslim background believers from all over our area for conferences on church planting. God was always faithful in providing the right persons to encourage us to face the challenges that lay ahead.

Section V

Growth and Retreat

Chapter 19

GROWTH

Living in *Dar Baker* "Baker House", which had now become *Dar Register* "Register House", had its blessings in Nazareth in the 1980's. Coming back after many long visits in the Arab villages in Galilee I was able to bask in the comfort and beauty of the garden, the arched veranda and enjoy our family. Each child had their own room and we had our master bedroom across on the other side of the house. We had our private living room, a larger dining room salon which doubled as a meeting and hand bell practice room, and a large kitchen with a stairwell leading down to the meeting hall, journeyman apartment and guest rooms in the basement. We were slowly developing the empty nest syndrome as our children grew up and out.

Chuck graduated from Chilhowie and transferred to Carson-Newman College near Knoxville, Tennessee. Jimmy anxiously packed and repacked his trunk to move to Louisville, Kentucky to enter the University of Louisville. Cheryl attended high school at the American International School (AIS) in Kefr Shmaryahu next to Herzlia, a northern suburb of Tel Aviv. All the children lived during High School at the "MK Dorm", attended AIS during the week, and commuted home on the weekends. They all had their circle of close Arab neighbor friends in Nazareth and classmates at the Nazareth Baptist School, as well as a contrasting set of friends at AIS who were the children of diplomats and English speaking businessmen in the country.

One of our bell choir members was the son of the Director of Social Welfare in Nazareth. I had become friends with her and the other social workers and shared concern over special cases of Arabs from the West Bank and Galilee. One day Selwa, a social worker, showed up at our door with a beautiful teenaged Christian Arab girl named Nawal. Selwa asked to come in with her. She sat down and explained that Nawal needed a home. Her mother committed suicide after she was born. Her father was unstable and unable to care for her. The Sisters of Charity in Jerusalem where she had been living were unable to control her. Selwa thought that our daughter Cheryl, being the same age, would be a good influence on Nawal. Rose Mary and I remembered that after the 1967 War we had investigated adopting an Arab child from one of the orphanages in East Jerusalem, but were prevented at the time. Taking Nawal in made our life very interesting! It required me to set some perimeters in our home, such as her not wearing short shorts. I explained that even though I was a happily married man I could not take such exposure! Fortunately, she dressed appropriately from then on. I consulted with a Christian Arab psychologist Dr. Sami Debini and he told me that in Arab society only capital punishment, not moral persuasion is heeded. One night in exasperation over some discipline we had to impose, she told me,

"I will just commit suicide like my mother. I'll burn myself!"

I told her, "You will not disgrace my family by committing suicide in our house. You will have to do it out in the street."

She quickly recanted.

Her father was another case. He told me when I saw him in the market one day, "I am going to take Nawal out of my will."

I told him, "If you do I will take your estate to court and take your money myself." He kept her in his will. The Baptist and evangelical community enfolded her in love and understanding. We will see the results shortly.

She and Cheryl used to attend the youth conferences in Ramallah and Bet Jalla. They were a contrast in Eastern and Western beauty and were formidable with the boys! Though Nawal came from very difficult circumstances, she spoke Arabic, Hebrew, French, German, Italian and English. She eventually graduated herself from high school, followed an older sister to Germany, married, had a daughter and son, and is now working with a welfare agency there to assist immigrant Arab women in difficult marriages. We consider her as one of the family.

Ray, Rose Mary, Cheryl, & Nawal, c 1980

Our newsletter of March 1, 1980 reflected these exciting times:

Spring comes early in Galilee, following heavy winter rains. The hills turn green, the poppies bloom red, and Mt. Hermon is white with snow. This with the deep blue sky on a clear day makes Galilee one the truly beautiful places in God's creation. It all beckons toward harvest, which reminds us of why we are here.

Since returning home from our furlough in July, Ray has been very involved with speaking in conferences and groups about his favorite subject—witness to Muslims. Interest in his new book is running high and the first printing is nearly sold out. He is continuing personal contact with individual Muslim friends and with others who are witnessing to Muslims. A stateside organization has filmed his ministry for Christian television.

Complementing this is his continuing ministry with churches and centers in the Arab villages of Galilee. Plans are being drawn up for the construction of a kindergarten-preaching center in Yaffa of Nazareth. $10,000 from the Lottie Moon Christmas offering will be used to begin construction along with the savings of local believers. In Rama, George Kazoura, who has worked with Ray for two years there, hopes to be ordained on April 25. They have been making evangelistic trips to nearby villages. In Cana of Galilee Ray has been helping missionary David Groseclose to translate for new members classes for young people awaiting baptism. Also Ray has begun teaching evangelism at our seminary extension course in Nazareth. Overall, the work among the churches and centers of Galilee looks very encouraging. The fields are white unto harvest and the laborers are being prepared.

The Nazareth Bell Ringers led by Rose Mary performed in Manger Square in Bethlehem on Christmas Eve and were seen via satellite on TV in Europe and the USA. It was a thrilling experience for her and the young people who performed. Her older bell choir group performed over Israel TV for the Arabic Youth Christmas Program. She is helping to plan a Palm Sunday march in Jerusalem for about 100 young people from our churches. Her bell ringers will accompany the group as they sing traditional Arabic hymns as they march from the Mount of Olives across the valley and up through Saint Steven's Gate into Jerusalem. Since both Eastern and Western churches will celebrate Easter together this year all denominations will participate together in the Palm Sunday event.

As all this happens our family continues to grow up and apart! Cheryl is in the 11th grade class president and on the student council at AIS near Tel Aviv. Honors English and History along with school play practice keep her very busy. We enjoy her weekend visits home but do not look forward to the day she leaves for college!

Nawal, the Arab girl who lives with us, accepted the Lord at an evangelical conference in August and is preparing for baptism. She is attending night school and job hunting. Please pray for her and us.

Chuck continues Chemistry major at Carson-Newman College and Jimmy has transferred from Louisville to Oregon State University in Corvallis where he is studying mechanical engineering. We naturally miss them both.

Continue to pray for us as we look forward to the harvest. Thank you for your many letters, cards, prayers, and continued giving through the Cooperative Program and the Lottie Moon Christmas Offering. Pray especially as we plan with local leaders and expatriate partners for bold missions in Galilee during the remainder of this century.

Our Christmas newsletter of 1980 evidenced continued growth:

"Good News"

Bad news seems standard for the Middle East! Iran-Iraq war, hostages, Khomeini, oil crisis, etc. But that is only one side of the news. Good news still rings out from the Holy Land – "Don't be afraid. Look here. I have good news for you!" (Luke 2:10) The good news of Jesus is making a difference in Galilee. It is being told by your representatives and by many faithful believers and it is bringing results!

One way it is being told is through the "Jesus" Film we recently acquired in Arabic. It is being shown all over Galilee and Israel almost daily. Well over 10,000 Arabs have seen it. Ray showed it in the middle of a Muslim village one night and a Hajj (a Muslim who has made pilgrimage to Mecca) came up afterward and said, "That is just like it says in the Quran, that Jesus was born of a virgin, healed the sick and raised the dead!" Another Muslim leader indicated to Ray after seeing the film that he wanted to be baptized. So that is good news through the "Jesus" Film.

Bells are ringing out good news through Rose Mary's "Nazareth Bellringers," She has four groups of young Arabs from the Nazareth Baptist School performing around the country. Many have accepted the Lord and Sahir, the leader was baptized with a group of 20 in June. Also, Nawal, the Arab girl who lives with us was baptized.

Evangelistic centers all over Galilee are telling the good news. To date there has been over 30 baptisms in Nazareth and the village centers this year. For the first time we heard a Muslim give testimony that "Jesus is the only Savior of the world" and go into the water for him! An Egyptian youth group visiting recently brought many to the point of decision.

It is good news that so many Arab young people are committing their lives and being trained to lead others to Christ. Five young men will be ordained as deacons in the Nazareth Baptist Church. Each is a committed witness. 15 young people are studying in the Christian Service Training Center where Ray teaches evangelism in Arabic.

You have helped share this good news in Galilee. How? Through your prayers and your faithful giving. You are helping to finish the building of a new evangelistic center in Yaffa of Nazareth through the Lottie Moon Christmas offering. You have helped provide hand bells and music for the youth choirs. Your Cooperative Program gifts week by week through your local church has provided us transportation (over $3 per gallon) as we visit centers in Galilee and witness to Muslims. You are assisting in the education of Chuck at Carson Newman, Jimmy at Oregon State, and Cheryl at AIS, Israel which has freed us for telling the good news. Thanks for helping us keep on. And remember, we are just in the beginning of the harvest. Many still have not heard the angel's story right here in Galilee.

Nazareth Bellringers performing at Baptist Village, 1980

Some high points of our fast pace in "Galilee Wanderings" stand out in our August 1, 1981 newsletter:

SUMMER HAPPENINGS IN GALILEE

We have been pleasantly surprised to discover that Ray was featured as "Missionary to Jesus Hometown" in the first day's missionary story in Vacation Bible Schools in churches all over the Southern Baptist Convention this summer. So we have been receiving a deluge of letters from children and teachers asking questions about our work and assuring us of their prayers. Certainly we need this encouragement as we begin our 17th year of service in Israel.

The beginning of the summer was especially busy with camp counselor training. Many of these are Arab young people who play in Rose Mary's bell choirs. Ray has packed up suitcase and typewriter to catch up on correspondence while accompanying Rose Mary to training and conferences at Baptist Village where camps are held.

Ray is coordinating the work of the Children's Evangelical Fellowship (CEF) in Nazareth while its director is on furlough in the U.S.A. At a recent training conference for CEF "5 Day Clubs" at Baptist Village an Arab teacher from Yaffa village accepted Christ as personal savior, as well as 15 campers who heard the Gospel during the training sessions. Now those trained are going throughout Galilee and parts of the West Bank leading Vacation Bible Schools. Pray that hundreds may respond to the Gospel message!

We are being assisted this summer by Lisa Richards, a BSU Summer Missionary from the University of Nebraska. Lisa's family is of Lebanese Druze ancestry. She has been working alongside Naomi Abu Ata, an Arab Baptist student, in Vacation Bible Schools in Galilee. We enjoyed having her live with us and fellowshipping with Cheryl.

Later this summer we will be in Cyprus for 10 days where Ray will teach for a training session of the Youth with a Mission (YWAM). Three Baptist young people from Galilee are participating in this training. Another young man from Nazareth will be leaving soon for the Baptist Seminary in Ruschlikon, Switzerland. Ray has been teaching these students missions and theology at our Baptist Training Center at the Nazareth Baptist School.

Our family is experiencing change this summer. Chuck joined the Marine Corp, finished basic training and is being stationed at Camp Pendleton near San Diego, Ca. Jimmy is employed in 2 jobs this summer in Oregon and is considering working for a semester.

Cheryl graduated from the American International School and received the art award for the senior class. She leaves in August for Carson Newman College in Tennessee to study art. We all stand in special need of prayer as the family disperses.

In addition to the above, Ray continues to supervise the construction of the Yaffa Baptist Center. Pray for him and the small group of believers there as they plan for the opening of this ministry in the fall.

Now both boys were in college and Cheryl was on her way. Chuck called one day from the States and indicated he needed $50. Before I could send it, Jimmy called and said he needed $500! I scrambled around to get his check off as soon as possible and forgot about Chuck. Several weeks later Chuck called and asked,

"Dad, what is your birthdate?"

I told him and asked, "Why?"

He said, "I am filling out some papers."

"What papers?"

"I am joining the Marines."

I said, "You mean you are joining the Marines because I forgot to send you the $50?"

He said, "Dad, I am starving. I have to do something."

We had a little talk about, "He who takes up the sword will die by the sword." These words were to haunt us in the not too distant future.

My father had been in bad health for some time. He remarried to Atha Mae Barwick of Florence, South Carolina a few years after my mother's death in 1971. Atha was a no-nonsense person and would not tolerate his drunken rampages. At one point, I had to intervene and tell him I would personally put him in jail if he treated her like he treated my mother! He claims to have injured his heart while separating two drunks who were fighting. I sometimes think he may have been one of them. It does not make me feel good to speak disrespectfully of him and causes me pain to do so. His grandchildren adored him and he and his Camero were their role models. He was a man of contrasts. Handsome, personable, and a hard worker when sober, but a dangerous monster after one or two drinks. He started a Scout troop for me every place we lived. He knew what was right and always counseled me to follow an honest path. However, the drinking, which started in his early college days in Newbury, SC in the mid 1930's, was his undoing. I learned years later from my sister Betsy, who lived with our Grandmother Agnes, "Nana" that he and mother had a "shotgun wedding". Mother's Uncle Bill Kendrick promised him that all his bills would be paid if he would marry her. It explained the late night arguments they used to have and the degrading way he talked to her. Life and finances went bad after all the supporting relatives died. Daddy lost our home and 40-acre farm outside Charlotte and another large property in Blacksburg, South Carolina to foreclosure while I was on my first term in Israel. He and mother had free phone service because her father retired from the New York Telephone Company. He used to call me in Nazareth while drunk and I had to tell him to call when he sobered up. I know it was because he missed me, which made it even harder.

I received a call from home in October of 1981 that Daddy was dying and asking for me. Not wanting a repeat of missing Mother's funeral, Rose Mary and I hurriedly took a flight to the States. When we arrived in New York, he was already gone. It was October 7, 1981. He was 66. Chuck came from Camp Lejeune, Jimmy from Louisville and Cheryl from Jefferson City, Tennessee for the funeral. It was one of the last times for me to see my cousin Billy Register who I spent summers with in Hartsville, SC growing up. Daddy was buried in Mount Hope Cemetery in Florence, South Carolina near the grave of his sister, my Aunt

Susie Perkins, who prayed for him to become a preacher. *Her prayers fell on me.*

While home, we visited my sister Betsy in the mountains of Boone, North Carolina, where she and her husband Dero Davis retired. Rose Mary and Dero were the introverts in the family and were upstairs enjoying some peace and quiet. Betsy and I were downstairs in the guest room talking. Betsy sat on the foot of my bed as we discussed family history. She lived with my maternal grandmother, "Nana," Agnes Brough, outside Charlotte in Oakdale, while in high school. She gently told me the family secret that unraveled the mystery of how Daddy never paid any bills and how I received a free education at the University of Virginia. It seems Daddy got Mother pregnant while they were students at Newberry College. Uncle Bill Kendrick promised to pay all Daddy's bills and send me to the best college in the country. He got Daddy a job at the Lake Murray Dam, since he was Vice President of the power company. So, I finally understood, now in my 40's, about the constant arguments between my parents and the drinking; how Daddy put all his bills in a drawer in the kitchen; and how Uncle Ernest put me all the way through the University of Virginia. Now that Daddy was gone the family secrets came out the closet! The Lord prepared me though his gracious love, to mature me enough to face the truth that should have been obvious to me long ago. As I quoted Rick Warren in the Preface, "There are unplanned pregnancies, but there are no unpurposed people."

Back to Galilee for the fall found me busy with the dedication of the Yaffa Baptist Center, near Nazareth. Yaffa was the traditional home of James and John, the sons of Zebedee who may have been the cousins of Jesus. It was a special event since the Mayor of the town, who was a Muslim and a Communist, stood behind the pulpit and said, "I admire the Baptists. They keep their word. They said they would build a kindergarten in my town and this is the proof!"

He remained a friend for years. He asked one day to see my Doctoral report, which was published in Arabic in Beirut. He wanted to use it to overcome the propaganda of the fundamentalist Muslim movement that opposed him in town. He told me he was disappointed that I was too soft on them!

The Yaffa Center Kindergarten became an experiment in self-support. We charged tuition from the beginning. The Ministry of Education trained our teacher and her helper. They used the then new idea of centers of learning in the same room with the children. The parents were willing to pay more since our staff was qualified. We were able to get maximum use of the building during the week with the KG and use it on evenings and weekends for worship and Bible study. The Inseir family, Monsour, his son Steve, Hanna his sister and Secretary of the Local Council, and Emad Khoury were active leaders. Emad dedicated himself to the ministry under the preaching of Dr. Roy Fish who came several times to conduct revival services in Yaffa. Roy was a real missionary preacher and loved to be out among the people. He was an encouragement to me.

Yaffa Baptist Center

All three of our children were now in the States. We decided to take a short furlough from April 1 until August 15, 1982. The FMB allowed us to bank time according to our length of field service. This gave us the flexibility to schedule furloughs according to work and family needs. The Leonard's in Kingsport, Tennessee again arranged for us to make contact with a family willing to let us stay in their home. This time we stayed in an old two story home estate on the east side of Kingsport. The house was like something out of the Adams family on TV! One night when I was out speaking, Rose Mary and Cheryl heard strange noises and saw uncanny movements outside. They were scared and kept the shades closed. Driving up in the dark, I discovered the cause of their alarm. A spotted Holstein cow was grazing outside! All you could see were her white spots floating around in the dark. The house had an unusual winding stairway up to the second floor. Hanging over the first landing was a large portrait of a stern looking man and wife, who were obviously the patriarchs of the clan. Their eyes followed you as you walked up the stairs! I came home from one of my trips to find the picture gone. The children had taken it down and hidden it in the closet. They only put it back up when the landlord came to inspect the house. There were strange noises in the walls. We assumed they were from squirrels that came in from the woods for warmth. The plumbing stopped up and I tried to open a valve in the basement but it was frozen closed. My good fortune! When we finally got a plumber out he followed the leach line down the hill behind the house. When he plunged a steel rod into the ground the sewage spewed out 10 feet in the air! It would have flooded the basement had I opened that valve. Despite the peculiarities of that country home the folks at First Baptist Church, Kingsport, Tennessee again proved themselves a wonderful family for us travelling nomads from the Holy Land.

We traded our Chevy Nova hatchback for a huge Mercury Marquis sedan for the trip with Jimmy and Cheryl in July to see Rose Mary's parents in Wenatchee and Lake Chelan, Washington. On the way, we visited my cousin Dr. Ken Cannon in Cedar Rapids, Iowa. Ken was professor of English at Coe College. He later revised my manuscript of *Back to Jerusalem, Church Planting Movements in the Holy Land*. In Denver, Colorado, we stayed with Gilman and Vonnie Hill. Gilman was an oil explorer in the Holy Land. He generously granted funds to the work of the Association of Baptist Churches in Israel, giving them the opportunity to expand church planting and development in the Land. After a wonderful stay at the Yacht Club on Lake Chelan where Rose Mary's parents lived, we headed back to Galilee to an empty nest and unexpected events.

Chapter 20

BEIRUT AND CAIRO

Jimmy transferred to Oregon State University in Corvallis to study civil engineering and computer science. Cheryl moved to Hofstra University on Long Island, New York to study art. Chuck continued to train with the Marine Corp. He was an amphibious assault vehicle driver. The Marines pulled him out of line in 29 Palms when they learned he was a native Arabic speaker and sent him to language school in Monterey, California. Rose Mary wrote home March 1, 1983:

> We just got word from Chuck that he has been transferred to Lebanon. He went on the U.S.S Guadalcanal. The weather has been unusually cold with snow in upper regions. The U.S. Marines were helping the Lebanese Army & Syrian Army to shovel off the Beirut highway and mountainous areas where over 50 people froze to death on the highways.

> Most likely Chuck will not be allowed out of Beirut but we are going to see about getting in touch by phone or perhaps going up there sometime.

Israel invaded Lebanon when we were on furlough in 1982. Our colleagues Ray and Bev Hicks were living in Turan village at the time. Ray said that one day the mountain across the highway from Turan opened up and tanks started pouring out! It seems the Israeli Army had one of its largest bases right there and it was the jump off point for the Lebanese invasion. For us it meant that the whole of Lebanon from the northern Israel border to Beirut opened up to us. For years we were a separate country at war and the only contact we had with our FMB Lebanese colleagues were in conferences in Cyprus or when stateside.

While at a conference on Cyprus, we met a Lebanese pastor whose mother was a Christian and father was a Muslim. He offered to take us to Beirut to visit Chuck. He drove down from Beirut one day in August and spent the night with us in Nazareth. Early the next morning he drove us north. We passed by Tyre and Sidon and then up to the outskirts of Beirut. There was a nervous stop at a Lebanese Army check post and then on into Beirut. The whole trip took about 5 hours. Chuck arranged to meet us in town. We parked at a traffic circle to wait on him. All of a sudden, a military jeep came barreling around the circle. Chuck was driving. Without stopping, he signaled for us to follow. He was not taking any chances of being a target for snipers. We spent the nights there in an orphanage run by a noted Armenian family. Homer Lanier and his wife Miriam worked there. Homer grew up with Chuck in Israel and Miriam grew up as an MK in Jordan. We could hear the coyotes, in Arabic *wawi*, howling at night, and occasional gunfire and shells hitting the mountain behind us.

The next day Chuck took us to the Marine base at the Beirut airport. We visited the PX. Standing at the door, watching everyone who came in, was a neatly dressed Lebanese Army officer, obviously a Shiite. In retrospect, I think he was casing the joint. Chuck took me up to the fourth floor of the Marine barracks where he was staying. He had his guitar lying on his bunk. He slept on the floor! Later we drove up into the mountains to Beyt Mary and visited with Wayne and Frances Fuller, FMB missionaries we met while in orientation at the University of Richmond in 1964. Frances directed Baptist Publications in Beirut. We ordered Arabic textbooks from her and she published my book, *Dialogue and Interfaith Witness with Muslims*, (Global Educational Advance) in Arabic. Our book orders had to be mailed through Cyprus and it took months and sometimes years to get them. Now here we were face to face! Their house is on the cover of Frances' book, *In Borrowed Houses,* (inborrowedhouseslebanon.com) Later we had lunch with Homer in a restaurant high above Beirut and visited the Baptist Seminary in Monsouria. On Sunday, we attended services at the Bikfeya Baptist Church. We also visited FMB missionaries, Ed and Ann Nicholas, formerly of Gaza. I attended a pastor's conference and the dedication of a new Bible Society building, which had been destroyed several times. One day when we were high on the mountainside above Beirut, we heard a terrible explosion and saw the dust cloud rise. Later we heard that an Israeli soldier was killed. Our life would not be the same after that memorable trip.

Back in Nazareth we kept our ears tuned to the news out of Beirut. Occasionally Chuck and Homer managed to get phone calls through to us, but the line kept getting worse in stages as the calls were obviously monitored. We had US Embassy friends who were classmates at UVA but they also had difficulty getting word from Tel Aviv to Beirut. One evening, watching the news on Israel TV I jumped out of my chair and told Rose Mary,

"There's Chuck!"

We saw him on TV after the US Embassy bombing in Beirut. He stood guard in front of the Embassy after the bombing. We heard later from him that he translated at the Beirut harbor for the removal of Arafat to Tunisia when a sniper killed a man standing right beside him. Arafat's men left Beirut shooting in the air in celebration.

On Sunday morning, October 23, 1983 I turned on the 9:00 AM BBC News broadcast. **The Marine Barracks had been bombed and there was a heavy loss of life!** I went into shock. How could this happen? How could I lose my eldest son? I remembered the words I spoke to him when he told me he was joining the Marines, "He who takes the sword shall die by the sword." I thought about the agony of heart that Dwight Baker, pioneer church planter in Nazareth after 1948, must have suffered when his oldest son, Bron died in an automobile accident. "Lord, how could this be?" God used this to teach me a deeper meaning to John 3:16, "For God loved the world (the cosmos) so much that he gave his only unique son," Until then I never realized the agony that God suffered when he gave Jesus up to death. There is no way to describe the heart wrenching pain of such a loss.

While I was in such despair, Rose Mary was upbeat! She had a dream about 6:00 AM that morning that Chuck was struggling, but he was all right. She received two calls that Sunday assuring her that Chuck was alive. One came from a Jewish mother of one of the Marines Chuck worked with. Her son took leave and came home to Israel that weekend. Another mother of an Israeli soldier called and said she also had a dream that Chuck was all right. However, nothing could console me. I was in shock and despair until about 7:30 that evening. The phone rang. It was Jimmy calling from Oregon to tell us that he received a call from a Lebanese army friend of Chuck's in Beirut to tell us that Chuck was all right! Chuck knew the building was going to be blown up and he moved into the office next door and was sleeping under a heavy oak desk when the building blew up. He ran out in his underwear and started digging through the rubble with his bare hands to rescue his buddies. Over 240 Marines died that day. The Lebanese Army friend asked him that afternoon if he had notified his family that he was safe? Then the friend called Jimmy to give him the good news.

Not a year goes by that we do not learn more about what happened in Beirut. Chuck understood colloquial Arabic and heard conversations on the streets of Beirut about the danger.

He warned his superiors that the building was in danger and was told,

"Son, that is not your area. We are taking care of it."

Obviously, they did not. I learned recently that they had requested permission to dig a tank ditch around the perimeter of the barracks and were denied since it would be viewed as a "hostile act." The Marine guard at the barracks entrance did not have an ammunition clip in his gun when the bomber drove his truck into the middle of the barracks and pulled the cord to detonate the explosives with a smile on his face. The guard was blown out of the building and survived to tell the story. The other men in Chuck's translation unit were Arabs recruited out of US colleges. They all took leave that weekend because they knew the danger. President Reagan took final responsibility for this needless loss of life, which I call "Pearl Harbor, Number 2." Every year we receive a call from Chuck on October 23rd. God spared him, and in turn me. Through the years friends in Nazareth would hesitate when asking me about my family because they had not gotten the word that Chuck survived. Chuck thought about a career in the military until this traumatic event. He got out of the Marines as soon as his tour was over and returned to Carson Newman College in Tennessee.

On November 20, 1977 Anwar Sadat, President of Egypt, surprised the world by visiting Israel. (http://en.wikipedia.org/wiki/Anwar_Sadat) God used Sadat, Menachem Begin and President Jimmy Carter to make an historic peace agreement between Egypt and Israel on March 26, 1979. I heard that God spoke to Sadat to fly to Israel and make peace. All three men were God-fearers and sensitive to the Scriptures. I was in Haifa at the time and got lost in the industrial sector of Haifa bay. I pulled my car off to the side of the road. Suddenly I noticed several limousines with police escort approaching. As the main limousine passed me a long dark hand waved from the rear window. It was President Sadat!

Sadat-Begin Comminatory Stamp November 20, 1977

The peace agreement between the two warring countries suddenly opened up travel for us to visit Egypt for ministry. A Christian Coptic Evangelical businessman visited us in Nazareth and invited us down to Cairo in 1983. The bus ride down through Sinai seemed endless, passing an isolated Army officer's town in the middle of the dessert outside Cairo. We stayed in a modest hotel on one of the main squares in Cairo. Looking out the window, we could see chickens, goats and other animals being raised on the rooftops. The trolleys and trains were full of people hanging out of the doors and sometimes on the roof. Driving was like a demolition derby! Our host recently bought a new car and it was already dented. Egyptian police do not stop you to give you a ticket. That could back up traffic and cause a riot. They simply take down your license number and you pay the ticket when you renew your license. The major traffic arteries were clogged at the crossroads. On every corner and in front of every church stood a white uniformed policeman. We felt the dirt from the dessert everywhere, in our clothes and in our food. Despite it all, the cheerful spirit of the Egyptian Christians was unforgettable. Rose Mary writes home about our second trip in 1984:

> We just got back from 3 weeks in Egypt on Sept. 28th so we have been out of touch all around. We had an unforgettable time- 2 weeks in conferences and the rest of the time sightseeing in Cairo & Alexandra. Latter was a beautiful city larger than Tel Aviv. Cairo is unbelievably dirty & crowded. I've never seen so many people and cars before. The fellow who invited us there provided young people with cars and mini buses to transport us & the other 14 young people from Nazareth. Cheryl was with us- she went 10 days before us to help out with secretarial duties for the conferences. We were appalled at the primitive conditions at the conference grounds, but after a few days of getting used to it we had a very good time with the Egyptian Christian people. We managed to keep healthy the whole time- better than last year. The young people all want to go back.

Our young people from Nazareth enjoyed their first time in Egypt, though there were challenges. Two of our girls were picked up by the secret police in Ismailia because they used the wrong Arabic expression for ice cream. In Egypt, the word is "ice." The word we use in Galilee is *booza*. Unfortunately, *booza* in the Egyptian dialect means *hashish!* So, we had an interesting interview with the Egyptian detectives to explain what the girls really meant. The two girls happened to be the most beautiful in our group, which may have added to the detective's interest in them. The encounter did give us an opportunity to share the Gospel with some very tough looking Egyptian detectives.

I also had an embarrassing experience. I was invited to a luncheon of religious leaders of the large youth conference in Ismailia. I wore a new grey Egyptian suit which I had just purchased and of which I was very proud. The tables we ate on were very narrow. They fed us a meal of rice and greasy meat on large round platters. I sat across from a very proper Egyptian bishop with a large cross hanging around his neck. As I cut my meat, the platter flipped and spilled the greasy meat and rice all over my new suit! When I got back to the hotel that night the doorman told me to take off the suit and bring it to him. He hand washed all the stains out, but the memory of the occasion lasted for a long time!

On one of the trips to Egypt, I was suffering from a kidney stone. I tried to flush it out in Galilee by drinking castor oil. All that did was make my skin smell like castor oil! Rose Mary and I took our first horse carriage ride. The joggling from that carriage on the stone street caused me to pass the kidney stone!

The locals warned us not to change money on the street. We learned the hard way. Rose Mary was shopping for some Egyptian cloth material. A young man came up and offered to change money at a very good rate. I watched as he flipped the cash as he counted. When we got to the store to buy the cloth we counted out the money. Instead of 113 dollars Egyptian, he had given us 13! We learned they have a way of folding the money so they count the same bill numerous times. The shopkeeper was angry we did not exchange the money with him. He told us the merchants do not cheat us because they want our business. It was a costly lesson.

The closest I came to being afraid in Egypt was when we rode the trolley from downtown to the suburb where we were staying. It was so crowded Rose Mary and I were separated by the jostling passengers. We did manage to get off together. It was an experience I would not want to repeat.

On our last trip, we made reservations for a hotel in Luxor from a travel agency in Cairo. We flew down and went to our hotel. No reservations! The clerk said they were not in the system. I threatened to sleep in his office until he got us reservations. He finally relented and gave us a room. We enjoyed the spectacular ruins in Luxor the next day and were happy to get a train back to Cairo.

The churches and believers in Egypt left a lasting impression of their devotion to the Lord. All I really knew about the Egyptians up until our visits in 1983-85 were the Friday evening Egyptian soap operas on TV that competed with our church meetings in Rama. Now we experienced their ongoing commitment to their faith in the midst of difficult circumstances. I had the privilege of visiting a young married group at Qasr al-Mubara Church where Munis Abdel Nur preached. I met him previously in Cyprus. I still have the clock presented to me as a gift after teaching on the book of Ephesians at a youth conference in Alexandria. The singing of the "New Life" choir that continues to encourage Arab believers inspired us. The church in Egypt still carries the light of the Gospel shared with them by the Apostle Mark in the first century. Despite continual pressure from the Muslim majority, they have meetings of thousands of believers in cave churches and conference centers around their vast land. The renewal in Egypt was part of a worldwide phenomenon as I was soon to learn.

Egypt played a dramatic and unexpected role in our use of the Jesus Film. I lent a copy of the Jesus Film to John Pex in Eilat. John was Dutch and his wife Judy was from Maine. He gave the film to a team to go down into Sinai and show it to the Bedouin. In the middle of the showing, the Egyptian police raided the place! They confiscated the film, arrested the team and put them in jail. Early the next morning there was a commotion in the jail. One of the team looked out the cell window and saw his partner running out through the dessert! The Egyptians kept the film for at least six months and I appealed to the US Embassy to try to get it back. One day I received a call to come down to the Embassy. The Egyptians returned the film!

The Embassy official who gave the film back to me said, "Ray, please do not show any more films in Egypt. We had to go to the highest levels of the Egyptian government to get the film back. They were using it to show to all their soldiers in training so they would know the topography of the Holy Land in case they invaded!"

In any case, we knew the Jesus Film, translated into Arabic, must have had a spiritual impact on some of those Muslim soldiers. Today the "J-Film," as we call it, is available on DVD in many languages and is still one of the best ways to share the Good News.

Amsterdam 83 and 86, Zeist and to the Uttermost Parts

The Billy Graham Evangelistic Association sponsored conferences for Itinerant Evangelists in Amsterdam in 1983 and 1986. To my delight, I received an invitation. I learned there that the Association represented a large segment of the parachurch mission organizations in the world. I was already familiar with the Catholic, Southern Baptist and other mainline groups. Amsterdam 83 and 86 were eye-openers. Over 10,000 evangelists from various organizations and nationalities attended. The training was informative and the worship inspiring. At one worship session, I was raising my hands and praising the Lord. A man from the Four Square Church in front of me turned and remarked, "What is this, a Baptist praising the Lord?" I told him that the Pentecostals did not have a corner on the Holy Spirit! He was an Iranian believer, Shah Afshar. We became lifelong friends. I made other friends from Sri Lanka and Turkey. These were confirmations that the Lord was bringing renewal not only to Galilee but also around the world.

I met Ruth Graham and Franklin Graham at the conferences. Ruth rode around in a wheelchair, but maintained her witty charm. Franklin led a workshop on relief. In later years, I assisted in importing Samaritan's Purse Christmas shoeboxes to the Palestinians in the West Bank. One of our former journeyman missionaries worked on the staff in Boone, North Carolina to co-ordinate the shipments.

Amsterdam 83 Plaque

The Zeist conference, June 27-July 1987, discussed critical issues in sharing the Gospel with Muslims. I enjoyed networking with many others who had similar challenges and concerns. It may have been one of the last times I heard Dr. Kenneth Craig, author of the *Call of the Minaret*. While in Zeist I visited the center of the Moravians who settled there in 1746.

There were many more trips to conferences in Cyprus, Jordan, Germany and Egypt through the years of my Galilee Wanderings. They gave us periods of learning and spiritual re-freshment and contact with others burdened with the sharing of the Gospel to the people of the Middle East. Returning from one particular trip to Cyprus, my friend Hamdy told me he had a dream about me. He said,

"I saw you beside a big rock and a stream."

We visited Kakopetria in Cyprus, and ate in a restaurant next to a large stone and a stream! Were we being watched? Or did he really have the dream? Take a look at these pictures!

Chapter 21

UCCI, The Jewish Messianic Movement and Interfaith

The United Christian Council in Israel formed in 1956 to represent Protestant Evangelical churches and organizations before the Israeli government and to champion the cause of religious liberty. Baptists were prominent in the formation and ongoing work of the UCCI through the work of Dr. Robert L. Lindsey, Dr. Dwight Baker, and Rev. James Smith who were my mentors. I personally enjoyed the meeting every year in November at the historic Church of Scotland Hospice on the shores of the Sea of Galilee. The sessions were peppered with the wit and ingenuity of the Scots, British, Norwegians, Danish, Finnish and occasional outbursts by Arab and Jewish participants. I was active on the Theological Commission and Scholarship Committee for many years. I became Chairman of the organization by default in 1986 since I was vice chairman and the chairman could no longer serve. I brought the Chairman's Message at the 30th Annual Meeting in Tiberius on November 4, 1986

A quick glance at the 30th Anniversary edition of the UCCI News reminds us that "we are surrounded by a great cloud of witnesses" who have led our group in the past. These men have candidly noted our achievements and our failures. Lest we get bogged down in retrospect, which could lead some of us to remorse, let us look at the present and future. I cannot escape the conclusion that something is on the move in our land. Everywhere I look I see evidences of growth and maturing in the evangelical Churches. One evidence is

that the facilities in which we meet every year are overcrowded. The
same is true of camp and conference centers in the country. Growth
is evident, not only in numbers of people attending meetings, but
in the increased maturity and initiative of a younger generation
of leadership arising in our fellowships. The words of Isaiah are
increasingly relevant for us, "Remember not the former things nor
consider the things of old. Behold I am doing a new thing. Now it
springs forth. Do you perceive it?" (Isaiah 43:18-19a)

He spoke not only in terms of renewal, but of imminent judgment. Renewal was promised as God poured out his Spirit in new
and fresh ways. We have certainly seen that in this land since the
1970's. Interestingly, revival can be observed in Islam and Judaism,
as well as in the traditional Christian churches. Judgment was
promised if men failed to repent of their idol worship and continued
to live in past sins.

I believe we will be judged if we ever let the UCCI become an end
in itself. This is particularly true if expatriate involvement stifles
local initiative. I do not mean by this that the expatriates should
pack their bags and leave. But increasingly they will have to take a
supportive role. I have maintained through the years that the only
way to see local leadership involved in the UCCI is for each member
organization or church to send local people as delegates and observers. Hopefully, we are beginning to see more of a balance this year.

Another area, which may bring us into judgment, is if we use
the UCCI as a platform for our own particular theological or political views. There has always been an "unwritten" understanding
that "we check our theological and political guns at the door" and
lay aside our banners and placards when we come together at the
annual meeting. A greater issue faces us as we meet as twenty different churches and organizations. That is, how can we become "one
in the bonds of love?" It is understood that a basic loyalty to the
Bible as the written Word of God and Christ as the living word of
God is accepted by all. There is room for Arab, Jew and expatriate
in our many expressions of the body of Christ. Let us remember as
we deliberate and fellowship that each is represented in this 30th
Annual Meeting. We must be sensitive to one another. If we fail,
allow forgiveness and reconciliation to take place.

God continues to do a new thing in the land. Do you perceive it?

Ray with Israel President Chaim Hertzog and Rev. Fuad Sakhni
President's Residence, Jerusalem, c. 1987

Having a high position in the evangelical community had its perks, especially in being able to assist other organizations. I was able to help Rusty Caraway who worked with Life Agape (Campus Crusade) in Jordan to get a visa to live in Israel. A member of his family needed special medical treatment that was available in Israel. He was able to use an unused visa from the Nazarene Church. Rusty and I published a shortened version of the "4 Spiritual Laws" in Arabic and the Bible Society in East Jerusalem did several printings of 5000 copies, which became an important tool in our work with Muslims in Israel and the West Bank.

The Israel Government struggled with the initial stages of a Bill of Rights and asked for our help on the issue of religious liberty. I and another UCCI partner at the meeting were late in getting to Jerusalem. When we walked into the conference room at the government office, the Israeli officials seemed relieved that we finally made it! In the discussion, which followed, a Rabbi called Baruch Maoz, one of the Messianic Jews present, a "heretic." Baruch answered, "I accept being called a heretic. That means I am still considered a Jew!"

The Narkis Street Baptist chapel was bombed and burned down in the 1970's. It was later discovered to be the work of Orthodox Jewish students. The church now met in a large tent. The tent was about three times bigger than the chapel and full every Saturday! Mayor Teddy Kollek tried unsuccessfully to get the pastor, Dr. Bob Lindsey, to move to another location near the Bethlehem highway. Building permits were being stalled. Bob was frustrated. I told him, "Maybe I can help since I am now the chairman of the UCCI."

He made an appointment with Mr. Zvi Levi, the District Commissioner, who was in charge of issuing building permits. Levi also tried to persuade us to move out of the present location since it was now surrounded by Orthodox Jews.

I told him, "Mr. Levi, the Baptists built their chapel on the Narkis Street property when it was on the outskirts of the city. The Orthodox Jews moved in later because they knew we were good neighbors. We plan to stay right where we are!"

Then I started talking Arabic with him. His face lit up with a big smile. He looked at Bob and told him.

"All the permits you need will be downstairs tomorrow to rebuild your church."

A book needs to be written about the growth of the Messianic Jewish church in Israel. Throughout history there were small groups of believing Jews in the Land. Some returned from Europe after the holocaust. However, the real impetus to the present movement began in the 70's with the Holy Spirit renewal. A group of Yeshiva students studied the Torah in Rosh Pina, the site of a British customs post at the foot of the mountain of Safad, the "city set on a hill" north of the Sea of Galilee. Through a series of revelations, this small group of men and women came to believe in Jesus as the promised Messiah. They came under severe persecution when the word got back to a fanatical Rabbi in Migdal Ha Emek, a Jewish town near Nazareth. He sent Yeshiva students to beat up the men and threaten the families. Sharon Geyer describes the attack in her book, *Daughter of Jerusalem*, pp. 169-174. One of the Messianic Jewish believers, Arieh Kline, brought his wife Mary to Baptist Hill in Nazareth for protection. They stayed for a while with our neighbors Dale and Anita Thorne until they could settle in Upper Nazareth. Other believers scattered to Tiberias and to Jerusalem. Everywhere they went they brought renewal to the existing fellowships. I invited Arieh to the UCCI Annual Meeting in Tiberius.

One day he asked me, "I have believed in Jesus and been baptized. Do I have to become a Baptist?"

I told him, "Only if you chose to."

Arieh reminded me that the early Jewish believers were not called Christians until Antioch. I told him he had our blessings whatever he did. The Messianic Jewish movement in Israel is bigger than any one denomination. They now have congregations of hundreds of members in Tiberius, Tel Aviv, Ramat Hashron, Nathanya, Rishon LeTzion, Haifa and Jerusalem and many other cities. I interviewed some of their leaders for the writing of *Back to Jerusalem, Church Planting Movements in the Holy Land* before 2000. These groups have doubled in size since then. I would never have anticipated my daughter would marry one of their leaders! More about that later.

One conviction I have always lived by is that the Gospel has to be taken to those outside the church. We cannot wait for the unbelieving world to come to us. The Lord gave me a love for those who do not see eye to eye with us about religion. I participated in the interfaith movement my entire career in Israel.

Israel has at least a hundred interfaith groups. The unbelieving Jews are always searching for truth and reconciliation since they do not know the Spirit Jesus came to give us. I found that many interfaith meetings gravitated toward Jews and Muslims who shared some common beliefs and antagonism to Christianity. I always thought that they should include an evangelical Christian perspective. Often a priest who did not share the 'born again experience' made the Christian presentation. I once attended an interfaith meeting of people trying to atone for the atrocities of the Crusades. There were no Catholics present! The one Muslim participant did not see the reason for the meeting.

One positive experience I had was with Dr. Bernard Reznikoff of the American Jewish Committee and the Hebrew Union College. Dr. Reznikoff was a fellow graduate of the Hartford Seminary Foundation. He became a true friend. He liked my book, *Dialogue and Interfaith Witness with Muslims* so much that he bought copies and sent them around the world to all the other AJC centers. Another was Father Stransky of the Tantur Ecumenical Institute near Bethlehem. The Vatican sponsored Tantur and housed numerous visiting scholars and ministers on sabbatical study leaves. He sponsored a conference on "fundamentalism" when the issue became popular in the late 1990's. During the presentations and discussions, a number of derogatory comments were made about Southern Baptists being fundamentalists. I finally stood up and said,

"I am one of them!"

Later after the meeting, Father Stansky pulled me aside and told me, "Ray, I want you to know that we Roman Catholics are also fundamentalists so you are not alone!"

Taking part in the many varieties of the interfaith and ecumenical movements in the Land added to the contrasts of my Galilee wanderings. In my later years in the Land, I attended a Sufi conference at Nes Amin on the road to Jerusalem. I met people who had migrated from the Christian charismatic movement to Sufism! I believe a key to staying on track with Jesus is to stay in the Bible. When we depart from the Bible we can get into all kinds is 'isms."

My friendship with Dr. Bob Lindsey gave me some unusual opportunities to discuss his research into the Greek, Hebrew and Aramaic origins of the New Testament. His work, some of it done in the "Scorpions Den" in Poriya, resulted in *A Hebrew Translation of the Gospel of Mark,* (Israel, 1969). We had long discussions about my work among the Arabs and about his theories of the early New Testament manuscripts. In his work, he determined that the Gospel of Luke was the earliest Gospel, which reversed much of modern scholarship on the New Testament being taught in the seminaries and resulted in the "Jerusalem School" of New Testament scholarship. One area we disagreed was on the speculation of the existence of an early Hebrew manuscript of Matthew. I heard that this Gospel is mentioned in early writings. Supposedly was in the possession of Waraqa Ibn Nofel, a mentor for the Prophet Muhammad, in the 6th century. Nevertheless, no Hebrew manuscript of a New Testament book has ever been found. In my experience with Israel Arabs, I understood that Arabs studying in the Israeli universities in Hebrew thought in Arabic! Therefore, it is very possible that the Jews of the New Testament period wrote in Greek, but thought in their native Aramaic or Hebrew language. Therefore, the New Testament, though written in Greek, was strongly influence by their native Hebrew or Aramaic. That explains the Hebraisms and Aramaic expressions in the Greek, and makes an earlier Hebrew Gospel unnecessary. It was to Lindsey's credit that he dedicated his life in translation of the Gospels into the modern Hebrew language so that Israelis in this modern age can understand the New Testament. Would that the New Testament had been translated into Arabic before the time of Muhammad! It would have changed the history of the Middle East. Evidently, the Quran was the first complete book written in Arabic, which became a codified writing after the time of Muhammad. Books are a special ingredient in my Galilee Wanderings, which leads us to our next episode.

Bob Lindsey doing research in the "Scorpion's Den"

Chapter 22

THE BAPTIST BOOKSTORE
EAST JERUSALEM

When Israel took the West Bank and East Jerusalem from Jordan in June of 1967, responsibility for the Baptist Book Store and the East Jerusalem Baptist Church fell upon the BCI. Rose Mary and I visited the Bookstore and Church on Easter of 1967 before the "6 Day War," and had lunch with Bill Hern who was the missionary working there with the Jordan Baptist Mission. In just two months, the political situation changed and East Jerusalem came under the control of Israel. I began to assist the BCI in relating to the newly acquired Arab work. The Baptist Bookstore was unique in that it ministered to the local people, the Arabic churches and to the tourists. It was also the only Baptist institution in the Middle East that made money rather than spending it! Christian tour buses used to stop at the store on Rasheed Street in East Jerusalem. The Bookstore made hundreds of thousands of dollars in income through the years it operated. This led to the dilemma of what to do with all the money. Dr. J.D. Hughey, our Area Director, decided to divide the money between Jordan and Israel. We received funds for the building of village centers. It was a great assist. However, there was internal division in the BCI over the use of the funds. Some felt the money would spoil the nationals and that the churches should only be financed by their own tithes and offerings. This opinion was at odds with the local Arab custom of having businesses on church property to support the church. I tended to side with the locals. The local Arab schoolchildren, mostly Muslims, would stop by the store on the way home from school and read from the Arabic Bible we kept open in the storefront window. Muslims and others would come into the store, buy Bibles and receive free Bible literature and tracts.

It was not just about money. There was another problem. The Israeli Tourism Department forbade the local Arab practice of giving commissions or kickback to tour guides. The BCI insisted on being up to standard on not giving commissions. They had an Israeli accountant audit the books and keep an eye on the operation. Two missionaries from the States worked successively at the Store, Wayne Buck and Tom Neighbors. Wayne was a tourist chaplain and Tom was a businessman. Then, in the late 1980's the local Arab pastor insisted that the store be placed under a board, with the local churches being in control of the store. I was made the Chairman of the Board. During this time, I learned several tricks that the local employees used to make additional income for themselves from the operation of the store. One was the "garbage can" trick. The stock clerk would throw a few items from the olive wood and mother of pearl stock into the garbage can during the work day. At closing time, he would take the garbage can out and empty it into the trunk of his car. He would sell the items in another location on his days off! I had the unpleasant responsibility of having to fire him.

One day I received a call from a local member of the Board informing me that there would be a called meeting of the Board in Jerusalem. I asked him about what? He told me to come and I would find out when I arrived. I drove to Jerusalem and was presented with evidence that the local Bookstore manager was accused of giving kickbacks from stock purchases. It seems that a neighbor to the local pastor came to him complaining that the manager failed to pay her a kickback for items she sold to the store. She met with the Board and presented evidence. The store manager was very popular with most of the American missionaries and they resisted firing him. A called meeting was held at Baptist Village where I presented the evidence. Some then became angry that I had not fired him earlier! I told them that the Treasurer of the BCI was the person responsible to fire the manager. It would save me another trip to Jerusalem. The next day, a Friday, I got a desperate call from David Dorris, the Treasurer. He said, "I told him he was fired and he laughed at me! He won't leave. What am I going to do?" I said I would come down on Monday and handle it. I drove down from Nazareth to Jerusalem on Monday and asked to see the manager upstairs in his office.

We sat down and I said, "Do you remember how many times I have shared with you and your wife about Jesus?"

He said, "Yes."

I asked, "Do you remember how many times I have defended you against allegations of your paying kickbacks?"

He said, "Yes."

Then I asked him, "What do you think I would have to do if I was presented with irrefutable evidence that you were paying kickbacks for stock purchases. You know I would have to fire you and you would lose all your compensation?"

He got up, walked to another desk, wrote out his resignation, and handed it to me!

As I mentioned above, the Baptist Bookstore was not all business. We used to put a large print copy of the Arabic Bible in the window, opened to the Psalms and other books. I noticed many times Arab Muslim students stopping to read the Scriptures. Muslims and others would come into the bookstore and ask for Bibles and literature. The downstairs basement next to the Bookstore served as the Chapel and meeting room for the East Jerusalem Baptist Church. I was saddened when the BCI finally voted to close the store. Little did we know that the *intifadha* (Arab uprising) and the Gulf Wars were coming and tourist traffic to East Jerusalem would all but stop, killing the income of the store.

Chapter 23

SALEH THE BEDOUIN

A narrative of my Galilee Wanderings would not be complete without a tribute to Saleh the Bedouin and many like him who were my traveling companions throughout the 26 years we lived in Nazareth. Saleh was from the Abu Raqeik tribe that lived southeast of Beersheba. Saleh claimed to have worked with the Israel Army Intelligence, The Israel Internal Intelligence (The *Shin Bet)*, and the Israel Foreign Intelligence Service (the *Mossad)*, all at the same time! They all used the Bedouin since they crossed the borders to Jordan easily and linked up with other Bedouin tribes in the other neighboring countries. Somehow, in his travels Saleh read the Bible and came to believe in Jesus. (It is a good possibility he got a Bible from the Bible shop in Beersheba run by the Sevanto family, since we often visited the Sevanto family who lived there.) Saleh's tribe rose up in opposition to him. He knew they were going to kill him. He told them he would save them the trouble. In an act of desperation, he doused himself with kerosene and set himself on fire. Those viewing this rash act managed to save his life. He fled north and settled in the Nazareth Hospital, sponsored by the Edinburg Medical Missionary Society. Dr. Hans Bernath and his wife Madeline took him in as one of their family. The hospital compound became his new home. He occasionally grumbled that his job as a handyman, sweeper and gardener was beneath his dignity. When he got his health back, he called the handlers from the three different intelligence services and invited them to dinner. None of them knew he worked for the other!

Through my friends Hamdy, Bevin Woodhead and others, Saleh must have checked me out and learned of my love for his kind of people. He started inviting me to take him back down to the Negev to visit his tribe. He slowly patched up his relations with them. He had a close relationship to his uncle, Sheikh Salameh Abu Raqeik. We would drive south through the back country, taking short cuts that Saleh knew from his tracking years in the army. Once we left the main highway southeast of Beersheba, we cut across dirt tracks in the rolling hills of the Negev desert. We sometimes had to build rock bridges to get our truck across the gullies. About five to ten miles off the highway we rounded a hill and came upon a group of black goat-hair tents of Sheikh Salameh's encampment. He always greeted us warmly. Toward evening, we would sit around a charcoal burner and sip strong sweet tea in small cups after a dinner of rice, bread and lamb meat called *mansaf*. We ate with our hands but they graciously would provide me with a large spoon, called a *zelifi*. Then we would settle down for the night on mattresses laid out on the ground.

Once I asked Saleh, "Where is the bathroom?"

With a sweeping gesture of his hand he said, "The whole dessert is a big bathroom!"

Sheikh Salameh once explained to me the reason they have to keep a charcoal fire going in their tents. The acrid smoke keep the mites from eating the goat hair. I used to come back to Nazareth with my clothes reeking of the pungent smoke odor. The sharp contrast between the slow pace of the dessert and the fast pace of city life always impressed me.

Saleh would always take me down the dirt path about a mile away from Sheikh Salameh's encampment to visit his sister. He said his sister had become a believer and was sympathetic to him. Saleh always talked to the Sheikh about his faith and gave me a time to share a short story from the Bible. Through the years, Sheikh Salameh's heart was touched and he received Jesus. He built a tent for each of his wives, divided each a portion of his flocks and lived with the youngest wife. He gave out Bibles to other leaders of his tribe. One day, several years later, Saleh was called in by an acquaintance of the intelligence community. They opened a closet and showed him all the Bibles they had collected! Amazing that the Jewish intelligence service would consider the Bible a subversive book! In later years when the fundamentalist Hamas movement gained momentum, they sent word they would pay to print Bibles for us!

On one trip to the Negev Saleh took me on a hike to explore two mountains mentioned in the Old Testament near Sheikh Salameh's camp. We found an ancient water tunnel with dust a foot deep inside the mountain. The Israeli Government eventually confiscated the land in the area for a military airbase.

One year in the 1980's Saleh invited my family and several other missionary families to a fantasia celebration at Sheik Salameh's encampment in the Negev dessert. They had horse races to entertain us. Our children never forgot the event.

Saleh and I used to have discussions on our long drives to the Negev. One day we passed a girl at a crossroads. He made a remark that he would like to have her. I told him that fornication was a sin. He disagreed. The Arabic translation of the Bible has a weakness and does not distinguish between adultery and fornication. It uses the same word, *zina* for both which can lead to an interpretation that sexual relations between the unmarried is not wrong. Saleh never invited me to go with him again. I know he was lonely. He tried many times to find a woman to marry him. He was in love with a single Bedouin lady who lived near the Nazareth Hospital in Galilee. When her family found out he was a believer they prevented the marriage and married her to another man. On one of his visits to his home in the Negev in his earlier days as a believer, his family paraded all the single women of the tribe in front of him. They told him he could have his pick if he went back to Islam. He refused.

Saleh's health deteriorated and he eventually passed away while I was home on furlough in 1985. I will always miss him, his dry sense of humor and occasional sharp insight. He once corrected me when I said the Quran teaches that Abraham offered up Ishmael. Sure enough, when I checked Sura 37, Saffat, The Ranks: 112 it mentions Isaac, not Ishmael. Despite the earlier strain in our relationship, Saleh eventually restored our friendship. I believe God used the separation to mature him. My diary entries indicated the impact Saleh had:

Friday, November 1, 1985

On arrival in Israel from furlough, I was saddened to hear that Saleh Abu Raqeik had died of a heart attack in August. It had happened after just a few days of sickness. Saleem Nassar was also very disappointed that the duty nurses had not called him when Saleh had asked for him. But I was happy to learn that Zahi Nasser had visited Saleh in the hospital and prayed with him before he died. Saleem carried the body to Beersheva for burial and visited Saleh's sister.

Friday, December 27, 1985

Had difficulty sleeping as I remembered old times with Saleh. Was nostalgic for the times we used to visit his Bedouin tribe near Beersheva. Remembered Sheikh Salami and his talks over the acrid campfire and nights spent in the tent. The mountain kingdoms in the middle of the dessert. The burned rocks where lightning had struck. Saleh's desire to share the Gospel with his people. Our giving Bibles to Sheikh Salami, which he gave to other leaders in the tribe. Later confiscated by the Shin-Bet. Saleh's strange ways about women and our argument, which broke relations. But he later warmed up to me. Remembered his occasional visits and even the times he used to attend church. He had wanted to establish a mission center to the Bedouins and build a school. Sheikh Salami had even offered land. However, the BCI simply could not afford such a project. He had loved a girl from a local Bedouin family but the father had married her to another man. Saleh always felt it was because he was a believer. Thought about the many times he had invited me and others to "fantasias" in the dessert. So much history when I was a 'young' missionary. Somehow, I wonder what it all meant and what it will mean in eternity. His tribe lost their land to new air force bases in the dessert. Hope to visit his sister sometime with Saleem Nassar. Life is so short, and I am half-way through my career. Will there be fruit? Sometimes seems so hopeless.

Remembered the two boys from the Atowni tribe who studied at the Baptist Village School and came to me one day to ask about a friend who became a believer. One is now a director of social welfare in Beersheva. So many memories. How to consolidate it all and see some reason for it all? Jesus help me to know how to pass it on!

Recording this brief tribute to Saleh the Bedouin, who expanded my Galilee Wanderings into the Negev desert, is one way to pass it on!

Chapter 24

THE SONG OF GOD

AND THE

NIGHTINGALE IN THE FIR TREE

By 1984, Chuck was out of the Marines and back at Carson Newman College. Jimmy was at Oregon State University and Cheryl returned to Israel from her time at Hofstra University. She came back to Israel wondering if she would ever get married. One weekend we were in Jerusalem and I planned to introduce her to a young Arab Christian man who just returned from Fuller Seminary. We were in the Bible Society Bookshop on Prophet's street while Rose Mary waited in the car. I introduced Cheryl to the young man and we returned to the car.

Cheryl remarked, "The Lord just showed me the man I am going to marry!"

I said, "Great!"

She said, "It was not the man you introduced me to. He was standing over in the corner with his back to me and I could not see his face. All I could see was his hair."

She worried all night about how she was going to marry a man she did not even know! The next day I dropped her off at a Messianic study conference at the Finnish School. I took her in to introduce her to the teacher. It was Ilan Zamir, a leader of the Messianic Jewish movement in the country. He said,

"I saw you and your daughter yesterday at the Bible Society bookshop."

He was the man the Lord told Cheryl she was going to marry! What happened after that is a story for a romance novel.

Cheryl decided to start studies at Emmanuel House in Jappa of Tel Aviv where Ilan was active. When she got there, the girl volunteers were all jealous because they knew Cheryl would be Ilan's choice for a mate. Things became obvious at a Campus Crusade Conference at the YMCA in Jerusalem where Bill Bright was speaking. The first night Ilan sat in the back of the auditorium on the other side of the building. The next night he moved over closer and the last night he sat beside Cheryl. Soon they were engaged. It was challenging from the beginning.

Cheryl grew up in the Christian Arab Community in Nazareth. Ilan grew up near Tel Aviv as a Sephardic Jew whose ancestors were from Libya. We met his widowed mother and asked her what she thought about her son marrying a gentile *goya*? She said,

"We are not complicated."

She meant 'they were not orthodox Jews.' Ilan became a believer after suffering from an undiagnosed illness in the army. As he lay in bed, he started reading the Psalms in Hebrew and began believing in God. Later, after he got out of the army, he went to Amsterdam, Holland where a lady missionary led him to the Lord. He sold Bibles in Spain. When he came back to Israel, he teamed up with another Messianic Jew and a Christian Arab believer and the three of them became an example to the whole country of "one new man in Christ." He witnessed to his family. His sister became a believer and his mother was open to the Lord. His sickness was a bigger challenge.

Familial Mediterranean Fever (FMF) is a genetic disease, which can be passed down to oriental Semitic males when both spouses carry the gene. Ilan had FMF. His mother tried many years to treat it though herbal medicine but Ilan relapsed into kidney failure. He ended up in the intensive care unit of the Hadassah Hospital in Tel Aviv in a coma. Rose Mary was sitting in the hallway when the alarm went off on Ilan's bed. His heart had stopped. The doctors and nurses ran into the unit. They prepared to give him electric shock to restart his heart. Rose Mary saw a man dressed in a white coat appear in the hallway, brush himself off, walk into the ICU and stand at the foot of Ilan's bed. They were about to give Ilan the electric shock when the man said,

"Wait. He is coming out of the coma."

They waited. Nothing happened and they were about to apply shock.

He said, "He is reviving now."

Ilan woke up. The man disappeared.

At the same time all this was happening at the hospital, Ilan's aunt, who was not a believer, came home from work and laid down for a nap. All of a sudden, she was startled to see angelic beings flying overhead.

She screamed, "Lord what is this?"

The Lord told her, "These are angels going to rescue someone in distress."

The next day Rose Mary checked the end of the hallway where the man in the white coat appeared, thinking there was a door. There was no door! Cheryl went into the ICU and began asking in Hebrew,

"Who was that man?"

No one knew.

Finally a little lady patient said, "It was an Angel!"

To this day we do not know who it was and assume the Lord sent a special angel to bring Ilan back to life.

Cheryl asked the doctors and nurses at the nurse's station, "Who was the doctor?

They answered with an embarrassed look, "We don't know."

Everyone became concerned about Cheryl marrying a man who had a life threatening illness. Pastor Sakhnini expressed concern.

I told her, "We do not object to your marrying a Jew, but we are concerned that he is sick."

She said, "Daddy, what would I think if I did not marry him and he lived another 15 years? I believe the Lord wants me to marry this man."

Ilan and Cheryl traveled to Nicosia Cyprus in May 1985 for a civil marriage and returned to Israel for their religious ceremony at Baptist Village on May 29, 1985. The Orthodox Jews controlled the Ministry of Interior in Israel. They would not allow the marriage of a Jew to a Gentile, unless they were married outside the country. Over 100 Arab and Jewish believers were there to celebrate. I will never forget her coming down the aisle with the whole congregation singing the wilting Hebrew tune from the Song of Solomon and the Book of Revelation;

"The Spirit and the Bride say, Come!"

Cheryl's name in Hebrew is *Shir El*, or 'Song of God.' Ilan's name in Hebrew means, "a nightingale in a fir tree," so the Song of God married the Nightingale in the Fir Tree! Their life together would not be without its challenges.

Rose Mary, Ray, Cheryl, Ilan and his mother Yudit Zamir c.1985

Ilan survived on dialysis two or three times a week. His life was bound by this necessity. The only solution was a kidney transplant. In spite of the high standards of Israeli hospitals, there were hurdles to overcome. The socialized medical system in Israel made it necessary to bribe a doctor to place you on the top of the list for a transplant. While Ilan was waiting for a kidney there was news that a doctor actually kidnapped a kidney because he did not get his bribe! Ilan knew of cases where the nurses extracted sexual favors before giving a patient dialysis. The solution came when the Arab and Jewish believers in the country raised the funds for Ilan to travel to Canada for a transplant. Nizar Shaheen, who became a believer in the Cana Baptist Center in Galilee, married the daughter of David Maines, director of 100 Huntley Street Television in Canada. David introduced a bill in the Canadian parliament to allow Ilan to receive a Canadian kidney. Ilan flew to London, Ontario and received a new kidney on October 17, 1988. Shortly afterwards Cheryl became pregnant and their son, Nathanael, was born in March 1990. Five years later their beautiful daughter, Moriel was born.

Ilan lived almost 15 years after the transplant. He built computers. He translated a series of devotional books from German into Hebrew. He recorded the New Testament into Hebrew for the Bible Society. He was founder and first president of the Israel College of the Bible. He spoke in the annual Arab-Jewish believer's conference on the Mount of Olives. He traveled the world representing native-born Messianic Jews at various prayer conferences, even to the "Prayer Mountain" in Korea. These same Koreans and others around the world were praying for him when the angel doctor appeared in the Tel Aviv Haddasah Hospital. Already God had raised him up from the dead at least twice through the power of prayer, once in Israel and once in Canada. In his last days, I visited him at the Hadassah Hospital in Ein Kerem, the home of John the Baptist, southwest of Jerusalem. He called for Cheryl to be with him. He passed into the arms of Jesus on April 1, 2001 as Cheryl sang to him the Hebrew tunes they loved so much. He was in the same intensive care unit that former Prime Minister Erik Sharon lay for many years.

I was concerned about how he would be buried since he was a well-known Messianic Jewish leader. Some radical Jewish factions were very opposed to the Messianics and made life miserable for them. To my amazement, the Orthodox Jewish burial society was very gentle with Cheryl and Ilan's family. They showed the family how to make the traditional tear in their lapel symbolizing the tearing of the garments in mourning. Ilan's body had been washed and wrapped in linen similar to the burial of Jesus. They laid him out on a stone slab and prayed the traditional

Hebrew prayers. Then they stepped back and let the family and
his Messianic friends say their prayers. Ilan was buried on Mount
Herzl in a stone grave and another stone placed over him, again
similar to the burial of Jesus. The Prophet Samuel's tomb can
be seen on the distant mountain to the southwest. Aside from
Jesus, Ilan was the greatest Jew I have ever known. It was my
privilege that our paths crossed so personally during my Galilee
wanderings.

Chapter 25

BEFORE THE INTIFADHA

AND

RETREAT TO GALILEE

The 1967 War not only opened up Christians from East Jerusalem, Gaza and Arabs from across the Jordan to renewal, it provided an open door for my friend Hamdy and me to visit all his relatives in the West Bank of Jordan (Judea and Samaria of Bible fame). England and the European powers determined country borders in the Middle East after World War I. They often divided families. The Israeli-Arab conflict created other artificial borders, sometimes dividing Arab towns down the middle. Now that the borders were all controlled by Israel it was a time of reunion for many Arabs in Israel with their kin in the West Bank. We made numerous trips to Silat al-Harithiya, El-Yamun, Tulkarm, Deir al-Ghusun and Yata to visit branches of Hamdy's family who were related to the three-time Prime Minister of Jordan, Mudar Badran. I was amazed to find some allied with the Hashemite Kingdom of Jordan and others aligned with the Palestinian Independence movement.

In Sila, we met an outstanding relative. The father was very knowledgeable and was a generous host. He held a high position in the local municipality and sent his sons to study in Amman. He was opposed to the Hashemite Kingdom and very pro-Palestinian independence from Jordan. I believe he was part of the village league aligned with Israel. He explained to me that the Israelis charged less tax than the Jordanians did when they were in control of the West Bank. I always felt honored to be in his presence. He treated us politely and listened attentively as I shared Gospel stories in Arabic.

Another relative in El-Yamun was of a different stripe. He had family who were in and out of Israeli prisons and always trying to pull some kind of deal. I felt a bit sticky in his presence. He was a sick man. He showed up at the Nazareth Hospital one day and told the Director, Dr. Hans Bernath, that I sent him for treatment. Dr. Bernath sent me the bill! I felt for the old man. He went home to Yamun and later died of his illness.

Hamdy's relative in Deir al-Ghusun was a remarkable man. He was honored by all around him. He had a family tree in Arabic which traced every Arab family and tribe back to Ishmael, Abraham and Adam. He read the Quran to me and I read the Gospel for him. He was well acquainted with Christians. All the listening ears of relatives around us were not so informed. One day I was sharing about the Holy Spirit and they actually thought it was a ghost! His son also opened his home to us. They shared with me their concern that the Israelis were controlling the water sources in their area. They feared they would not have enough to grow their crops. I pray we will see them in heaven someday.

This man's adopted son was a successful merchant in the city of Tulkarm. He welcomed us many times and introduced us to town officials. On my last visit, he introduced me to the police chief in the area. He read the Bible and treated his workers with respect. His business is connected to retail outlets in Europe and America. I was surprised to see famous name brand labels on his merchandise. Now I know they are produced in the West Bank.

Ray visiting in West Bank Home in 1987

Hamdy eventually married one of his daughters to a young man in the village of Yata south of Hebron in Judea. We attended a wedding there. They were an entirely different group of people from those in the north. I did not feel the warmth and hospitality there like that of Tulkarm area. He later married another daughter to a believer in the Nablus area.

Hamdy's relatives made return visits to his family in Galilee. Few understand that during the period between 1967 and the beginning of the *intifadha* or Arab Palestinian uprising in December 1987 the borders were open to travel and commerce. Palestinian Arabs from the West Bank and Gaza worked regularly in Israel. I saw them build their homes, which were more elaborate than the homes of Israelis. They were the builders, gardeners and laborers that undergirded much of the infrastructure in Israel. With the coming of the violence of the *intifadha* this all stopped. Also with the return of Arafat to Gaza in 1994 and the rise of the Palestinian Security Services (PSS), it became very unwise for an American and even Israeli Arabs to visit friends in the West Bank. A normal part of the *intifadha* was to attack cars with Israeli license plates. Also, the PSS would mark any families we visited for interrogation. I simply turned our efforts back to Galilee, not only for our own safety, but also for that of the families we visited.

Ray with Druze leader on Mount Carmel, 1987

Life was not dull in Galilee. Hamdy's extended family and acquaintances reached into many of the Galilee villages. I called them my "parish" especially those around the valley where Hamdy's village lay as an ancient Roman outpost guarding the trade routes. One such village was the home of one of Hamdy's sisters who was married to *Hajj Biss*, Hamdy's nickname for his brother-in-law who went on the Hajj to Mecca every year. Yes, every year! Sometimes more than once, for the big Hajj and for the lesser Hajj called the *umra*. He had a regular tourism business to accompany Israeli Arab Muslims on the Hajj to Mecca. Hamdy suspected he worked for the Israeli Security Service to keep an eye on them. If so, they did not pay him much since he had an outhouse that was a rickety shed with a hole in the ground! We had many interesting conversations in his living room or *diwan*.

In the next village down the valley lived a Bedouin family I met at the Nazareth Hospital. The widowed mother was very smart and enterprising and raised her children to be the same. I was able to give her son a small scholarship grant for college, only $100 a year. He never forgot it and welcomed us into his home whenever we visited. On down the road in the center of the village lived the local imam or leader of prayer in the local mosque. He had a very intelligent daughter who I also recommended for the same $100 scholarship from our ABC-BCI scholarship fund. She later graduated as a pharmacologist and married another graduate from the village. One afternoon her father invited Hamdy and me for dinner. I took Judge Wajdi's advice and let the imam tell me all about Jesus from the Quran and traditions. He went on and on about "Jesus and the three thieves" a story about Jesus taking justice on a young thief who stole from his friends. He told me also about the Muslim tradition that God placed Jesus appearance on Judas and they hauled Judas away screaming that he was not Jesus and crucified him! I heard the same stories dozens of times all over the Galilee. Finally, after supper and enjoying a good meal, as we reclined on the pillows on the rug, he looked at me and said, **"Now tell me how Jesus really died!"**

I then had the opportunity to explain from I Peter 3:18 and 2:24 how Jesus was "put to death in the flesh but made alive in the Spirit" and how "he bore our sins in his body on the tree" and other scriptures that his image was marred by torture and our sins. (for a more in-depth explanation see, Dialogue AIFWM, pp 43-51). He thanked me for explaining it so clearly. We will wait for heaven to see the results.

Hamdy's village guarding the Netofa Valley

Down the dirt pathway through dusty fields was a large town of probably over 10,000 Muslim souls sprawled up the side of the mountain. One of Hamdy's sisters was married there to a very intense Muslim farmer. At the *Eid al Adha,* Feast of Sacrifice, I was able to share that Jesus was the *dhabith al-athiym,* "The Great Sacrifice" that God offered for our sins. The

Muslims believe that Abraham offered up Ishmael, not Isaac. As I mentioned earlier, my friend Saleh corrected me on this. The Quran in Surah 37: does not mention Ishmael being the sacrifice, but gives a blessing to Isaac. It does say in 37:107 that the son was redeemed by a "great sacrifice." I used this as a picture of Jesus. This man had a daughter who never finished high school. She became the religious fanatic for the family. She did all the praying and arguing and finally married a devout Muslim man. I found this common that one person in the family would do the praying for the rest of the family.

On over the hills above the Notof valley was the town of *Deir Hanna,* where Sabri lived. Sabri was a graduate of the Nazareth Baptist School and always opened his home to us. He had several very intelligent children. Sabri for many years served as the secretary of the Local Council, meaning he was the Government representative in the village. We spent many enjoyable afternoons and evenings in his home. He was always open to hear from the Word.

On down the road you come onto the town of *Arabi*, a center of political resistance to Israeli land confiscation in Galilee. Hamdy's sister married a local car dealer. In later years, he built another floor on his house and married another girl from the same town. We were able to observe the dynamics of multiple marriages first hand. He always respected us, but with reserve. Hamdy's sister went home for a few days when her husband brought his new bride home. Then she went back. He treated her as the "senior wife." I believe she was a believer, as evidenced in her patience and openness to hear the Word and teach her children. One day they paid us a social call to our home in Nazareth. We observed how each wife took turns sitting with the husband in our living room while the other helped prepare refreshments in the kitchen with Rose Mary. Hamdy's sister took the younger wife under wing and taught her how to cook and to be a good wife to the husband.

This was not the way it happened with Hamdy's other sister (he had many sisters!) in the little village of *Ein al Assad* on the side of the high mountain near Rama in Upper Galilee. Her father-in-law was a gracious old man with handlebar mustaches. He was a refugee from a village destroyed near Safad in the 1948 war. We used to spend whole days and evenings in this home looking out over the "Sea of Olives" part of which he cultivated in the valley made famous by James Michener's book *The Source.* I used to tell Bible stories using Child Evangelism flannel graphs. He and his wife would listen intently. We made trips up into the village to the spring where a mountain lion used to drink. (Yes, the Assad family in Syria means "the Lion" in Arabic!) He had a son who was the ticket puncher or "control" on the bus route between Safad and Acre. The son fell in love with a Bedouin woman on the route and tried to bring her home one day as his second wife. Hamdy received a call to come immediately. The old man wanted us to take him to the police station in Carmiel, the nearby Jewish settlement town to make a complaint against his son. We drove down to Carmiel and the police loaded a paddy wagon with officers with automatic rifles.

On the way back up the mountain I thought to myself, "Lord, I came over here to tell people about Jesus. Are you going to let me get killed because some man wants to bring home a second wife?"

The police told us to stay back down the road and wait. We watched as they approached the house with drawn weapons. A few minutes later, they came back and said, "Problem solved."

Hamdy's sister withdrew her complaint against the husband. She was willing for him to have a second wife. We learned later that the husband would have divorced her if she had not consented. The upshot of the situation was the father finally kicked the son and his Bedouin wife out and he had to find another place to live in another town. I respect the old man for protecting the honor of Hamdy's sister. They stayed with the father-in-law. Her son and daughter eventually both became believers.

Down the road, turning south across a deep ravine and winding to the top of another mountain you pass the tomb of one of Salah al-Din's (Saladin's) generals, Abu Hejer. We used to visit a relative of Hamdy's in a nearby village. He told us about a lady in his village who used to live in America. When we visited her we found out, she became a believer in the USA. She attended a very radical Pentecostal church but left when the married woman pastor took up with another man in the congregation. The lady we will call "Sarah" did not think this was the way Christians should live. She returned to Israel and married a local merchant. She always felt encouraged by our visits. We found recently that there is another believer in that town, so the circle grows.

The next town, which is a small city, is Sarah's hometown. I received word that a city official wanted to see me. He told me that he had a vision of Jesus and received healing from a type of blood cancer. He shared this good news with other officials in the region. He made Jesus' healing power a popular topic in the area. He eventually passed away, but painlessly and still bearing his testimony of the one who healed him, not only physically but also spiritually. I was touched by the gentle spirit of his widow and sons.

On the road out of Nazareth to Shefrarm stands a Bedouin town, "The Broken Well." Some of the inhabitants serve as trackers in the Israeli Army and have good incomes. A young married woman there tried for many years to have a child with no results. She and her husband were very discouraged. Evangelist Elias Melki was preaching on Middle East Television out of Cyprus. As they watched his program on TV he told them that Jesus would give them a son. I guess it was a gift of prophecy, since he was in Cyprus and they were in Israel! They knelt down in front the TV, laid their hands and the screen, and the wife got pregnant shortly thereafter! I had many pleasant visits in their home sharing their joy of a growing family.

Not all my visits were so positive. I used to visit a Sheikh who was an Al-Azhar University graduate. He lived on a remote road on the mountain behind Nazareth. Late one afternoon we were discussing the death of Jesus. He denied that Jesus died.

I quoted him a verse of the Quran, 3:55 where it says, "God said, 'O Jesus, I will certainly put you to death and raise you up to myself.'"

The Sheikh said, "That does not mean Jesus was put to death. It meant he only went to sleep!"

I replied, "Dear Sheikh, I hope you do not go to sleep like that tonight!"

When I got home, I had severe stomach cramps. I think he poisoned my coffee! Rose Mary's ladies were having a prayer meeting in our living room. They prayed for me and the pains went away!

We took a much-deserved furlough to the USA in April 1988. Little did I anticipate all that would happen during that time. I related a little about it in our November 7, 1988 newsletter:

"Home Assignment-1988"

We settled into Knoxville until the end of the year after a "whirlwind" furlough. The Foreign Mission Board granted us an extended furlough and leave-of-absence so that we could assist our son Chuck and Barbara to finish their final semester at Carson-Newman College. Ray will work part-time as an assistant in the Enlistment Department while Rose Mary baby-sits grandson Jaime, soon to be two years old.

After arriving on April 1 in San Diego, we spent time with Rose Mary's mother in Yuma, AZ, then took part in James' wedding to Diane Lyszczasz (pronounced like 'delicious') near Philadelphia in May. Then we attended the Southern Baptist Convention in San Antonio in June and returned for the wedding of Rene Kale, Ray's niece in Spartanburg, SC. The weddings brought our children and Ray's family together for the first time since 1981. Late July and August found us at WMU Week, Glorietta, NM, studying TESL (Teaching English as a Second Language), visiting James and Diane in their new home in Oceanside, CA, participating in a Muslim Ministries Seminar in Colorado Springs and visiting Rose Mary's sisters and mother in the Northwest. You can appreciate our relief to finally "settle" in Knoxville for the fall!

We divided our time between the east and west of the USA to get in all the family events. In Yuma, we stayed in a rented mobile home near Rose Mary's mother. I finished the manuscript of **Clothed in White,** The Story of Mavis Pate, ORN, while Rose Mary traveled with her family for the weekend in Laughlin, Nevada. I used a Kapro Computer with the floppy disks. I started the manuscript earlier in Israel where I took off a week and borrowed the house of BCI colleague David Smith who was on furlough. I found it very hard to work on book manuscripts when there were other demands distracting me. I needed down- time.

When we finally got to Knoxville, we faced the divorce of our oldest son. His wife warned us that she was going to divorce him.

She told us, "You can go the easy way, or the hard way."

He kept his boy for a while. We got an extension of our furlough to help him through the difficult transition to a single parent. The FMB had to keep us on salary due to some stipulation in Virginia law regarding our retirement and medical coverage. I worked with the Enlistment Department interviewing new candidates for mission service in East Tennessee. The Arlington Street Baptist Church graciously extended our time in their missionary home. **I learned again through all this that Southern Baptists are a great family for their missionaries.** The tragedy is, the first child of many of our missionary colleagues have experienced a divorce. It was like a societal plague. God graced Rose Mary and me with 59 years of marriage, but it does not make the pain any less for those who have endured the breakup of their home.

My simplistic view is that God hates divorce and Jesus gives only one reason for divorce and that is "hardness of heart." I encourage younger couples to be patient. I tell them, **"Marriage gets better after 40 - 40 years of marriage!"** Men and women both go through changes of life. We have to pray that both of us are not down at the same time! If we have patience, we are actually married to a different partner every 5 years. All the cells in our body renew every 5 years. Therefore, be patient and you will have a new partner if you stick with it. Real joy in marriage comes from satisfying the other partner, which sounds a lot like the Gospel.

We moved back to Nazareth in early 1989 and began part-time Hebrew studies in the ulpan in Upper Nazareth, the Jewish Israeli immigrant town on the hills above lower Nazareth, the Arab town where we lived. We studied on Sunday and Tuesday afternoons. I was in a class ahead of Rose Mary. Most of the students were either Russian or Argentinean immigrants. One day they were discussing a business in Upper Nazareth and it was obvious they did not want me to understand what it was. Then I realized it was the ammunitions factory. Many of them worked there. They were supposed to keep it secret!

Rose Mary also taught 1st grade reading and math to the daughter of Sonny and Sissy Rogerson, new FMB representatives who moved up from Bet Jala near Bethlehem where they studied Arabic to begin work in Me'iliya a Christian Arab town near the border of Lebanon. The Rogersons were from my native state of South Carolina. It was a joy to be involved in their orientation.

Rose Mary also continued her work in the library of the Nazareth Hospital as she relates in a letter home on January 23, 1989:

> I'm back in the library job + Ray is running around tending to business in the village Baptist centers, meeting, etc. I haven't gotten the bell choirs back together because the students have exams the last half of January. They managed to give 5 or 6 performances during Christmas, directed by Fadi Ramadan, the fellow who has been helping me. His father is the minister in Turan village.

Later she shared about our social life on Baptist Hill with our missionary friends, on May 2, 1989:

> We are sending this letter with our neighbors, the Ellers, who are returning to Bristol, TN for a 4-month furlough. Their only child, Karen, is graduating from Wake Forest University next week.

> We had a barbequed chicken supper last Monday to celebrate Ray's (54'th) birthday and ended up with 22 adults & children, all our missionaries from Haifa + Galilee area, in our back yard. Ray did the actual grilling & made homemade ice cream. I did the BBQ sauce, marinating of chicken legs and thighs (40) pieces, and setting up tables & chairs, drinks, etc. The other 5 families brought potato salad, baked beans, slaw, salad, & cake.

Our BCI family in Nazareth for a barbeque, The Ellers, Hicks, Thornes, Registers, and Journeymen Tom and Terry and Mike Lee c. 1989

Balancing family, mission business and ministry was always a challenge. I was responsible for keeping up the property of the Baptist House and handled the petty cash for all the other BCIers in Galilee. Since the Israeli currency was worth about ¼ of a US $ dollar, the accounting was very exacting. In fact, we had to be accountable for the last ¼ of a penny! Every time I went on furlough my accounts were audited, and most of the time I ended up putting in my own money to make the books balance. The house was always a challenge as well as a blessing to live in. The roof had to be tarred and whitewashed every summer. Pipes burst inside the cement walls and had to be repaired. A spring broke out under the downstairs steps so I engineered a drainage system to keep the downstairs meeting room from flooding. The garden had to be maintained. One year I put in a drip system to conserve water and Im Sami, the gardener, got mad and pulled it up! When we finally had to let her go she danced all the way to the bank since Israeli employment law dictated a sizeable compensation fund. Keep in mind, much of this had to be done in Arabic or Hebrew so it increased my language skills. All this made 1989 a busy year as indicated in our newsletter of December 1989:

"Where had the year gone?"

Someone said that when you are older, time goes faster! That certainly it is true for us in 1989, our twenty-fifth year since appointment to Israel in 1964.

In early October, we received a desperate call from a young woman in a Bedouin village near Nazareth. She fled from her home with her six young children (ages 1-8) because of a blood feud in her husband's tribe. Her husband left the country. When Rose Mary saw her plight she said, "Bring her home." So, for a month they lived in the downstairs journeyman apartment while Ray assisted them to make contact with the welfare department.

We met "Maria" this summer through our ward, Nawal, who visited us from Germany. "Maria" was born in Valparaiso, Chile, raised in Austria and married her Muslim Arab Bedouin husband ten years ago when he studied German in Austria. She converted to Islam, returned to Israel and raised six children. We enjoyed many times of sharing about God's love and will with her and the children before they moved back to their village recently.

Because of this new exposure to the Bedouin tribe, Ray became involved in the "sulha" or peace process with neighbors of "Maria."

We learned about the power of evil and the influence of the occult among the Bedouin women through this experience. The women used the occult to gain power over rival wives and relatives. It got so bad in this tribe that young men murdered their own cousins. Every year to the date of the killing another person would be killed in revenge! This happened among cousins who lived across the road from each other. They burned each other's houses. Demon spirits tormented one woman and she could not sleep. We prayed with her and she found relief. I will always remember the advice of Walter Wasserman, veteran German missionary to the Arabs, when I asked him how to approach the Bedouin. He said, **"Ray, they need to know the basics of life from the Ten Commandments, so teach them the basics."**

Going into 1990, we faced new challenges and decisions. We were rattling around in the large, beautiful house we raised our family in for nearly 25 years. Now there were other couples with growing children who needed the house more than us. We got together with our neighbors, the Ellers and tried to come up with a feasible plan to divide the house between us, but it was not financially viable. Events yet unknown would provide a solution.

Along about this time I came to the reality check that I would never become an Arab. No amount of language, cultural adaptation, and human effort would change the reality that I spoke Arabic with a "southern" accent. **I was an expatriate doing the best I could to adapt to the local culture, but there was always the tension of being part of an American organization in a very volatile area of the world.** This new realization gave me the release that I needed to follow the Lord unhindered by my personal ambitions, which may not have always been realistic. I simply accepted with joy and adoration that the Lord privileged me to live in his Land to live and work among his people who were both Arabs and Jews.

Part of my reality check was trying to reorient young men who returned from study abroad into the ministries in Galilee. The goal was for them to assist in the growth of the local churches that they left. In every case, they ended up leading a rebellion against the pastors who help send them out for training! There is something built into the Arab culture that mitigates against submitting to or sharing authority. I sometimes think it is the **"Ishmael-Esau" complex**! Amazingly, God uses this to expand the church through division, since each of these men ended up starting their own church or moving to other denominations.

Another reality check was in the area of church development. The limitations of finances and time taught me in Rama and Yaffa that it took about 10 years to establish a new church using the standard method of gathering a group, discipling, baptizing, renting facilities, purchasing land, building a building and developing congregational leadership. There was ongoing tension with my BCI colleagues over budgeting and policy for church development. A better way had to be found. It was to come in the not too distant future.

My cousin Sarah Perkins Steagall visited us in March of 1990 from Raleigh, North Carolina. She typed my Doctoral report for Southeastern Seminary in 1976 on an IBM Selectric typewriter without any mistakes. This and her work with the Department of Agriculture and friendship with Senators Jesse Helms of North Carolina and Strom Thurmond of South Carolina gave her an intense curiosity about Israel. Our newsletter of November 1990 indicated the heightening tension in the area:

ANTICIPATION

Muslims all over Galilee are talking about the second coming of Christ. Ominous political events in the Persian Gulf and tragic explosions of violence between Arabs and Jews in the Holy Land lend urgency to the anticipation. One Muslim tradition says Jesus will return before the year 2000! Ray sat with a Muslim Sheikh recently who confirmed that the Quran says that Jesus is coming again. The Lord allows us to remain here at this crucial time to encourage Muslims and others to receive Jesus as their Savior, before he comes as their judge. They listen as God adds his explanation points in the daily news.

Baptist Brothers meet daily for prayer at 5:00 AM at the Nazareth Baptist School to pray for revival. The Lord adds to his kingdom daily as people respond to the Gospel. We anticipate the real spiritual harvest at this crucial time. Added is the anticipated completion of the new Nazareth Baptist Church building, an addition to the Cana Baptist Chapel, and a pastorium and foster home for the Rama Baptist Church. Ray will survey the Galilee area to anticipate opportunities for outreach in the 1990's.

One special answered prayer was the recovery of our son-in-law, Ilan, who delayed his return to Israel because of hepatitis. We made an unexpected trip to London, Ontario, Canada in October to help him recover. We enjoyed seeing Cheryl and our new grandson, Nathaniel (8 months). Chuck drove up from Marietta, GA with Jaime to see us during his semester break. Also we made a week's trip to San Diego to visit James and Dianne and Rose Mary's mother in Yuma, AZ. Ilan flew in for a short visit at the end of October but returned to Canada to remain under doctor's care for another six months.

We anticipate the publication of Ray's new book in January:

CLOTHED IN WHITE

The Story of Mavis Pate, ORN

By Broadman Press ($8.95)

The publication of Clothed in White was a story in itself. Broadman could not publish a book about a missionary nurse without the endorsement of the Woman's Missionary Union. Finally, after several years of negotiations the WMU agreed to place the book on their monthly study agenda if Broadman would publish it. It was almost a twenty-year process in getting her life into print!

Clothed in White-1991

The publication of **Clothed in White,** The Story of Mavis Pate, ORN, in 1991 by Broadman Press gave me high exposure in Southern Baptist churches. Broadman's advertisement illustrated Mavis' life and sacrifice:

Clothed in White

Ray G. Register Jr.

Meet a Louisiana girl who faithfully chronicled her experience as a missionary in Pakistan, the Gaza Strip, and other Eastern locales. Through this book that recalls her life by lacing her letters with bridges of narrative, you'll see how she fearlessly exchanged the white uniform of an O.R. nurse for the glistening one awarded to those slain for God. And you'll see how God weaves His perfect plan through plain people. Like you.

To many of us, overseas missions is the ultimate in saintly service. A tireless task performed by people who never doubt themselves, never get homesick, and never struggle with their faith.

But it's time we changed that image.

Mavis was a lady with an adventuresome spirit. Her calling was not to go preach and evangelize in the typical fashion, but to represent her Father's love through the comforting touch of a nurse's hand.

And while her weekly letters home mirrored her resilient courage and compelling personality, they also revealed how the gripping fingers of depression, fatigue, and frustration did their best to defeat her.

Her personal ministry ended to the seething staccato of sniper's bullets. But her legacy, which endures through the friends and co-workers who were touched by her life, is a riveting testimony of someone who understood what missionaries are.

They are simply human beings who happened to serve a limitless God. Just like you do.

Events in the Middle East made the publication timely as seen in our newsletter of April 1991:

"A TIME FOR WAR AND A TIME FOR PEACE"

We want to thank each of you personally for your many calls, letters and expressions of concern during the Gulf War. The Lord gave both of us peace about staying in Israel several months before the war. Remaining provided unforgettable experiences.

Ray taped up windows in the house and sealed off an inside hallway against possible gas attack. Rose Mary stored canned goods and food. On January 16 at 2:00 AM, we had our first "Scud" missile attack! Scrambling for the sealed room, we put on gas masks. We both had difficulty breathing so we were grateful that the gas threat never happened. We heard and felt the thuds as the missiles hit in Haifa and Tel Aviv. (Also, sonic booms as Patriots broke the sound barrier!) As the war dragged on and missile attacks came more frequently we moved our sealed room to the bedroom so we could stay put when the siren sounded!

The war improved our Hebrew vocabulary. We quickly learned "azaka" (siren warnings), "heder atom" (sealed room), "masakot" (gas masks), and "tileem" (missiles). We pampered ourselves with sweet rolls and watched TV while waiting for attacks. Searching the Scriptures, we found a prophecy in Isaiah 26:20 about entering sealed rooms! Rose Mary predicts that Israel will be attacked according to Ezekiel 38:11 next time. It is a miracle that so far so few Israelis were killed, that she did not fight and the war ended on Purim, the holiday commemorating the salvation of the Jews from the wrath of Haman in the Book of Esther.

We restricted our work to daytime. Meetings changed to the afternoons so that families could be home in the evening in time for "Saddam's visits". We were caught outside two evenings during missile attacks. It was strange driving past cars with people staring at you in gas masks! People in Nazareth were surprised we stayed but it gave us rapport with both Arab and Jewish friends. Our greatest concern was for families that stayed in the Tel Aviv area. TV & CNN made the war as close to you as to us. We hope all your loved ones returned safely.

Now that "peace" has come we are back to schedules and planning outreach into Galilee for the 1990's. One church, Kefr Yasif near Acre, is taking on a five-year project of opening new ministries in Northern Galilee. Pray for this outreach. We assisted the Jack Hodges family, formerly of Gaza, to settle into Nazareth for ministry to young marrieds. Nurse Gerry Bowen from Gaza is on temporary assignment to the Nazareth Hospital where Rose Mary works. Pam Rhodes, new appointee from women's work studies Arabic in Turan village. Pray for these and others from the Arab countries who evacuated due to the war.

The Gulf War in 1991 was a departure point for our ministry to Muslims. It freed the Kurdish areas of northern Iraq, which allowed Americans to enter that area as aid workers. We received a request for Rose Mary to go as a nurse. I would go as her translator. She began to update her nursing skills and I studied Iraqi Arabic with Mr. and Mrs. Bashi at Baptist Village. The Bashis were Iraqi Jewish believers from Baghdad. We had our tickets purchased to fly to Diyarbakir in Turkey when the word came that the United Nations would not permit us to enter the area. So, we were in the moving mode with nowhere to go!

I learned during this writing (2014-15) that Rose Mary still suffers from PTSD from the Gulf War, every time she hears a noise while sleeping. The toll on our younger missionary couples was significant. **Several of those who separated during the war, that is, one staying and the other leaving, ended up divorcing. It revealed to us the importance of families sticking together through tough times.** Despite the war and turmoil around us God began working in dramatic ways as we recorded in our November 1991 newsletter:

"POSSIBILITIES"

Rose Mary said, "You can't do it. It's not possible. Your nerves won't take it!" But I am doing it. I could not resist—teaching *Masterlife* Discipleship training twice a week in Arabic— Wednesday evenings in Nazareth and Friday evenings in Shefrarm, a large town between Nazareth and Haifa. A born-again Catholic layman who lives there and ministers to drug addicts and young people from broken homes asked me to lead Masterlife for believers who meet in his home. Pray for these 20 young people and adults in Nazareth and Shefrarm to be leaders of New Testament churches in the future.

We just finished a new training program for Entry Orientation Counselors (ENOC) to assist newly appointed Southern Baptist rep-resentatives in language and cultural orientation in Galilee.

Our daughter Cheryl, and her Israeli husband, Ilan Zamir and their son Nathanael will move back from Canada to Israel in November. Ilan will serve among the Jewish believers in the country. Also, Nizar and Ellen Shaheen will be back from Canada where Nizar works in Christian Television and Arab Evangelism. Nizar is from the Cana Baptist Center and will minister to the Arab congregations of Galilee. Pray for Ilan and Nizar as they seek God's will for their future ministries.

We plan to move further north in Galilee after the first of the year to assist in church development and outreach. Our big house in Nazareth will then be available for Jack and Shawn Hodges and their three children for their family enrichment ministry. Pray for this major transition after 25 years in one house. We are grateful to Southern Baptists who provided this beautiful home for us, and feel now is the right time to make a move.

1992 promises to be a year of great possibilities in Galilee. Churches are growing and people are responding to the Gospel in exciting numbers. Our biggest problem is lack of space for meetings, especially in Haifa and Acre. Much depends on your prayers and faithful support through the Southern Baptist Cooperative Program and especially on your sacrificial gifts to the Lottie Moon Christmas Offering for World Missions.

The IMB provided resources for our ongoing training at leadership conferences in England. On one of these conferences, they encouraged couples to take the Gallup Strength Finders survey. Then Rose Mary and I sat and compared our strengths. This was very helpful. I always resisted her suggestions until I realized that one of her strengths was "arranging." She always thought ahead and had things arranged in her mind. I was a "wooer" or salesman, always trying to convince someone to do something. Our strengths were the characteristics that caused the most aggravation for the other! At another conference, they taught leaders to be followers. They blindfolded me and led me through a maze with some unknown person taking me by the hand. I had to trust this person. When we finally got through the maze, they removed the blindfold. **My guide was none other than Avery Willis, the author of "*Masterlife*!"** I will never forget his firm and gentle hand leading me through that maze.

We were on vacation in the Hula Valley in northern Israel during August when the Lord released us to move out of the

Nazareth house. The Hodges were camping at Horshat Tal, one of the headwaters of the Jordan River.

As we were driving along one day, I said to Rose Mary, "Why don't we stop by the Hodge's campsite and offer them our house! We can find a smaller place in a Galilee village."

She said, "Fine!"

Therefore, we did.

The Hodges were also from North Carolina. We felt bonded to them and their lovely children from the time we knew them in Gaza. They evacuated from Gaza due to tensions from the *Intifadha,* Arab uprising, leading up to the Gulf War. They accepted our offer. We began the healthy and arduous process of downsizing from a mansion to a 3-bedroom apartment in Kefr Yasif, the traditional hometown of the Jewish historian, Josephus. The gracious members of the Local Church in Kefr Yasif and their leader Joseph Odeh adopted us into their family for the transition. God again provided for our Galilee Wanderings.

Chapter 26

JOSEPHUS' TOWN AND THE IIBS & ATS

Kefr Yasif is one of the most highly educated Arab towns in Galilee, along with Rama and Nazareth. The Russian Orthodox had a training school there in past centuries. The town boasted of four vibrant churches, the Greek Orthodox, The Arab Episcopal, The Plymouth Brethren and the Kefr Yasif Local Church, the latter being part of the Association of Baptist Churches since the renewal in the 70's. The Pentecostals also had a meeting in town. There was a smaller Muslim population. The town was surrounded by two significant Druze towns from which occasional tribal wars broke out against the local Christians, usually sparked by rival football teams, or unrequited love. Being so close to the Lebanese border we had daily Israel Air force jets diving over us on bombing missions into Lebanon against the PLO and Hezbollah. There was a Jewish settlement to the north where Rose Mary held Bible studies with a Christian friend married to an Israeli. I spent my time leading up the International Institute of Biblical Studies (IIBS) and assisting at the Baptist Bookshop at the Al-Jazzar Mosque in Acre. Yes, in the Al Jazzar Mosque. It was probably the only Baptist Bookshop in the World on mosque property! Dr. Dwight Baker my predecessor in Galilee had a Druze Sheikh friend from nearby Abu Sinan village who leased him his store in the Mosque!

The move to Kefr Yasif in the northeast of Galilee near the border of Lebanon stretched out over several months as I hauled loads of books in our van to my new office in the back of our downstairs apartment in the "Ghantous" complex. Our new house was located at the beginning of the town, which enabled me to slip in and out to the south without having to drive through town. We lived in the downstairs apartment to the right under the apartment of Terez Ghantous, a nurse. Across the complex lived Suad Ghantous who graciously oriented us and informed us of any developments in the area. Her landlord husband was the elder brother in the Ghantous family and ran a garage in the nearby city of Acre. On the driveway out to the street was a dental clinic. I had a cap on a molar installed by the friendly Arab dentist who studied in Romania. On the street lived a Muslim grocer whose faith grew in intensity after going on the Hajj to Mecca. Rose Mary had frequent conversations with the grocer's wife. This devout Muslim questioned her about why she was not a Muslim. Rose Mary answered her with Bible quotations letting her know the source of her faith.

When I drove into town on a bypass from the south to the Post Office I passed by an ancient cemetery with Hebrew inscriptions on the tombstones. One day I filled up gasoline at the service station at the entrance of town and gave the attendant a copy of the Jesus Film.

He cheerfully told me, "I was an actor in the film!"

The move to Kefr Yasif added to the contrasts and variety in our Galilee wanderings as noted in our newsletter of May 1, 1992:

"PERSONALITIES"

On March 1, 1992, we moved from Nazareth to Kefr Yasif, a village near Acre in northeast Galilee. Kefr Yasif reputes to be the home of Josephus, the Jewish-Roman historian in the time of Jesus. Today it is a village of about 6000 Arabs of Christian and Muslim background, surrounded by Druze villages and Jewish settlements. We live in a downstairs apartment of a four-family compound of Christian (Greek Orthodox) Arabs surrounded by an olive grove and

Ghaly of the K.
Association du
ranging our sm
wives, and acc
a variety of nev
the night, gees

Some specia . . . .
are:

An orthodox Muslim official who saw Jesus in a vision
after evening prayers and claims he cured him of lung cancer. He preaches to his Muslim friends, using the Quran as a
prooftext!

A young Druze friend who loves the Lord and seeks new
ways to share his faith with his relatives

A Muslim housewife who came in contact with the Lord in
the USA and is trying to adjust to life back in the Galilee.

A bearded Greek Orthodox priest who enthusiastically studies the Bible and encourages his friends to do the same.

A Christian Arab construction worker who just received
the Lord after being an unfaithful husband for eight years and
now wants to be reconciled to his wife!

Rose Mary reflects on our new life in the north in a note
home, referring to the school vacations:

They get out for both the Muslim & Christian holidays here in
Kfar Yasif. Ray has gone for the day to greet Muslim acquaintances
on the last day of their Ramadan fast. Today is a feast day so he will
come home well fed. He has spent the entire month arranging his
office, putting up shelves in laundry room and getting faucets in
working order. He spoke at an ecumenical type Lenten service at the
local Episcopal Church Wed. on subject of repentance.

I'm enjoying getting used to chatting with the women neighbors
& drinking Arabic coffee with them mid-morning. Two of the wives
of our close neighbors are Nazareth girls. I may start working some
in our Baptist Book Shop in Acre. I had to quit the volunteer librari-
an job at the EMMS Hospital.

Kfar is the Hebrew word for village. In Arabic, we pronounce it 'kufar yaseef"

We hardly settled into our new home in Kefr Yasif before we returned to the States for furlough July-December 1992. We stayed in the missionary residence of the Eastside Baptist Church in Marietta, Georgia to be near Chuck who was studying at the Life Chiropractic College. Our friend and former BCI colleague in Jerusalem, Wayne Buck, was pastor to seniors at Eastside. It was a very active furlough as indicated in our newsletter of November 1992:

> "Stateside assignment" has been a full and enriching time. It included rest, recreation, renewal and much travel. Our main reason for furloughing in Marietta was accomplished. Chuck finished the Doctor of Chiropractic degree at Life College. Two weeks later, he received a call from Dr. Small, a chiropractor in Tel Aviv, to come to Israel and train for practice with him. Now we have two "children" living in Israel!

> We enjoyed the experience of innovative worship at Eastside Baptist Church in Marietta, what time we were in town. They provided us with a beautiful "Lottie Moon" furlough home.

> Together we experienced "Jericho" missions week and Fall Festival of Marriage at Ridgecrest, furloughing orientation at MLC and nostalgic visits to the University of Virginia and Washington, DC, Raleigh, Wake Forest and Charlotte, NC. Ray traveled to mission's conferences in Tifton, Georgia, Upstate New York and Plano, Texas. We shared together in a world mission's conference in Atlanta and in Hartsville, South Carolina, Ray's ancestral home.

> The general mood in the churches we visited was upbeat. We experienced intense interest in missions and the Middle East. Commitment to world missions is encouraging.

> Never has there been a time when your support for the Lottie Moon Christmas offering and the Cooperative Program was more essential. Opportunities for sharing the Gospel in the Middle East, Europe, and the Russian republics (many Muslim) and Asia are limitless and demand our best giving and going.

> Continue to pray for us as we return to Israel and Galilee on January 5, 1993.

I asked him if h   s? He told me, "I
s Pate to the refugee camps to treat patients.
w a Christian is supposed to live!" Her memory
ty years after the Lord allowed her to be taken

f Local Church called an Egyptian pastor, Ashraf
Ghal   hraf was not only a gifted preacher, he had an
evangelist's heart. He and I started a new meeting in Shefrarm,
a large Arab town between Nazareth and Haifa. Several young
businessmen from the town invited us to open these meetings.
Jabour Baba offered the downstairs of his home for a meeting
place. Munthir and Dena Naoum, business leaders, encouraged
the meetings. Yusif Odeh gave his backing. Some of the participants in Masterlife training from Naim Barhoum's center attended. We ran into some opposition from our Baptist Association
leadership because we did not call the center "Baptist" but used
a generic name. The center later applied and was accepted into
the membership of the Association of Baptist Churches.

Association of Baptist Churches Leaders c 1997
Ray, Rev. Philip Saad, and Rev. Yusif Odeh (RIP) in front.

This new approach resulted in growth as indicated in my newsletter of June 1993:

"Bringing in the Sheaves"

So far, since the beginning of summer, our local churches and
centers in Galilee baptized 28 new believers, most in the Jordan
River. In one baptism, a medical doctor, formerly communist, gave
his testimony. He made fun of believers who were praying for a
patient in a coma. He told them, "Make this man well and I will
become a believer!" They prayed and the man awoke, healed! In
another baptism, a Muslim and a Jew were baptized together. Last
week we witnessed the baptism of a former drug addict along with
his mother and sister. Following periods of spiritual dryness, these
new commitments prove God's faithfulness to the struggling ministries in Galilee.

The Lord led us to visit a Muslim family last week. A year ago,
the father received healing from lung cancer after seeing Jesus
in a vision. When we arrived at his home, a copy of the Quran
and the Bible sat on the coffee table. He told us that every night
Muslim leaders from various villages in Galilee invite him to give

his testimony and tell about the Bible. He invited Ray to speak at a "halqah" or circle of leaders next month on the subject of "repentance." Pray for this opportunity.

This week a Muslim neighbor returned from the Hajj, the pilgrimage to Mecca and Medina. We heard the bleating of the sacrificial goat tied outside our kitchen window that night before he arrived. The next day his family slaughtered the goat. Pray that we will have opportunities to share with him and his family about the "Great Sacrifice" of Jesus on the cross for their sins.

We travel to Cyprus June 13-20 to attend an International Institutions Conference. Ray will serve as interim director of our Theological Center and assist in piloting Decentralized Theological Education in our area. Pray for the right persons to participate in this project, which could revolutionize theological training in the Middle East.

Our son Chuck practiced chiropractic in Tel Aviv for six months and returned to the USA in April to visit his son Jaime in Knoxville and to take state board license exams. He began work with the Kale Chiropractic Research Foundation in Spartanburg, S.C. as international representative. He plans to be in Moscow for six months. Pray for him in this new venture.

Nathanael, our three-year-old grandson, remains a source of joy when we can get up to Jerusalem to visit our daughter Cheryl and Ilan. Ilan is president of King of Kings Colleges and is in good health. Thanks for your prayers for them.

Our time in Kefr Yasif provided the ideal setting for the launching of the International Institute of Biblical Studies, the "IIBS." Dr. Weldon Viertel and other IMB-SBC missionary educators in the Caribbean developed the multilevel curriculum that allowed pastors and church leaders to study on-site rather than having to leave their homes and churches to study in a seminary. Students were able to take courses from the certificate to Master's level depending on their academic background and the amount of course work. We used Arabic textbooks from our Baptist Seminary in Beirut and those developed by the Assemblies of God and recognized by seminaries worldwide. I taught one of the first courses in Kefr Yasif. The experience in the CSTC and Masterlife in former years was very helpful. Though the IIBS never achieved recognition, students were able to transfer credits to the Bethlehem Bible College and the Nazareth Seminary that developed later.

Another educational adventure in our Galilee Wanderings in Kefr Yasif was the Academy of Theological Studies, the "ATS." Isam Hussein, Director of Broadcasting for the Voice of Israel Radio in Arabic started the ATS to provide training for religion teachers in the Arab schools in Israel. Isam was from a Druze family in Rama where I pastored in my earlier years. He enlisted me as the Director of the ATS while he served as President and Founder. We traveled together around Israel Arab towns visiting Arab Muslim and Christian teachers who taught religion in the public schools. Many studied the ATS correspondence course in Arabic, which advertised in the local Arabic papers. Occasionally we held conferences in Latrun in cooperation with Solomon Duhne and Ross Byers from the Assemblies of God.

ATS Board Meeting, 2002

At one particularly memorable conference in Latrun, we had a number of Muslim believers in attendance. My mentor Judge "Fredrick Wedge" taught at the conference. My friend Hamdi from Galilee also attended. What makes it memorable is that **Hamdi snored so hard at night it shook the stone walls of the ancient Crusader building!** Everyone had to flee the building and sleep outside. None of us got much sleep at that conference, but the fellowship was great.

Response among Muslims did not go without detractors from the Christian community. For years, I advised and encouraged the work of Gerald Derstine, a Mennonite pastor who turned Charismatic. Groups of Muslim Bedouin and Druze responded to his teaching when he took tours to Israel. I met and counseled with several of his leaders. Gerald was high profile and wrote about the believers and "miracle" stories, which attracted attention. It became apparent that an enterprising local Arab leader had fabricated one of the stories. Gerald kept on through the years despite setbacks.

The Theological Commission of the UCCI, on which I served, decided they would investigate the truth behind some of the stories and the number of Muslims Derstine claimed to be believers in the villages. I discussed this with him and found he counted a Muslim as a believer if they stopped going to the Mosque on Fridays and read the Bible. I told Gerald that we normally would call these "inquirers." I warned the committee that doing an investigation of the movement would hurt the real believers. It would expose them to the public and cause them harm. One curious person had already gone to one of their towns asking about them, which resulted in a kindergarten they operated being closed. The committee would not take my advice, so I simply resigned.

Several weeks later, I received a call from Ray Hicks in Cyprus. Ray had been a journeyman and was now family counselor of the FMB-SBC personnel in our area. Ray asked me, "What is going on?" The chairman of the UCCI committee had privately expressed concern to Ray that I was no longer communicating and was concerned about my mental state! I assured Ray that I was all right, but I objected to the committee exposing the Muslim believers to possible persecution. Ray backed me up and that was the end of the matter.

The only Protestant Evangelical Church, which conducted Sunday morning services in Kefr Yasif, was the Arab Episcopal Church. Reverend Hani Shihadi pastored the church. We knew Hani and his family for many years before our moving there. He lived in the Ghantous apartment before we moved in. In the process of renewing our acquaintance and attending his Sunday morning services, He asked me to speak in his church to a joint Christian, Muslim, and Druze meeting on the subject of "Repentance." Following is a portion of the speech in my Arabic handwriting, with credit going to my late teacher, Isam Nurideen Abbasi, for the beautiful Arabic script he taught me. This particular section refers to verses from the Quran on repentance:

١٩٩٣

"التوبة" الى الدكتور راجي ريست ... أبو شاكر تيم ياسف
إن التوبة موضوع من المواضيع الرئيسي في الكتب السماوية
و هي الأساس و بداية الإيمان و جوهر علاقتنا مع الله
و الآخرين.
في القرآن الكريم نجد ليس اقل من ٧٦ آية عن التوبة !
و منهم في سورة التوبة (١٠٤/٩) الم يعلموا ان الله هو يقبل
التوبة عن عباده و يأخذ الصدقات و أن الله
هو التواب الرحيم
و في سورة النساء (١٧/٤) "إنما التوبة على الله للذين يعملون
السوء بجهالة، و ليس التوبة للذين يعملون السيئات.
و عن الله سبحانه في سورة الشورى (٢٥/٤٢) هو الذي يقبل التوبة
عن عباده و يعفوا عن السيئات
و في سورة طه (٨٢/٢٠) "وإني لغفار لمن تاب و آمن
و عمل صالحا ثم اهتدى
و في سورة الأنعام (٥٤/٦) من تاب من بعد ظلمه و أصلح
فإن الله يتوب عليه
إن الله غفور رحيم
و في سورة الفرقان (٧٠/٢٥) و من تاب و عمل صالحا
و إنه يتوب إلى الله متابا
و إلا من تاب و آمن و عمل عملا صالحا
فأولئك يبدل الله سيئاتهم حسنات
و كان الله غفورا رحيما
و هناك آية أخرى التي تثبت أن موضوع "التوبة"
موضوع رئيسي في رسالة القرآن الكريم !

Arabic Message on "Repentance" by Ray in Kefr Yasif, 1993

Our Galilee wanderings among the Muslims was soon to take a dramatic turn as seen in our newsletter of December 1993:

"The Fullness of Time"

The year 1993 was unforgettable. Never in all our lives would we expect to find ourselves in Moscow in August. We visited our son, Chuck, and Norman and Martha Lytle, veteran Baptist Representatives who transferred from Israel to Russia. We experienced "culture shock" in that vast country and mammoth city where we neither read nor spoke the language. Riding the underground Metro, visiting the Kremlin, and touring beautiful Saint Petersburg were highlights. We worshipped in the crowded Central Baptist

Church in Moscow. Ray preached (along with four others!) in North Saint Petersburg, where a growing church baptized 300 last year. We also visited the new Evangelical Baptist Union headquarters that Southern Baptists had a small part in building. (Our former IMB partner in Israel, Norman Lytle took part in this.)

While in Moscow, we met one of Chuck's translators, "Tanya," a graduate and tutor of English at the Moscow Linguistic University. We met her parents and at a five-course Russian meal in their home. Chuck and Tanya married on November 18 and will visit the states for Christmas. So, some of you may meet the newly-weds before we do! We are happy for them and ask that you continue to pray for Chuck as he endures the Russian winter and develops Kale Chiropractic Clinics in Moscow.

Returning to Israel in September, we found the country in the midst of a peace settlement with the PLO! All the major highways are being widened in anticipation of traffic from the surrounding Arab countries. Already it affects our work. Several years ago, Ray gave a box of tracts to a friend who distributed them in Samaria. About a year ago, a young man from "World A" found a tract in the glove compartment of a used car he bought. He read it and believed in the Lord. He followed the Lord in believer's baptism recently and others like him are requesting baptism. ("World A" is the vast unevangelized Muslim majority in the Middle East). Pray for Ray as he encourages these believers.

Years back, Rose Mary directed the handbell choir in Nazareth. One of her students, Fadi Ramadan, recently returned from Bible College in France and now works with Child Evangelism and directs the bell choir. His team comes to our village to share the Gospel with children. The bell choir performed for a recent Association woman's day of prayer. Rose Mary feels a sense of accomplishment to have a capable, dedicated young leader to take the "reins."

Remember us and the nearly 4000 Southern Baptist representatives who share the Gospel around the world through the Foreign Mission Board. Please give generously to the Lottie Moon Christmas offering and Cooperative Program. We work in "World A" along with hundreds of colleagues in the Middle East. Do not be surprised that in the "fullness of time" the harvest is ripening.

To make life more interesting I acquired a little red Ford Fiesta from a neighbor. The FMB only provided one car per family and I was always out running around and leaving Rose Mary with no way to get around. She was having Bible studies with a friend in a nearby Jewish settlement and trips to Nazareth to help with the bell choir. I drove the little Ford to help part-time in the Bookshop in Acre. The poor little Ford would hardly make it up the slight hill to Kefr Yasif. It overheated frequently and I sold it for a loss to some young person in Rama.

Providing Rose Mary with more freedom paid off when we baptized a Chinese lady attending one of her Bible studies. Women's work was prominent in Galilee. Rose Mary, along with Anita Thorne and Fida Ramadan initiated a large gathering of Arab and Jewish women monthly, which developed, into the **Annual Golani Forest** family meetings of several hundred Arab and Jewish believers, which continues to this day. The Galilee Women's Meeting was the first to consistently bring Jewish and Arab believers in Jesus together into each other's homes and meeting places.

My Galilee Wanderings took an unusual turn with a knock on our door one day in Kefr Yasif. It was Reverend Paul Treat, an American married to a Jewish lady, Francine, in the nearby resort town of Nahariya. Paul started out in his earlier years in New England as a Presbyterian youth worker. Then he became a Unitarian Universalist. Finally, he became a Jew. He converted every time he married a new wife.

Paul sat down in our living room and told me,

"Ray, I have come back to Jesus and I needed to tell someone!"

He told me he started a nonprofit interfaith organization called the Center of Religious Pluralism.

He said, "I cannot give a direct witness for Jesus since I am now a Jew. But you can be my Christian representative and tell them all about Jesus!"

I traveled with Paul all over Israel attending interfaith meetings as his Christian rep. One time we attended a meeting in Ein Hod, an artist colony. The woman hosting the meeting had a more than life-size mural of the goddess Diana (or of herself!) over her mantle. A member of her group was the curator of the Haifa University. Another woman dominated the meeting. Paul later told me how upset he was that a woman dared to become a leader over the men in the group. Paul was a conservative at heart, but tried to appear liberal. He had a son in the states who is a conservative evangelical pastor. Paul and I had many deep and challenging discussions about our faith. He is now with the Lord. I miss him and his wife Francine who always welcomed me into their home.

Paul was a champion of Jewish-Arab relationships and yearned for peace between the sons of Abraham. Thinking of Paul led me to a nostalgic letter home in May 1994:

"Holding On"

Thirty years ago this month the Foreign Mission Board appointed us to Israel. Some might ask, "Why have you held on so long?" Looking back, we can see the benefits of holding on. We can also see the costs. History unfolded around us. The country grew under our feet and the population doubled. We lived through three Middle East wars. The membership of the small Association of Baptist Churches grew from 125 to over 700 baptized believers. We assisted in training and encouraging local pastors who now lead most of the ten churches and centers in Galilee. Though many still struggle toward self-support they gave over $70,000 in local offerings last year.

The Lord provided us a beautiful home on a forested hill overlooking Nazareth to raise three uniquely gifted children. The young people who gathered in our home for the bell choir and youth groups now take the leadership. We shared in a Book of Acts renewal in the 70's, which still impacts our lives. We witnessed a dynamic Jewish believer's community grow from its beginnings to over 30 congregations and gave our daughter in marriage to one of its leaders.

We came to a new understanding of Psalm 91 and John 3:16 when our eldest son narrowly escaped death in Beirut. The Lord or his angel raised our Israeli son-in-law up from his deathbed as a result of worldwide prayer. Three dear parents died in our absence. We saw the Lord give life to a few scattered Muslim friends across this land. We spent most of our 37 years of marriage in the Land of the Bible. Both the marriage and the Book get better every year! You may ask, "Did you ever think of giving up, quitting? Numerous times! But the Lord who called us impressed us to stay. Also, the thought of hundreds we know and thousands we do not know praying for us kept us holding on.

Presently, Ray holds on to the hope of starting the Masters level theological program when Arabic textbooks arrive. Also, we pray for the situation to stabilize so that we can minister to Muslim believers more effectively. Rose Mary continues as a leader of the Galilee Women's Group of Christian Arab and Jewish believers. We enjoy the slower pace of village life.

What's ahead? If Southern Baptists keep on holding on in the Middle East we anticipate a great season of harvest. The Lord is doing something unique in the Muslim world. We see the first fruits even now despite severe persecution and opposition. Also, the small Arab Christian churches show new vision for outreach and deserve our continued encouragement.

When are you going to retire, and where? How can we answer such a question when we have children scattered from Jerusalem to Moscow and San Diego, Rose Mary's mother in Arizona and sisters in the Northwest, and Ray's kin in the Carolinas?! The Lord continues to give us health and fruit for our labors. So we hold on to 2000! The Word is I Corinthians 15:58.

We left a great cloud of witnesses behind in Kefr Yasif. When I first arrived in Galilee in the late 60's I visited Kefr Yasif and met Saleem Shihadi, "Abu Fawzi", a large, soft spoken retired policeman. Abu Fawzi knew Majiid Ka'awar in Jordon in earlier years before 1948. **Majiid's mother, a devout believer, had a vision in the 1930's of the establishment of the State of Israel along with the stigmata of Jesus on her body.** The Arab believers in Jesus were prepared for the event. Revival broke out in Jordan and in Galilee as a result.

I had the privilege of knowing Fawzi, his son, and Hani Shihadi, his grandson who pastored the Episcopal Church when we lived in Kefr Yasif. Other strong men for God followed the wave of faith, Gerias Deli, Isa Said (Abu Hanna), Raja Gerias, Salim Helwey and Yusif Odeh who opened the door for my stay in their town. My Galilee wanderings could appear to some to be by chance, but God uses even what we may look at as chance for his eternal design. An office cleaning at Baptist Village to the South introduced us to our next adventure, or wanderings.

Our home in Kefr Yasif, August 1995

Section VI

New Directions

"Down South in Dixie"

Chapter 27

CHURCH OF SAMARIA

On one of my many trips to the south, the Baptist Village office staff told me they were cleaning out their cupboards and found some literature in Arabic they did not need. They did not want to destroy it and asked me what to do with it. It just happened that my friend David Ortiz from Ariel settlement in the West Bank near Nablus passed through in a Volkswagen "Bug" that day. Many Arab laborers from the West Bank villages worked as gardeners and construction workers in his town. We filled the front trunk of that VW Bug full of the discarded Arabic literature and David went all over the villages giving it out! Shortly he had Arabs contacting him for more information. One Arab Muslim from near Nablus found a tract in the glove compartment of a used car he bought, read it and became a believer. As the word spread and more young Arab men became interested, the taxi driver who carried them to meetings became a believer. Before you know it we had about 12 young Arab Muslim Palestinians who were believers in Jesus! I marveled at this new experience in my Galilee Wanderings in a letter to Jim and Betty Smith on March 15, 1995:

> For the first time in our career, we are baptizing Muslims. A scenario only you two will understand. A Puerto Rican American from New York married to a Jewish believer, living in a Jewish settlement in Ariel, witnessing to and winning Muslims to the Lord for me to baptize! He is bringing me an herbal doctor, sheikh today to the Acre Bookshop at the Al-Jazzar Mosque to talk about baptism. My

friend Hamdi is working on an archeological dig nearby and wants to meet him. Only in Israel!

David would call me and say, "Ray. Meet me at the Jordan River. We need to baptize "Ahmad" who has become a believer."

Then in a few weeks, he would call again and say, "Muhammad" has become a believer. "Meet me at the Jordan."

David Ortiz and Ray baptizing believers from the Church of Samaria, 1995

We had a meeting of the new believers in the ruins of a Byzantine church on Mount Gerizim in Samaria, and it was there they chose the name, "The Church of Samaria." We would meet sometimes at David's apartment for discipling and at other times under the olive trees in the orchard near a believer's home. Each one came with mixed motivations and a varied history of contacts with Christians. I jokingly named them "the Dirty Dozen." We had to teach them not to hit on the women when we took them to Christian meetings. When we took them to Baptist meetings, we would tell them ahead of time,

"These are like the Sunni Muslims They follow the teachings of the Bible without much emotion."

When we went to Pentecostal meetings, we would explain,

"They are like the Sufis. They dance and clap and make lots of noise!"

Baptist Village Congregation was open to having the Muslim background believers attend their services on Saturday morning if I would sit with them and translate from English into Arabic. The only condition they made was that if we had Bible study they asked us to sit outside under a tree. Many of the "Mbbs" had not broken the habit of smoking! An Arabic tract we shared with the Muslims, in addition to the "Four Spiritual Laws" of Campus Crusade, was a little leaflet on the "Sin of Smoking" called "The Cigarette Talks", published by All Nations Gospel Publishers in Pretoria, South Africa. I used to tell my Arab friends that the cigarette was the West's secret weapon to destroy the Arabs since so many of Arabs smoked. Cigarette companies could sell overseas without cancer warning labels.

What an international experience to meet with Filipinos, Russians, Americans, Israelis and Muslim background believers from Samaria! The only downside was when the political situation prevented the Mbbs from coming down from Samaria as indicated in our newsletter of December 1994 from Kefr Yasif:

"A CLEARER VISION OF PEACE"

The euphoria of peace between Israel and Jordan vaporized with the massive Tel Aviv bus bomb in October. Hope rallied again with the signing of the peace treaty on October 26. Our nerves have taken a roller coaster ride since the massacre of Muslims at the Tomb of Abraham in Hebron last February. The only thing that keeps us steady is a clearer vision of what the Lord is doing in the Middle

East. The gathering of the Galilee women's group, both Arab and Jewish believers in the Lord, the day after the bombing gave hope to that vision. They met in total peace and unity, reinforcing our experience that Jesus is the only way to true peace in our area.

In August, we were delighted with a short visit from Chuck and Tanya from Moscow. Then we traveled to Norway to attend the European Baptist Federation Conference in Lillehammer with over 3000 Baptists from Europe and Russia. Vacation time in Oslo, Geranger fiord, and Bergen renewed our spirits. We returned to Israel in time for an "Experiencing God" conference led by Henry Blackaby.

The International Institute of Biblical Studies (I.I.B.S.), Israel Branch, began classes in Nazareth and Kefr Yasif in September. Ray directs this decentralized theological education program in Israel. Many years effort went into developing the IIBS, which enrolls about 20 Arab students at present.

Rose Mary disciples two new believers related to her Galilee Women's Group using the "Survival Kit." These ladies came to the Lord through the witness of a vivacious Mexican-American friend who lives near us.

Ray continues to act as a roving "sheikh" for a group of Muslim believers that have grown to ten. Each one is winning one and sharing their resources in a way reminiscent of Acts 2:43-47. He returned sobered from his last trip. A rock smashed the windshield of the truck in which he was riding, narrowly missing the driver's head. They took a wrong turn into an unfriendly village.

Believing in Jesus was not without a cost for the Muslim young men of the Church of Samaria. The brother of one of our believers was jailed by the Palestinian Authority. He simply disappeared one day. After some inquiries, we found he was being held in PA Security headquarters in Tulkarm. I mustered up the courage to visit him one day. I can remember no one wanted to go with me since the PA interrogators were not noted for their compassion. I somehow made my way through the various checkpoints and found the building where he was being held. I told the guard I wanted to see the brother on behalf of the church in America. After a few minutes, the Chief of PA Security in the town came out to see me. He told me he would have to be present during the visit. When he brought the believer out we embraced in the usual manner of Arab friends. The PA Security Chief was surprised I knew Arabic and was friends with the believer. After we met a few minutes and I determined he was in good health, the PA Security Chief asked to see me privately.

Ray sharing the Good News with a Muslim on the Mount of Olives, July 2001

He asked me, "Where were you when I was being held in an Israeli jail? No friend came to see me!"

I asked him if he was a believer then? He said, "No."

I said, "That was the reason. If I had known you were a believer I would have visited you too!"

I reference the brother's older brother in another letter home from Kefr Yasif in July 1995:

MILESTONES

"The Lord gave and the Lord hath taken away. Blessed be the name of the Lord!" Job's reaction to what God allows expresses our feelings about milestones we passed this year. Ray celebrated his sixtieth birthday in Jerusalem on April 26 with family and a few select colleagues. Cheryl and Ilan with Nathanael and cute baby daughter Moriel acted as hosts. Chuck and Tanya from Moscow graced us for a short vacation. We missed many of you, but hope you will be there for his seventieth, Lord willing!

Another milestone was the passing of our beloved senior colleague and brother in the Lord, Dr. Bob Lindsey. He died in Oklahoma on May 31st at age 78. Bob made a lasting impression on our life and career in Israel. He played the part of spiritual mentor during the renewal in the 70's. He challenged us to keep on evangelizing for the Lord and planting his church in this land. Visits with him and Margaret always involved intellectual challenges and spiritual blessings.

The baptism of new believers always marks a milestone in our work. The last few months witnessed the baptism of both Muslim and Jewish believers in the Lord. One Muslim young man suffered a period of systematic interrogation and torture by those who understand life only in terms of political affiliations. When they realized he had nothing to offer them and pressure came from other believers, they released him. The first thing he requested on being set free was to be baptized. His ordeal clarified his commitment to Christ. He followed the Lord in believer's baptism in the Jordan. Pray for this young man and his family for protection.

A lady from Rose Mary's Bible study group requested baptism. We contacted the local Jewish believer's fellowship and had the privilege of participating in her baptism and witnessing the baptism of several Russian believers with her in the Sea of Galilee. Pray for Rose Mary and her ladies as they witness to their families.

The first academic year of the International Institute of Biblical Studies, Israel Branch, ended in June with about 25 students completing courses in four locations in Galilee. The IIBS provides continuing theological training at all levels for laymen and pastors. An engineer, an international soccer coach, a priest, a correspondent, several teachers and other professionals study with us. Christians from many denominations, along with Muslims and Druze receive new insights into the Bible. IIBS and interfaith contacts led to requests for Bibles from a Catholic Christian college and an Islamic College. Pray for the translation and publication of programmed textbooks into Arabic that this work may continue here and around the Middle East.

I loved the work with the IIBS in Galilee and the exposure to so many different peoples and communities in the Land. It was encouraging to see how an academic approach to the Bible was a drawing card to such a variety of professions. It was not without its challenges. Financial indebtedness carried over from commitments made in the past put a major burden on budgeting and staffing. At the same time, I was spending a growing amount of time and travel assisting David and others in discipling the growing group to Muslim believers in Samaria and the South. An appeal came from a pastor in the city of Ramla next to Lod, ancient Lydda, between modern Tel Aviv and Jerusalem. He took a short course on witness to Muslims that I taught at the Assemblies of God church in Haifa.

He called one day and said, "Brother Ray, we need help with the Muslims in our area. Come down and help us. I will find you a house to live in. We are praying for you to move down here!"

I explained the move to our BCI colleagues, David and Marsha Smith in a letter on February 13, 1996:

Hi Ya'll,

Sorry I have not written but too much is happening. There is a friend who sticks closer than a brother. In this case, your Forenbord 1099 stuck to mine so I am sending it to you!

We are moving to north Ramla at the end of the month. No way in a letter to tell you why! Our landlord is a retiring army man who speaks Lebanese Arabic, and our next-door neighbors are from Uzbekistan. It is a new housing project (a cottage) in a new Russian settlement.

We planned originally to move to the Carrell's house behind you at Baptist Village, but several in the BCI opposed us being there...so you fill in between the lines.

The IIBS survived a financial and administrative onslaught last year and I will be turning things over to David G. before furlough in July. We still have about 25 students. I thought at age 60 I had endured most of the trials of life, but learned different.

In answer to your E-Mail enquiry, you are always included in my work with Muslims, as a friend and colleague. We have meetings with David Ortiz's group next door to you at BV. I will disciple and follow-up the new believers. I look forward to continuing partner-ship with you in this work. But, for about a year and a half one of us is on furlough!

The Spanish congregation in south Tel Aviv joined the ABC this year. Pastor Thomas and his group raised $3000 to fix up a meeting place on the roof of his house. You and Marsha can really help in relating in Spanish. What dynamic services they have. So, the ABC connection is another reason for my move.

The mayor of Kefr Kassem and a busload of Muslim fundamen-talists attended a prayer conference with Rabbis for Human Rights and Arab pastors last month at BV. I was the duty "goy" who turned on the Sabbath lights.

Pray for us in this move. Wish I had you all around to teach me Hebrew.

Our new address will be Baptist Village. See you in July. We leave on July 25 for furlough.

I have deliberately not dwelt on mission politics in my "Galilee Wanderings." However, I chafed under the constraints of "consensus" which was the prevailing operational mode at this time in the life our Southern Baptist mission organization. God used it to steer us away from living at the Baptist Village conference center. It was all about to change.

Chapter 28

RAMLA: ARAB CAPITAL IN THE JEWISH HOMELAND

The New Directions

I find it very amazing that the only city that the Muslims built when they conquered the Holy Land in the eighth century was Ramla! Ramla, as indicated by its name, was built on the sands about 10 miles inland from the Mediterranean on the road to Jerusalem. It had no water source, so the Arab Muslim conquerors built a canal from the ancient city of Tel Gezer about five miles further east. With the water, they filled huge cisterns. One was under the ruins of the White Mosque next to the Ramla Tower. Another is located a few blocks away. You can still row around in boats underground. The only modern landmark in Ramla is a large cement factory you can see for miles. The town is largely populated by Jews from the Arab countries and new Russian immigrants and is the center of Karaite Judaism in the country. The Israeli government moved in a remnant population of Muslims, many Bedouin, after the Six-day war. The town is unique in the Middle East since the Franciscan Church building has a steeple and cross which are higher than the mosque minaret! *Wikipedia* records that Napoleon used the hospice there as his headquarters during his Palestine campaign in 1799. The hospice is named after Nicodemus and Joseph of Arimathea. I began my ministry in Israel in Rama in Upper Galilee in 1965 and ended it in another town that claims Joseph of Arimathea as its native son!

Ramle Pool of Arches, (Courtesy of Touchpoint Israel)

My Arab pastor friend called me to meet him at a new home he found in a suburb of Ramla and talk with the landlord about renting. Rose Mary and I walked through the house with the Jewish proprietor and the Arab pastor interpreted from Hebrew to Arabic for us. When we got through the tour, the landlord started speaking to me in Arabic! His family was from Morocco and he was fluent in Arabic. He had just built the house in a new suburb of Ramla on the border of Lod (ancient Lydda) and was planting an ornamental garden. He wanted tenants who would take good care of the house. The next-door neighbors in the villa-duplex were a family from Uzbekistan. About half the residents of the new suburb were recent immigrants from the southern Russian provinces or "stans," Uzbekistan, Kazakhstan, and other stans we never heard of! Our Hebrew was about as weak as theirs, so we could fit in naturally. We moved in at the end of February 1996 and I put my name on the mailbox, "Dr. Ray Register." We had people knocking on our door thinking we were the Russian veterinary doctor in the house behind us!

It turns out that the house in this new Russian immigrant suburb was a great refuge for our ministry with Muslims. Muslims could visit without the prying eyes of suspicious family and friends. Ramla was only a 20-minute drive to Baptist Village where a Muslim believing family was given refuge after the father had been interrogated and tortured by the Palestinian Security Service in Jericho. We gathered the Muslim believers there on a weekly basis to study *New Beginnings*, a programmed Bible study we published at the IIBS. Several other believing families lived in the Ramla-Lod area. Therefore, I spent lots of time assisting with their problems and trying to encourage them in their new faith.

An additional benefit was Rev. Bayuk Bayuk from the Episcopal Church in Ramla retired and lived only a block away. During our years in Ramla, we attended the Episcopal Church, which Rev. Samuel Fannous pastored. We knew Samuel and his family when he was a young man when I used to help Rev. Bayuk with Child Evangelism in the late 1960's. His organist Subhi Hissin used to visit our neighbors in Nazareth and was a musician friend of our son, Chuck. Our doctor in Ramla was a nephew to Sister Eidie Khoury who worked at the EMMS Hospital

Bookshop in Nazareth. So, our acquaintances of 30 years in Galilee helped us adjust to life in the south much quicker.

It took some time to get used to the harsh attitude of the Jews of Ramla, compared to the softer attitude of Galilee. Everyone seemed to have a chip on his or her shoulder. One day we were in the Barclay's Bank and Rose Mary needed to sign on an account. As we were standing in line, a man pushed his way in front of us. Rose Mary confronted him in Hebrew for his rudeness. It turns out he was an Arab from Nazareth who rented his home to one of our fellow Baptists! He apologized but it was a little embarrassing.

Another time I was mailing a package at the local post office in Ramla. People were crowded around me. I laid my money on the counter to wrap the package. I felt a mild breeze and discovered my money was gone! I went to the local police station to complain. They assigned a young officer to drive me around town to see if I could spot anyone from the crowd at the post office. He spoke to me only in Hebrew. When we got back to the station to write up the report he looked across the table and said in Arabic, "Mr. Register, you do not recognize me. **I know you. I have been watching you to see how you react**. You visited in my home in Galilee years ago and told my people about the Bible!" It turns out he was a Druze neighbor of my friend Hamdy's sister in northern Galilee.

While in Ramla, we enjoyed evening trips to Jappa of Tel Aviv to watch the sunset. Jappa is the ancient city where Jonah fled from the call of the Lord. They have a miniature stature of a whale at the entrance of the Old City. Artists spread their paintings out on the sidewalk in Jappa near the municipal archeological museum. We bought a beautiful painting of the sea waves, which now hangs in our living room. Rose Mary calls it "Grace upon grace." I summed up our life in Ramla in our newsletter of May 1996:

"NEW BEGINNINGS"

On March 1, 1996, we moved to Ramla to minister to Muslim believers in the central part of the country. The Lord gave us confirmation that it was time to concentrate on this area. The thirty years in Galilee were fulfilling and fruitful. Many faithful workers continue to reap the harvest and develop churches there. Ray spent hours on the road every week visiting and encouraging the "Church of Samaria" made up of Muslims living in Israel and the West Bank. They and others requested that we move to the area to disciple them in the Arabic language. We use "New Beginnings", a programmed Bible study designed to help new believers grow in Christ and share their faith with others. We meet weekly with ten Muslim believers. Much of our time is spent visiting with these families and inquirers. They face unique problems in their new life as believers in Jesus and need your prayers.

Ramla is a mixed Arab and Jewish city established by Muslims in 716 beside Lod, the biblical city of Lydda, halfway between Tel Aviv and Jerusalem. We found a new duplex for rent in a suburb called Kiryat Menachem-Afeka. Our neighbors are from Uzbekistan. All signs in the nearby shopping center are in Hebrew and Russian. Rose Mary enjoys the new house and being only twenty-five minutes from Cheryl and the grandchildren. They stay with us when Ilan travels.

Ray promotes the ministry of the International Institute of Biblical Studies (IIBS) and the Association of Baptist Churches (ABC) in the Coastal Plains area. The ABC added a Russian and a Spanish congregation this year bringing membership to nearly 1000. The IIBS survived a major financial crisis due to an unexpected 25% increase in teacher's salaries. Nineteen students finished courses in four centers in Galilee. David Groseclose returned from doctoral studies in the USA and will take responsibility for the IIBS while we are on furlough.

Our furlough, or "home assignment", runs from late July 1996 until April 1997. Ray will be visiting professor of Missions at Southeastern Baptist Theological Seminary for the fall semester. Then we will spend Christmas until Easter with Rose Mary's mother in Yuma, AZ and our son James in San Diego. James works as an associate scientist with Agouron Pharmaceuticals on a cancer therapy project. Chuck and Tanya, in Moscow, are now parents of a baby daughter, Margarita. We are now the proud grandparents of four grandchildren.

Our new duplex in Ramle, 1996

One of the many benefits of being a representative of the Southern Baptist International Board was a flexible furlough schedule, which was gradually introduced through the years as finances became available. In the beginning in the 1960's we had to stay on the field for 5 years and take a one-year furlough. Then it went down to four years and one year home. Finally, the FMB-IMB instituted a flexible furlough system, which allowed you to bank days of furlough for days served overseas. That way, families could plan their furloughs around the needs of their children and for special occasions. The IMB changed furlough to "home assignment" which emphasized rest, recreation and relating to our supporting churches and families back home. The final benefit came when the IMB allowed us to take a yearly month's vacation at our own expense, which provided time for family emergencies, and trips back to the USA. We shared the variety of experiences during our time home are in our newsletter of April 1997:

BACK TO JERUSALEM

We will be back in Israel by mid-April when you receive this. Ray will serve as leader of a church planting team for Muslims and Rose Mary as leader of the Arabic Language Strategy Team of the Baptist Convention in Israel. Ray continues as director of the International Institute of Biblical Studies (IIBS), Israel Branch.

We spent an enjoyable time in Wake Forest, NC in Fall 1996 where Ray taught Arabic and missions courses as the Fletcher Visiting Professor of Missions at Southeastern Baptist Theological Seminary. Relations with students, faculty and administration were very affirming. Chapel services were like revival! Ray presented the first half of his new book, *BACK TO JERUSALEM* to the class in Current Topics in International Missions. The book gives an up-to-date orientation on what God is doing in the Holy Land today to build his church.

We took several memorable trips to Charlottesville, VA for the BSU reunion and Rose Mary's nursing class reunion at the University of Virginia. We spoke in our sponsoring churches, Suffolk First Baptist and Great Bridge, Chesapeake who continue to generously support us through the International Mission Board. We also enjoyed visiting family, friends, and churches in the Carolinas, Tennessee, Georgia and New York.

Christmas found us in San Diego at son Jame's for a family re-union with Jaime from Knoxville; Cheryl and Ilan from Jerusalem with Moriel (2) and Nathanael (6), James and Diane, Rose Mary's mother, Mary Emma Rich (88) and us. We were all together for the first time in eight years and it was great! The memorable event ended with a trip to the San Diego Zoo with Jaime before he flew back to Knoxville.

Our time in the States ended with a leisurely stay in Saguaro Estates in Yuma, AZ in a singlewide trailer around the corner from Mary Emma. Ray finished the manuscript of *BACK TO JERUSALEM* and sent it to several publishers for review. Pray that he will receive a positive reply so you can order soon! He spoke in churches of the Yuma Baptist Association who graciously provided rent for our trailer. Rose Mary spoke at women's meetings and enjoyed cooking, shopping and attending church with her Mom. We both enjoyed the heated swimming pool!

Please pray for us as we return to Israel. We face unprecedented opportunities and challenges. There are those who try to use the delicate situation of the peace process to gain concessions from the government to place restrictions on evangelical Christians. Jesus alone gives the peace that passes all understanding, and for that cause, we return.

Southern Baptists in the USA were embroiled in the conservative resurgence about this time. Some liked to call it the "conservative takeover" of the denomination. I liked to call it a "back to the Bible" movement. I had good friends on both sides of the controversy which made it somewhat like experiencing a family feud which for some ended in a divorce. What made it particularly galling for easterners is that leaders like Dr. Paige Patterson from Texas became the president of our seminary in North Carolina. Despite my misgivings, I found Dr. Patterson and his wife to be very gracious hosts to us when we returned to the "new Southeastern." The **Biblical Recorder** published my reaction to a very caustic criticism of the changes at our seminary in the section on **Tarheel Voices** in the fall of 1996:

The other side of Southeastern Seminary

In response to Robert Brooks' "Wake up: a call to freedom" in the Oct. 12 issue of the Recorder, I would like to present the other side of Southeastern Seminary. I believe I speak with some credibility having grown up in Pritchard Memorial Church in Charlotte and received both my B.D. (M.Div.) and D.Min. degrees at the "old Southeastern."

Returning on furlough after more than 30 years of missionary service in Israel, I have not found the situation as Robert Brooks describes it: "propagandized pastors," "monarchial bishops," "religious tyranny," "no cooperation" and "no dialogue." Quite the opposite, I found Southeastern's campus in an atmosphere of spiritual renewal.

Instead of complaining about poor salaries and difficult deacons and cracking off-color jokes, I hear the "new Southeastern" students talking about their latest witnessing opportunity.

I was instructed as a faculty member to present all sides of an issue but to come down on the side of the truth, contrary to the "no cooperation, no dialogue" portrayed by Robert Brooks.

I am renewing acquaintances with many of my former professors from the "old Southeastern." All those I know retired and were not fired as Brooks implied would happen when the fundamentalists get control. If fundamentalism means spiritual renewal, evangelism and many of the 1,353 students here volunteering for missions, then more power to it!

By the way, I have not heard one of the "new Southeastern" faculty or administration, from the president on down, say that "they alone know the truth." The Bible is regarded as truth at Southeastern.

No, Robert Brooks, you are not a "one-eyed mule," but neither are they.

Ray Register

Wake Forest

One of the great privileges of living so long in the Holy Land was meeting men of stature who nurtured my personal and spiritual growth. I mentioned earlier my relationship with Dr. Robert (Bob) L. Lindsey who was a Hebrew scholar of note and my spiritual mentor through the Holy Spirit renewal. Another was Judge "Fredrick Wedge," of the Sharia Law Court of Joppa of Tel Aviv who helped me understand the Muslim mentality and who prayed for me daily. Then on the Jewish side was Dr. Bernard Resnikoff of the American Jewish Committee in Jerusalem. Dr. Resnikoff was a fellow graduate of Hartford Seminary. He liked my Doctor of Ministry thesis, **Dialogue and Interfaith Witness with Muslims**, so much, that he bought multiple copies and sent them around the world to the other directors of the AJC offices! I treasure a letter I received from him on June 16, 1997:

The American Jewish Committee

Dr. Ray Register

29-B Ben Eliezer, Kiryat Menachem

Dear Ray,

Upon my return to Jerusalem following an extended visit back to the good old U.S. of A, I found 2 striking pieces of mail from you.

The first was an invitation to attend the Register 40th anniversary celebration at the Baptist Village. You and I go back a long way and I would have been pleased to join your many friends to celebrate with you. I'm sorry I missed it. I wish you both well and let us look forward together to the 50th.

The other letter tells me you now teach the Bible in Arabic to the people of the West Bank. What a splendid idea. The more people who study and live on the teachings of the Bible, the faster will come to the day of full peace.

I must tell you that I often talk about you – or about us, in my public lectures. You are going your way and I am going my way, but, lo, our relationship is characterized by mutual respect and, I am pleased to add, admiration. You see? It is possible!

Sincerely, "Bernie"

Dr. M. Bernard Resnikoff, Director Emeritus

Dr. Resnikoff passed away about a year after writing me this letter. I expressed my condolences to the AJC in a letter on August 30, 1998:

I was saddened by the death of my dear friend Bernard Resnikoff. His death is a great loss for both the Jewish and Christian community. I will always remember his encouraging words as an elder fellow graduate of Hartford Seminary and his help through many situations we faced together through the years. Please express my condolences and those of the Baptist Convention in Israel to his family.

Not all my relations with public officials were so cordial. In the process of developing the Church of Samaria, I needed to meet with representatives of the Palestinian Authority to plea for the Arab Muslim believers who were being harassed and jailed on a regular basis. One such meeting took place on December 8, 1997 in East Jerusalem as recorded in my diary:

> Charles Kopp arranged for a meeting with Ziad Abu Ziad, legal advisor to Arafat. He is a lawyer in E. Jerusalem and one of the co-editors of the Israel-Palestine Journal. He cancelled the first meeting because the PNA had a called meeting. He was almost an hour late for the second meeting. He is a very sour man. My intent was to show him we could assist the PA through theological education, so I showed him various literature I used in Christian-Muslim dialogue. He asked me if I wanted to debate the matter on the basis of religion or politics? I was not sure of his intent. He said I had said Baptists separated religion from politics, so I said, "Religion." He asked me if I read the Quran and what is the penalty in the Quran for people who leave Islam? I said, "Some interpreted it as death." He said, **"The Palestinian State is an Islamic State under Sharia law and the penalty for converts is death."** My work as an evangelist is a threat to the security of the Islamic State. I told him they were worse than Saudi Arabia and if they keep putting their people under such pressure, they will rise up and throw them out. I told him the western countries would not support the PA in such repressive measures. He said no country would withhold funds from the PA on the basis of religion. I told him there was a bill in Congress to withhold funds from any country that practiced religious persecution. He said that any country who tried to put pressure on them could "go to hell!" Charles was very surprised at this. I told him "You see what Americans are paying for." Abu Ziad said MB* was in prison for political reasons and not for religion. I told him I only wanted one thing from him. He asked, "What?" I said, "A permit to preach in the Nablus prison, because we would have a church there!" He cracked a faint smile at that. I told him if he could give me any evidence that MB had been guilty of spying or land dealing I would shut my mouth. He said people only come to us for money. He said no one read the literature I gave out, but since he was an intellectual, I could leave it for him to read! The visit was a real eye-opener for Charles and me! Abu Ziad sends his son to the Anglican School. He is classmate of Charles's daughter. I heard later he tried to take his son out, but the son opposed him.

We received word several weeks later that five other prisoners in the Nablus prison received the Lord! One man died the same night that MB witnessed to him. I mention the unusual growth of the Church of Samaria in our letter home in February 1998:

Arabs, Jews and Jesus

Saturday was a long day. Ray picked up his friend "Joseph" and his son-in-law, "Antoine" and drove two hours to the Jordan River for their baptism. This brings to 15 the number of Muslims who joined the "Church of Samaria" in the last two years. Each came to the Lord through their own personal study of the Bible, contact with Christian friends, or the witness of believers in their family or friendship circle. After the baptism, they visited family in Nablus, the capital of Samaria, and then drove down to Tel Aviv to attend worship service at a Spanish Baptist Congregation where Ray spoke on "The Whole Armor of God" and spiritual warfare.

We partner in ministry to Muslims with David and Leah Ortiz, members of Brooklyn Tabernacle in New York. They live in Ariel, a Jewish settlement near Nablus and carry on a compassionate ministry to Muslims, Jews and expatriates in the area.

Our friend Shakir, for who many of you prayed, suddenly moved back to his home in Samaria. He pulled his children out of the Christ Church School in Jerusalem in the middle of the year. Pray for the family in this time of re-adjustment.

Our son-in-law, Ilan Zamir, Messianic Jewish leader and President of King of Kings College in Israel has been critically ill for the last month in Haddasah Hospital in Jerusalem. He was paralyzed by spinal taps and bleeding internally from amyloidosis, a complication of FMF (familial Mediterranean fever). His recovery is slow. He, Cheryl and the family receive the prayer support and encouragement of thousands around the world. Rose Mary often helps with the home and the children while Cheryl and others care for Ilan. A German single lady helps with the home and the children, which is quite a relief. Arabs, Jews, and all are united in prayer for them.

Many ask about the effect of changes at the IMB (formerly FMB, SBC) on us. We have worked for 33 years to encourage a church planting movement among Muslims in Israel-Palestine. We welcome the changes as we continue to mentor and encourage others as we participate in the gathering of Arabs and Jews into the Kingdom. We appreciate your prayers, support and encouragement.

The change of the Foreign Mission Board to the International Mission Board ushered in a "New Direction" in our work.

Southern Baptists finally came to the conclusion that they could not win the world single-handedly but needed to coordinate with other Christian groups with similar beliefs and goals. We started calling them "Great Commission Christians" or GCC's. It was a breath of fresh air for us. We had long chaffed under the system of a top-heavy organization whose decisions were handed down from above, and whose funding was going disproportionately to institutional development. Endless hours of our time were spent on traveling to various committee meetings where members in our group were making decisions for other members of the group. It was not conducive to efficiency nor to interpersonal relationships. I record my response to the New Directions in my diary on December 18, 1997:

> BCI meeting at BV with Mike Edens. He and David Groseclose presented the strategy for the "new way" at the IMB, which is basically church planting movements among unreached peoples groups. I do not see our specific work changing much since we have been involved in this for over 30 years. They are looking now for "Strategy Leaders" who will do unreached peoples surveys and motivate church planting movements. Some have asked me if I see myself in this role. My response is that I am doing the work without the title. I believe the IMB will bring in younger people to do this work, since it is patterned on the CSI model. The new approach is like hunting with a rifle and targeting specific peoples groups. My response is that it depends on what you are hunting. Sometimes the shotgun is necessary, particularly if you are hunting birds!

We spent much of our time teaching and assisting Shakir, the taxi driver who drove the "dirty dozen" around Samaria. He had become a believer, but apparently brought much baggage with him to his new faith in Jesus. Our friend, Norma Archbald, author of *The Mountains of Israel*, tried to get him to the USA because she knew the temptations and pull of the old life were too much. There was an apparent strain between him and his wife, the reasons of which would be revealed later. In the beginning, he was imprisoned and tortured in Jericho by the PA

Security Services. Later, when they released him, we were able to find shelter at Baptist Village for his family where we had good "New Beginnings" session with the family and other Muslim background believers.

Ray teaching "New Beginnings" at Baptist Village, July 1996

Finally, he found a rental property in Ramla before we moved there. The BCI and others generously offered to pay for his rent, and I made my first admitted mistake in my ministry as noted in my diary on December 27, 1997:

> Today Shakir had to pay his rent. He came by with Barnabas* in the morning to pick up the check. I heard later that Shakir moved out and went back to the West Bank. I put out the word for Shakir to call me. He called the next morning to tell me the landlord would not put in doors as he promised so he moved out. He said he would meet me to house hunt, but he never showed up. I called Bob Bradley to tell him to stop the check at the bank. Several days later he called back to say Shakir had cashed the check. It seems the Bank misunderstood Bob and thought he wanted the check "stamped!" So Shakir ended up walking away with $2500 in BCI money and

another NIS 2000 from Barnabas and $200 from me I had lent to Barnabas. Barnabas was mortified and broke. This is the first time in my career of 33 years I ever gave a check directly to a person in need. I should have gone with him and given it to the landlord. Shakir ended up pulling his children out of Christ Church School in mid-year. and leaving all the Bibles and literature I gave him in the apartment. Apparently the landlord threw them away. I learned from Merwan that Shakir had been seeing a man from Sarta'a who lived in his apartment building. Evidently, a relative of his moved back from Jordan and gave him protection in the village. I have a hard time thinking Shakir staged the whole thing, but after the visit with Abu Ziad, it looks entirely likely. What a patsy I feel like!

Several days after this major setback the Lord brought his angels to cheer me up; Dick and Louis Thomassian from Huntsville, Alabama. Dick's father was Armenian and his mother a Christian Arab. Dick had a heart of love for the Arabs and Jews and was a major encourager to us. They formerly spent several months ministering with us in Nazareth. We ate supper with them at the Hyatt Hotel in Jerusalem and I was able to end the year on this positive note on December 30, 1997:

> It has been a good year, unequaled in new experiences and opportunities and I may look back at it as one of my quality years. **I am nearing the end of my reading of the Quran from cover to cover in Arabic.** The final chapters being shorter and more endurable. The Muslim email networks I am on give opportunity for new information and sharing with others. Horizons for ministry are now more unlimited than ever. Despite all this, it will be the year that Princess Diana died, a tragic and wasted event. This world order is passing away and God' patience is running out.

Somewhere about this time, Mike Edens who lived many years in Cairo and was our encourager in Church Planting made me a proposition I could not refuse.

He asked me, **"Ray, do you think you could stay on the field another three years before retirement?** We need you to stay around and lead up our outreach to the Muslims."

On one of our visits to Egypt Mike took me on a tour of Al Azhar University in Cairo, which included a spectacular view from the top of one of the minarets. His offer was an affirmation of the direction of our Galilee wanderings in the future.

February 1998 found me in Winderswil, Switzerland for the 98 DAWN Europa Conference. DAWN stands for "Disciple a Whole Nation." I assisted DAWN in doing a country survey and they invited me to attend to learn more about their work:

> The venue was as spectacular as the conference itself. We stayed at the "Credo," an evangelical conference center just outside Interlaken, nestled at the foot of the Swiss Alps. The first meeting, Saturday, we drove into Thun to attend a youth rally at a converted warehouse. It was filled with singing and clapping Swiss young people. Wolfgang Simpson, one of the dynamic pastors who attended the conference, gave the upbeat message.

> The next day, Sunday, we took a train and tram ride up to Muerren, above the snow line, which overlooks the three highest mountains in the region and is just below "the Top of Europe" where a James Bond movie was filmed. I will never forget the little wooden chapel in Muerren dedicated to Anne Morehead, who as a young bride, was killed by lightning in 1865 while climbing a nearby peak with her husband.

> Back to the conference: Monday through Wednesday was marathon meetings, interspersed with delicious meals, led by Wolfgang Fernandez from the DAWN headquarters in Colorado Springs. I knew "Wolf" through Dr. Steff Nash who used to work at the Nazareth Hospital and is now a DAWN volunteer for the Middle East living in London and member of Ikthus Fellowship. Dr. Theo Kunst of Holland led a special study on "An Evangelical Theology of the Church,". He illustrated his study by overheads of churches that had become museums, clothing stores, and finally and tragically his own church which was sold to the Muslims! He proposed a dynamic view of the church that would not die when society moved outside its walls, but would live again inside the homes of believers. Throughout the conference the triangle of CELL GROUP, CONGREGATION, and CELEBRATION appeared to be the pattern that fits modern mobile society. This coupled with worship, community and mission resonated with things I discovered in ministry in the Middle East. The conference placed particular emphasis on cell groups as providers of fellowship and facilitators of cp movements.

Country reports indicated a decline in attendance in Catholic and Protestant churches in Europe, with the notable exception of Romania, which is experiencing a church planting movement. On the other hand, thousands of "Alpha Groups" or home meetings are springing up throughout Europe. I gave the Israel country report near the end of the conference after the presentation from Egypt. I find the methods of survey used by DAWN simple and thorough and am encouraging their use for a new survey being done in Israel. They will establish a benchmark to determine growth in establishing churches and areas where churches need to be planted.

DAWN was good preparation for the experiences ahead with the Muslim believers.

Chapter 29

BARNABAS,
THE CIGARETTE TALKS,
AND THE FOUR

Before Shakir left, a visitor in his apartment snitched my number off his mobile phone when Shakir was in the bathroom. Later he called me.

He said, "Shakir did not want me to talk to you, but I got your number from his phone. We need to talk. I used to be married to a Christian woman in Beirut. I could not understand what her priest was speaking about in Greek, so I need you to teach me the Bible in Arabic. I want to know how to be a Christian."

I agree on one condition.

He asked, "What?'

I said, "Whatever I teach you, you have to teach someone else."

When we met, I learned this man was married to three wives. One in Israel, one in the West Bank, and one in Gaza! Between them all, he had 15 children. He smoked three packs of cigarettes a day, one for each wife! He was constantly broke, trying to support these multiple families. At one time in his illustrious past, he served as an Israeli policeman in the West Bank where he grew up. With the connections he made he became what I call a "fixer." He could fix permits, applications and official documents for anyone who could not maneuver the complicated bureaucracy in Israel, especially for West Bank Arabs who did not know Hebrew. A fix usually cost the client about $500. However, he got the job done. His father was from Turkish ancestry from the Ottoman times and his mother was an Arab. That meant he had a temperament equally disposed to thinking as to feeling and he had a gift of strategizing. Finally, I met a Muslim who wanted to be a believer and who had the natural talent of acting on his beliefs. Remembering the advice of my theology professor, Dr. John Eddins at Southeastern Seminary, we began to learn the Christian catechism, that is, the Sermon on the Mount. My friend, who we named "Barnabas", would come by my house two or three times a week and we would spend time reading and explaining the Scripture. We first went through the *Four Spiritual Laws* in Arabic. He confessed Christ and was baptized. He went down to the Ministry of Interior and changed his religion from Muslim to Christian on his ID card! When his Gaza wife who was a fundamentalist Muslim found out, she took him to the Muslim Sharia Court in Jaffa of Tel Aviv and sued him for divorce. He had to scramble around to come up with the dowry or *mohar* to pay her off. Despite her opposition, her daughter become a believer! His West Bank wife, who was the oldest and bore him eight children, was sickly. He was about to send her to a hospital in Jordan thinking she was going to die. We prayed for her and she got well. She and her grown children who were scattered throughout Samaria and the West Bank became believers! The youngest wife who he now lived with in Israel also became a believer. Her brother who was a Muslim Sheikh kicked her out of his house. His two sons became believers!

Barnabas immediately began to keep our bargain. He went out daily and shared his new knowledge and faith with other Muslims. He quickly ran into violent opposition. He had several cars burned and windshields smashed. He was severely burned by a Molotov cocktail thrown into his car. I remember after a trying time he hung his head and said, "Despite all the problems I face, I have learned one thing."

I asked, "What?"

He said, "To tell the truth!"

We had talked many times about how it was natural for the people in the Muslim culture to lie to one another, but Christians told the truth in love. I warned him that I would always check up on him to see if he was telling the truth. I reflect on lying in my Diary in July 1988 after returning from a short vacation in the USA:

> What a difference to get back here to all the fairy tales of the Muslim believers after having a fairly normal month in the States! These people all lie. It is hard to know when they are telling the truth. Maybe it is just the kind I am working with. I am trusting God to do the changing.

He absorbed the tract on *"The Cigarette Talks,"* and tried his best to quit smoking. He started taking the tract to the schools in the West Bank and giving it out to students who smoked. The tract became a sign for the believer. His daughter in Gaza showed it to her teacher and the teacher asked,

"Where did you get this?"

She found out later that the teacher became a believer years ago but kept it a secret.

We had a great trip back to the USA in July 1998 with the usual stopover in Zurich to "decompress" from the pressures in Israel. We celebrated Rose Mary's mother's 90th birthday in Portland and visited our future home in Escondido, California. The International Mission Board affirmed our work as I indicated in my Diary on August 21, 1998:

> So much has happened. I was appointed Strategy Leader for the Israeli/Palestinian unreached people group and chairperson of the

Muslim evangelism training team for the NAME area. We attended a marathon retreat for SL's (Strategy Leader's) in Cyprus and about all Rose Mary and I had time to do was take an evening walk after supper. The New Way people seem more intent than ever to squeeze in meetings every minute. It was a good review of what is going on around the Middle East. I made contact with SIL people and got storying tapes on the Bible in Arabic. Met two couples who came to the area because of having heard us speak in the USA

The Lord kept sending interesting people to us in 1998 and expanding our contacts with new Muslim back ground believers. One such person was the Ustaz or "Teacher" in Arabic as noted in my diary in August of 1998:

My new believer Barnabas led to me to the *Ustaz*, a teacher of Arabic and former teacher of Islam. He also has three wives and 15 children! The *Ustaz* has more potential than Barnabas for studying the Word, and although they are friends there is a great deal of competition between the two. Barnabas made contact with the women in Halhul that Linda Finamore cultivated friendship with during her month's project there. The *Ustaz* keeps telling me of various tricks Barnabas is playing to get money from me. I am waiting for the opportune time to confront him with all of these, and several others I have picked up on. So far, he and the *Ustaz* have led me to six other inquirers. The *Ustaz* used to live next door to Arexi, an Armenian nurse who is a believer in Jericho and has been open to the Word for 30 years. I took Rose Mary over to meet his wives last week. Barnabas has continual problems with money, and keeps trying to catch up, but never does. He seems to get into debt to every new believer who comes along through some scheme of offering to help get permits, licenses, etc. and taking money from them.

I am teaching the mbbs that smoking is robbery and lying. It steals health, money and witness. They cannot tithe because they burn it up on cigarettes!

We started a Bible class using *New Beginnings* in Arabic at Baptist Village for the mbbs.

I took Barnabas and the *Ustaz* to attend the Haifa Church summer conference. They enjoyed the good preaching of Nizar Shaheen, but suffered in the heat. Two weeks later, we attended the ABC Youth Conference along with a carload of Muslim believers with David Ortiz from Samaria. There were 10 mbbs there, along with 130 youth from Galilee. One girl from Kefr Yasif invited her pen pal from a Muslim town whose brothers came and were friends of David Smith. They had already heard about Lisa Hoffman's (David's niece) coming.

When I finally got up the nerve to confront Barnabas about all the accusations of the *Ustaz,* we resolved the issues, but he went immediately and talked to the *Ustaz* who became furious with me!

The fall of 1998 witnessed a number of Muslims baptized by Barnabas with subsequent attacks on him and his cars and occasional threats against us. It started when he called me and said there were a number of Muslims who wanted to be baptized but if I showed up they would be arrested and interrogated by the Palestinian Security.

I told him, "You baptize them!"

He asked, "How?"

I said, "Just like I baptized you."

I noted in my dairy on October 27, 1998, "Banabas baptized eight people in in a rock quarry. I gave him my blessing. **Maybe cpm started today**!" He baptized another 8 in November. I almost ran out of baptismal certificates! One of the women believers near Hebron became critically ill with kidney failure and needed a transplant. The other believers collected NIS 16,000 (about $5000) to get her admitted to the hospital. A male believer from another town donated his kidney for her to survive. She lived over a year and when she finally passed away, most who attended her funeral were believers. The Muslim leaders who officiated at her funeral finally left and the believers had their own committal service for her.

When I got back from a training conference in Cyprus, I sat down with Barnabas to tell him all the new strategies I learned.

He said, "Wait a minute. Let me tell you some of the things I have been thinking about while you were gone."

His plans were better than mine! Our newsletter of November 1998 reveals his energy:

"Get Out the Bible"

"Get out the Bible and read with me!" said my Muslim friend. It came as music to my ears. Usually we had talked about his family and financial problems. Now he hungered for the Word, which indicated spiritual growth. This man, who had three wives and 15 children now trains as a witness to his Muslim family and friends scattered all over the Holy Land. He leads Bible studies in four locations. Daily he has to overcome ingrained habits from multiple marriages, intrigue, chain smoking, and habitual lying. He come back after trips and says, "Teach me more. I have to have something new to give them." Now we read the Psalms and the Gospel of John. It has become a new habit. His friends who received the Word have had their home burned and their windshields smashed. He has developed a pastor's heart toward them and studies a Bible correspondence course to be able to feed them better.

Rose Mary encourages his young wife to help her to cope with a husband who is always mobile and always spending his money on other people. The wife travels with him many places since the Lord has opened up ministry to Muslim women and their families. We try to help the man to love and provide for his wife as a partner in the Lord and to help the wife honor her husband and not see him as a banker. It is a challenge since this is a new paradigm for a Muslim couple. We act as role models in many ways.

We now serve as senior partners on a ministry team with Bill and Dena who work out of our former Galilee home. Bill is an expert mechanic and Arabic student. Ray also mentors Scott who serves at the Jesus House of Prayer in Jericho. Both of us encourage Lisa who lives in a Muslim village and teaches ESL. Pam, now on home assignment in the USA, serves as our prayer coordinator and liaison with our Arab Christian churches to encourage them in outreach to Muslims. Pray for them.

Our daughter Cheryl is working and is also studying as a tour guide while Ilan is in Canada for medical tests and a short sabbatical. We enjoy being close and being grandparents to Nathanael and Moriel who grow more handsome and cuter every day. Your continued prayers for their family are much appreciated.

Our big event of the year was a vacation trip in July to celebrate Rose Mary's mother's 90th birthday in Portland along with her aunt's 85th. Chuck flew in from Moscow, his son Jaime from Knoxville and James and Diane from San Diego.

Think of us as you pray and as you give to the Lottie Moon World Missions Offering. It, along with the Cooperative Program remains the financial lifeline of our ministry and that of over 4000 other representatives around the world.

Ramle fellowship, 2000, (Moriel, BCI partner David Groseclose, Hassan, Ray, Barnabas, Lydia, Cheryl, & Rose Mary)

A major departure in our Galilee Wanderings occurred that September 1998 when we had to close the IIBS training program in Galilee. The then Chairman of the Association of Baptist Churches protested that our main teacher was too Pentecostal. When I tried to resolve the dispute, he accused me of being Pentecostal also! It was a struggle over control of the property that had housed the training center for 34 years. I explained in my dairy on September 8, 1998:

Amazing at the same time, the IMB closed our Cyprus office without telling me. So we were hit with a double whammy. Bethlehem Bible College was supposed to come into Galilee with a program, so I decided to make the break. The new emphasis at the IMB is on unreached people groups, so the Christian Arabs are no longer a target. I regret very much the 25 students we left half way through their degree programs. I plan now to combine with the Academy of Theological Studies who are motivated to reach Muslims and Druze.

It is encouraging looking back that the Association took up the cause later with the establishing of the Nazareth Evangelical College in our former home and carried on the cause of theological education that Dr. Dwight Baker, others and I championed. (see www.**nazarethseminary**.org). The break allowed me to concentrate more time and energy on the development of the infant Muslim believer's movement and encouraging our new personnel working with Muslims, especially Scott Bridger and Bill Harrison at the Jesus House of Prayer in Jericho and Lisa Hoffman in Tira, near Baptist Village. Lisa ended up writing an orientation manual for new workers, *Figtrees and Durbekky's.* Another Journeyman missionary Carrie Nichole (Niki) Taylor settled later into the difficult work at the House of Love Foster Home in Rama. Carrie later went to Iraq where her husband was killed and she was wounded and in an ambush in Mosul. Carrie authored *Facing Terror* (Integrity, 2005). Bill Harrison later returned to the States and co-authored *A Pedouin Life* after visiting us in California. Scott Bridger became the Assistant Professor of Islamic Studies at Southern Baptist Theological Seminary in Louisville, Kentucky and published his PhD, *Christian Exegesis of the Quran*. He is now Associate Professor of Global Studies and World Religions at Criswell College in Dallas, Texas.

The new success in church planting with the Muslims led to persecution as noted in my dairy on January 16, 1999:

Barnabas and Lydia are discouraged since their car was destroyed after stoning in Hebron while we were in Cyprus. Lydia cashed in three gold bracelets to make the down payment on a used van. She complains that Barnabas did not buy clothes for the children either at Christmas of for the end of Ramadan. **He spends all his money running around for the new believers.** These people are always at their financial limit. I feel a real obligation to help them since they are winning family and friends to the Lord. He is going to Nablus today to baptize a group that Lydia won last week. I have come to the point now that I have to draw on my own resources, or trust the Lord to send the money from other sources. Anyway, we are still not lacking in anything we need. Believers are coming in so fast now that we are taxed to keep Bibles available and I get writer's cramp from so many baptismal certificates! Why am I complaining?

Chapter 30

BEGINNING OF THE HARVEST

My experience with the Muslims believers was not as I would have envisioned. Little would I imagine I would be working with a man who had 3 wives and 15 children! He was now living with the youngest wife. The Gaza wife divorced him and the elder wife lived with her children. My diary of March 25, 1999 explains some of the new reality and showed that church planting movements are "messy" as had been predicted:

> Just filled in my 100th baptism certificate for Barnabas! I wonder what we are going to do when it gets up in the thousands? I have so many questions about what is going on, but am having to trust the Lord that all this is genuine. If it is not, then they are the greatest actors I have ever known. He told me if he were a cheat, he would be driving a nice car and live in a big house! I help him only with benzene and some repairs to keep his cars going.

> This is a people intensive work. We sit and read the Scripture, a Psalm and part of John's Gospel nearly every day. I give to him and he gives to others.

> I have to do Strategy Plans, personnel requests and keep up with Barnabas and the grandkids at the same time. I am glad Rose Mary is hanging in with me, though it is hard on her.

> God is good. I learned several valuable lessons from reading Leviticus and II Corinthians on the computer. One thing about the fat. They kept down their cholesterol by sacrificing all the fat on the altar. Also about giving. It is meant to maintain equality among the believers in material things. We sure are doing this with our Muslim believers. We have an IAM Fund which some of us are putting our tithes into. I have to pray for how to include the mbbs!

Another highlight of the year was attending a leader's conference in England where the Lord blessed me with one of his surprises. April 10-15, 1999:

> Strategy Leaders Conference at Pilgrim Hall near Ukfield, South Sussex, England. An inspirational training time. Alitalia was late taking off and we nearly missed our connection in Rome. Our bags arrived two days late so we had to borrow underwear from the neighbors across the hall. We stayed in an old manor house about ½ mile down the road from the Pilgrim Hall which was an estate mansion built about 100 years ago. It even sleeted one night. We learned about the E-Myth Revisited and a lady who opened a pie shop. Amazing how her small business experience was applied to our work as strategy leaders and starting a church planting movement. **Avery Willis taught on the Book of Acts and I heard a Southern Baptist say that you could be filled with the Holy Spirit a number of times.** One day they blindfolded us to teach us team work. Someone led me down through the pasture almost to the highway. **When we got back and took off our blindfolds I found out it was Avery!** I kept the blindfold as a souvenir. It was a time of great affirmation and information. We witnessed to the Pakistani taxi driver coming over and later sent him some websites for the study of the Bible and the Quran.

The euphoria of these days was mixed with sorrow. **David Wu, a Korean student at the Columbia Bible College** in my birthplace, Columbia, South Carolina had used me as his research model and had me write a life history he used in his missions class. He and his wife were in Jerusalem studying at the Holy Land Institute, Jerusalem University College. An asthma attack struck David on May 22, 1999 and he stopped breathing. He was pronounced brain dead at the Bikor Holim Hospital in Jerusalem. The doctors and nurses encouraged me to work with David's wife to get permission to harvest his organs as I indicated in my diary:

> I went to the hospital each evening to visit. His condition did not improve. His blood pressure fluctuated on Monday, but stabilized on Tuesday. I met and talked to an Arab lady and another family from the village next to Ramat Rachel. They said, "The Lord is with that man," referring to David. The Jewish lady next to him asked his

friends to sing hymns to her also. The presence of all the believers was a real testimony to the staff and patients. Many Koreans and Chinese came, among whom was David's pastor from Houston, TX. He pastured a church of 1,500 Chinese and said there was a church of 1,000 in Kazakhstan. Some were Muslims. He knew Brenda Poon and knew of Leo Bruce.

Thursday, May 27, 1999-John Steinmetz called in the morning to tell me that David Wu had died at 8:30 in the morning. They would have a memorial service for him at the Jerusalem University College on Saturday at 2:00 and David would be buried in Houston TX later. **David had won over 80 Chinese to the Lord during the four months he lived in Israel.** He wrote my life story for his mission's project at Columbia Bible University in Columbia, SC, my birthplace. I picked him and his family up at the airport when they came to Israel and he was reviewing *Back to Jerusalem.* He left his wife Ruth who was 12 years younger and three small children. He was 40. God bless his memory!

The Lord blessed during 1999 with a major grant for the Academy of Theological Studies from a private donor. Mike Edens of the IMB approved funds for our outreach project with Muslims. We even had a request from the Islamic College in Israel to send them English teachers! In addition, Patrick Sookdeo of the Barnabas Fund provided major funding for our work among the Muslim believers. Patrick, himself from Muslim background, made an interesting observation. He was quite concerned about the negative impact of "contextualization" and the confusion it has caused in work with Muslims. He said almost every Muslim church had split over the issue. Also, **he felt strongly that every Muslim believer should be discipled in a tradition, which would replace the traditions of Islam**. Otherwise, the Muslim would eventually return to Islam. I often wonder how many of these conflicts are caused by the expat who carries their denominational divisions with them overseas. I observed in Nazareth that some local pastors were stuck in the same theology and leadership rut as when they first became a believer, while our denomination back home had moved on many years ago. Things were moving so fast in the development of the Muslim believers that no one was able to settle into a tradition, as indicated in our newsletter of June 1999:

"The Bee Hive"

Our friend came by one day and said, "I never dreamed there would be so many people hungering for the Gospel. They are like bees swarming out of the hive. It is impossible to catch all of them." I suggested that he does not need to catch all of them. But, each one he does catch he should teach from the start to catch another and they others. So, what I teach him, he passes on to others. There are over ten groups now scattered around the country. Opposition and persecution cause them to scatter and form other groups. This way, the supposed enemies of the Gospel have become its unsuspecting promoters. Pray for the leaders who are rising up in each group.

Our latest crisis is running out of New Testaments, Bibles, tracts, and baptismal certificates. *Also, the apparent lack of funds for itinerant expenses is frustrating. Our friend, who travels out daily to tend his flocks, has lost three cars by rioting, accident and breakdowns. This does not stop him, his family and friends from sharing the Gospel. This is the first time in our career that we can foresee what could become a real church planting movement among this unreached people group in our area. Members of our team are reporting equally exciting experiences all over the country. We are postponing "retirement" to encourage this movement in any way possible. Pray for the harvest force and for necessary provisions.

We took two trips to England this year for training in business management and leadership. The upgrading of our skills and the freedom to operate has renewed our vision for what the Lord is doing. On a personal note, we visited the shop in London on Regent Street near Piccadilly Circus where Ray bought our china and crystal 42 years ago while in the Navy.

Rays second cousin from his mother's side, Kendrick Cannon and his wife Martha visited on Ray's 64th birthday in April. Ken, a retired Professor of English from Coe College in Cedar Rapids, Iowa, is helping Ray to revise his book, **Back to Jerusalem.** Pray for publication by the turn of the millennium.

*We have replenished our stock!

We replenished our stock of Arabic Bibles by regular runs to a settlement near Jerusalem where the son of Kaarlo Sevanto kept a shipping container full of the precious books. His father used to supply me Bibles from his home in Tiberias on the shores of the Sea of Galilee. Mr. Sevanto told me one time that the leading competitors to the printing of the Bible were the cigarette companies! They used the same thin paper for cigarettes as for the pages of the Bible. The miraculous story of how God provided those Arabic Bibles is told in Sevanto's life story, **Kaarlo Syvanto-Pioneer**, Forty years in Israel.

One of our main prayer supports during these fruitful years came from the "Prayer Tower" at the CFI (Christian Friends of Israel). I would periodically drop by the CFI to update the ladies who prayed there on the progress of work in the Arab villages of the West Bank and Galilee. The interchange with them confirmed the experiences of Barnabas and Lydia, as did the work of "Smiley Marbles" who led a correspondence ministry to over 1000 Muslims in the same area. Ray Sanders, the CFI Director, and his wife and staff were instrumental in providing financial as well as personal and prayer support to our work among the Muslims.

In August, we had the privilege of hosting a visit by "Nik Ripken," an IMB colleague who was doing research on Muslim background believers. He served in Somalia where most of the believers were martyred due to their association with expatriate nonprofit organizations. It was good to have his more objective feedback since few I knew had experienced the direct work with Muslims and the subsequent persecution they experienced. He interviewed Barnabas and a new believer. He said 60% of the Muslim believers he interviewed married foreign women. Also less than 25% of the believers were women making it difficult for Muslim believers to find suitable mates. He was very much in favor of training and turning over responsibility of church planting to local believers as quickly as possible for a church planting movement. Nik eventually published ***The Insanity of God: a True Story of Faith Resurrected.*** Later, controversy swelled around the whole idea of the "insider movement" which advocated Muslim believers remaining in their Muslim communities until sufficient numbers became believers in order to provide protection for each other.

In October of 1999, I traveled to Egypt to attend the DAWN Conference for the Middle East at Moon Beach in Sinai about 5 hours south of Cairo. I notice that the Egyptians erected a mosque about every kilometer along the road since the Israelis gave Sinai back to them. The main theme of the conference was house churches and Wolfgang Simpson held forth bombastically. He gave me a copy of his book ***Houses That Change the World.***

Wolfgang Simpson and Ray exchanging books in Turan, May 2001

There were about 15 at the conference including brothers from Malaysia and Indonesia. I roomed with a Cairo business-man. Another from Cairo worked with the late Munis Abdulnur. We experienced an encouraging and inspiring time with lots of prayer support. When I returned to the Tel Aviv airport, the Israeli security called my daughter Cheryl in Jerusalem to verify my story. She told them to let me come home to see the grand-children! When I got home, I found that Barnabas had written up his own program for training leaders in Arabic! He is always one-step ahead of me.

Immediately afterwards I found myself embroiled with an IMB leader from our England office who asked me to assist in evaluating the use of our BCI properties in Israel. He proposed six possible options for the use of Baptist Village. One was to let the seminaries use it for training students. I replied that would be a great idea. It would encourage the students to get involved in the Middle East. Then He said that would defeat the purpose! I said it would get them acquainted with the Arab and Jewish believers. Then he said it would defeat the purpose if we started sending students to the USA. He turned my approval around and used it to defeat the idea! So, in the end, our BCI administrator and he decided to close Baptist Village for two years since it only served the Arab Christian community. (That was a shortsighted view since it also served the Messianic Jews.) I told them it would be a great blow to the Arab Christian community. I was in a dark mood over the whole meeting. He seemed to be determined to do as much damage as he could before he returned to the States to teach missions! He thought I was the one living in the past in the old paradigm. I challenged him not to go back to the RLT (Regional Leadership Team) and tell them I did not share their vision. I knew of no other way than to stand up to him, although obviously it did little good. Later I learned that they refused to authorize emergency relief for our persecuted Muslim believers because they were West Bank Arabs! **It was the end of the honeymoon with the New Directions**. Bureaucrats are bureaucrats whether from the old or new paradigm. The old control factor creeps in and destroys trust.

We had an affirming visit from Dan Hitzhusen from Global Missions Fellowship (now e3) with a group from California and Texas in October 1999. GMF had a streamlined church planting program that worked very well in many countries among Muslims. **Along with CEF I found GMF (e3) to be one of the best outreach programs**. At the same time, the Muslim believers were coming under increased pressure. A believing sheikh south of Bethlehem had his crop storehouse burned and lost his store of wheat, hay, barley, and animal food. The believers from the Hebron University collected funds to help him. He along, with a PA Security man who became a believer, eventually caught the two 16 year-old boys who committed the act as they tried to burn the stores of other believers. At the end of October, we were up to close to 260 baptized believers and increasing at 30 per month, sometimes whole families. Lydia was holding a Bible study for 20 women in her sister's home in the West Bank. As 1999 ended, I reflected in my diary:

> November 17, 1999-I am finally clearing my desk to begin working on *Back to Jerusalem* again. I was stuck for a year with an agent in Atlanta who took over $300 from me and never did a thing! In the meantime, I have benefited in reading about house churches and spiritual warfare. The whole idea of house churches is shaping itself before our eyes in the Muslim believer's movement. Our greatest need now is for more men like Barnabas to spread the movement. At present, we are only one heartbeat away from imminent disaster if anything happened to him. Keeps you humble and praying.
>
> The Lord taught me something about being the first-born when reading Numbers 8:15. The Lord set aside all firstborns of the Levites, the Sons of Israel and the children of Egypt as his for his

service. This included both Jews and Gentiles. It is a responsibility
to be a servant and wave offering (?) before the Lord and his people.
What a heritage! He has placed on me a privilege and responsibility
only He can sustain.

Our newsletter of February 2000 summed up the twentieth
century for us:

THE NEW MILLENNIUM

The rain falling outside hopefully is a sign of God's blessing on
the new millennium. We have been taking care of our daughter
Cheryl's two children, Nathaniel (9) and Moriel (4) during a two-
week teacher's strike, while she works as a cake decorator and
completes studies for the Ministry of Tourism tour guide's course.
Their father, Ilan Zamir has been on business in the States and just
returned with a severe cold. In July, we visited with our son Chuck,
his wife Tanya, and our beautiful Russian princess granddaughter,
Rita, along with Vladamir and Tamara, Tanya's parents in Moscow.
We missed James (Jaime) in Knoxville but hope to make up for it
next year. Grandchildren are a blessing and a challenge!

A great part of 1999 was taken up in preparation for **the
Summit for the New Millennium at Opryland in Nashville,**
in December. Nearly two hundred fellow Strategy Coordinators for
the 10/40 Window (from Indonesia to Morocco) met with representatives from churches across the United States to share the vision
for church planting movements among unreached people groups.
Ray spoke in our sponsoring churches in Virginia on the way there
and visited his sisters and cousins in the Carolinas afterwards. Rose
Mary flew later to San Diego and we spent Christmas with James
and Dee in our newly expanded house in Escondido. Rose Mary's
mother, Mary Emma (92) and her sister Charlotte and husband Red
celebrated with us. We began the process of helping Mary Emma
to find a retirement home in the San Diego area so we can be close
in the years to come. Ray had an unscheduled operation to repair a
hernia, which slowed him down a bit for the "vacation." We returned to Israel in time to celebrate 2000 by watching fireworks on
TV.

The challenge of the new millennium became clear as Ray
traveled Israel recently with Linda and her husband Jimmy from
Houston. Linda is a prayer supporter of the ministries in the Holy
Land. We were overwhelmed by the challenge of praying for villages and towns where up to one million Israeli Arab Muslims live.

Many have no known believer living in them. Will you join us in this prayer effort? If you will commit yourself to this, please contact us by email and we will send you periodic updates of ministry developments. We are already seeing the beginning of a harvest, and the Lord promises blessings beyond our imagination in the years ahead.

As mentioned above we spent an uneventful New Year in Israel without a glitch for Y2K, which was a big media hoax. It is a miracle to live into the NEW MILLENNIUM as a 64-year-old man who feels like he is 20 except for a very subdued sex drive! God is good. We watched TV as the year 2000 circled the globe. Only He knows what blessings and trials face us in the future. We trust in him.

Chapter 31

BACK TO JERUSALEM-2000

We returned to Israel from our trip to the USA on January 2000 to find Barnabas in the hospital for treatment of blocked arteries. At least it slowed him down a bit and even caused him to finally quit smoking. Instead of staying home or going off to rest, he went out and baptized 10 new believers! One of the problems we ran into with the 300 who were now baptized is that they would not baptize each other. They wanted to wait for Barnabas to do it for them. They were either too immature in faith or scared of the PA Security or Hamas if they got caught. I dreamed if we had 10 like Barnabas, we would have a church planting movement! I attended a conference in Bethlehem in February and reported the work that Barnabas was doing. Another brother said he had ten times that number of believers in the West Bank, which for me was confirmation of what Barnabas reported. **I had a dream one night and it was like I was awake, that I would see a great turning of Muslims to the Lord in my lifetime**. It was overwhelming. It can only happen if God does it, since humanly speaking it is impossible.

In March 2000, I finished the manuscript of **Back to Jerusalem,** Church Planting Movements in the Holy Land, to send to WinePress Publishing in Enumclaw, Washington. In the process, I got the index stuck in the footnotes and my computer froze up, causing me great consternation.

Rose Mary asked me, "When are you planning to write another book?"

I asked, "Why are you asking?"

She said, "When you do, I am planning to leave!"

I finally sent it in ready or not. Every time I tried to correct it, something else went wrong.

Our son-in-law, Ilan, got back from a trip to the USA with a bad cold. He had several unfortunate episodes in the hospitals in Jerusalem and ended up at the Hadassah Hospital in Ein Kerem. I visited him and he wept and asked to see Cheryl. She went to the hospital in the midst of her studies and poured her heart into helping him. He was finally transferred for physiotherapy to Mount Scopus Hadassah and I visited him several times before leaving for a Strategy Leaders conference in Ashburhnam, in South England. Soon after I returned, Ilan was in the intensive care ward in Hadassah Hospital, Ein Kerem. They had him hooked up to a respirator and he suffered intensely. **He passed away at 1:00 AM on Friday, April 7, 2000 in the same ward that they kept Arik Sharon alive for many years.** The whole ordeal he suffered reminded me of Isaiah 53 and the agony Jesus went through. He was buried on a hillside overlooking the Jerusalem hills with Samuel's tomb in the distance. The Orthodox burial society did a sensitive work in helping the family through the burial. The rabbi tore the lapels of the nearest of kin as a sign of mourning. They wrapped Ilan in a linen shroud with a prayer shawl over it. He was laid on a stone slab for a short service and then taken to the grave. His mother wept and screamed uncontrollably the whole time. Some Russian woman kept praying over him for him to "Rise!" We were all overcome with grief.

At noon, the believers gathered at Yad HaShmona for a memorial service. Elisheba and her husband provided music. Many friends from around the country came and I greeted them all. I spoke some words about Ilan's accomplishments, which surprised some there. He knew a number of languages, was a linguistic and computer expert, the President and Founder of the Israel College of the Bible and President of the Messianic Alliance. He had been a giant in our midst. I lost a friend who was a great man, despite his weaknesses. He knew the Messianic heart. He was only 42.

Ilan Zamir preaching in Turan Baptist Church, c. July 1989

WinePress published **Back to Jerusalem** in time to use it for my class in "Current Topics in International Missions" at Southeastern Baptist Seminary in Wake Forest, North Carolina. The IMB sent me on special assignment so it was not counted as furlough time. Altogether about 400 copies of the book sold during my time in the States. I spoke in six states and interviewed with several AM radio stations.

We were very encouraged by the hospitality of the Dr. and Mrs. Paige Patterson at Southeastern and our old friends Dr. and Mrs. George Braswell. I was pleasantly surprised while standing in line in the Southeastern chapel for the book signing of Judge Pressler's book, *A Hill On Which to Die,"* to turn to the page where he says he has no problem with Charismatics because they take the Bible seriously! **Charismatic has never been the issue for me. Bible study, soul winning and church planting have been my passions long before the Charismatic movement ever came along.** However, I cannot deny the life transforming experience in 1971 five days after my mother died. It literally changed my life! Along with my salvation experience at age 16, call to missions at Ridgecrest in 1955, and marriage to Rose Mary in 1957, it has been the pinnacle of my spiritual pilgrimage. My three books so far, on witness to Muslims, on Mavis Pate, and on church planting have all come as a direct result of that experience in 1971.

Back to Jerusalem published in 2000

I looked to the future in my newsletter of December 2000:

FOCUS ON THE FUTURE

Our hearts and minds are focused on our return to Israel after special assignment to Southeastern Baptist Seminary. Ray taught Arabic and Current Topics in International Missions to students in the church planting program who will be serving in the Middle East. We were in almost daily contact with family and colleagues in Israel during the latest conflict. Last reports were that all on our team there are safe and having more opportunity to share Christ's love with the people. Our daughter Cheryl and the grandchildren have moved to a new home and are trying to cope with the tensions around them.

In reflecting on the churches we visited during the fall of 2000 in the USA, I saw two things. First, despite the growing support of the Cooperative Program and the Lottie Moon Offering our people are still not financially sold out to missions. Most are not giving beyond their comfort level. **The Lord is sending signals with the bombings in Beirut, the Gulf War, the Cole attack, immigration and growth of Islam in the USA, but most simply have not gotten the point that we are in a war, which will require total sacrifice or ultimate capitulation.** Secondly, Southern Baptists of the old school are divided over non-essentials like women clergyman and are using the CBF to send a signal to the new conservative leadership. Missions is the loser. The woman pastor issue is really a non-issue since most SBC churches will never have a woman pastor, much less a woman senior pastor. It is just a way that the losers are making a problem for the winners. I wonder what it will take for Southern Baptists to wake up? Even the Sunday School Board, LifeWay bookstores and the rest of the mammoth Nashville system are operating on the profit motive, and not that of sacrifice for getting the Gospel to the world.

When we got back to Israel, Barnabas and Lydia came over and we read Acts 3 and prayed together. They reported they now have believers in 20 locations with over 100 families. That is about 25-30% increase over when we left. They want to concentrate on Israel now because of the new *Intifada* in the West Bank. We loaded up his car with tracts and New Testaments for Beersheba. This guy will not quit! On top of all his other problems he was hit broadside financially by a PA friend who passed bad checks to him and now Barnabas is paying back the bank for about $9,000 in overdrafts. A hard lesson to learn!

In February, I visited Ein Ibrahim near Megiddo with Cal Nathan who was teaching English in Baka. Ashraf, son of the head of the English department at the Islamic College invited us to visit his home near Umm al-Fahm, one of the largest Muslim cities in Galilee south of Nazareth. We were able to visit in a number of homes and pray for his father who was sick with prostate problems. I cannot believe that after 30 years the Lord has opened Mus Mus and Umm al Fahm to us! Ashraf took us to the top of the mountain of Umm al Fahm and we saw many villages around that I had visited with the Nazareth Hospital staff (Im Abdu, Bevin Woodhead, Salim Nassar) when I first came to Nazareth in 1966.

As the work developed, Barnabas started paper work to form a non-profit organization to give us a broader base for administering funds to the outreach projects. We had several kindergartens in the West Bank and gave basic scholarships to students, and assisted families whose homes were burned out by Muslim radicals. It would also give us a legal way to assist in the work after we retire. I chaffed under the continual changes of administration and policies for funding but was encouraged by Rose Mary as I noted in my dairy on February 14, 2001, Valentine's Day.

> I bought a card at Steinmatskies about how my computer was so overloaded with love that it crashed! That added to my depression this month, in addition to ongoing problems over budget and missiology. I got diverted from my thought about the computer crash and forgot to mention how tremendous it is to be married to a smart, beautiful, patient and talented wife who has tolerated me for over 40 years of marriage. I do not know what I would do without her and hope I never have to! Aside from God's gift of salvation and calling, she is the greatest thing that has ever happened to me, along with the infilling of the Holy Spirit in the 70's. She keeps trying to encourage me by telling me that the people in England need me

more than I need them and that I am doing a good job with what I have to do it with. She thinks I worry too much!

We had a positive meeting with John Brady from our England IMB leadership in Ramle on February 23. There was a good number of our Muslim believers present considering the dangers of traveling from the West Bank. I was encouraged to keep on with my approach of dealing with the whole family in evangelism. We were able also to encourage Barnabas to train up leadership to relieve him of the burden of all the baptisms.

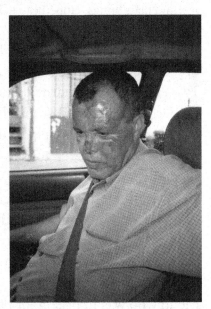

Both Barnabas and I have been warned to keep a low profile. The sheikhs in Ramle have been talking about us. A friend in security told Barnabas not to go back to the West Bank more than once a month. The "bad check" friend came looking for us several times with PA men with him under the pretense of wanting to be baptized. Later in March, Barnabas went over

Barnabas burned, 2001

to Jordan to visit family. The police stopped him and searched his car. They accused him of being an evangelist. He talked his way out if it by telling them his cousin was the Minister of Communication and he drove a taxi in Amman before the patrolman was born!

On April 7, 2001, we traveled to London on British Airways to attend the Strategy Leader Conference at Ashburnham Conference Center near Battle, England. Our Gaza colleagues, the Fitzgeralds were honored since it was their last SLC before retirement. We could not decide if we would be back next year since we were leaving Israel in April of next year so Mike Edens decided for us. They had a short service for us. I note a most significant activity at this conference in my dairy:

> We did the Strength Finders survey by Gallup and got the results to study. I learned from this that my strengths were: Learner, Communication, Connectedness, Wooer, and Maximizer. Rose Mary's were: Connectedness, Maximizer, Arranger, Empathy, and Relator. It explained to me why Rose Mary always tries to arrange and plan things. Hope I can affirm it rather than bristle and discourage it!

When we got back from England, Islamic fundamentalists firebombed four homes of our Muslim believers near Bethlehem. Two children were burned, one girl "Susie" was burned severely on her face, legs, and stomach. Barnabas went to a PA security friend and asked his help in apprehending the perpetrators. A local Muslim believer took responsibility to buy necessities to rebuild the houses and furnish them. We learned shortly that the Palestinian Security caught the two men who firebombed the homes. **They were Shiites and had been under orders from Iran not only to burn but also to kill the converts!** They gained information on the believers through calling Christian groups advertising the Bible and from Barnabas' PA friend who was in prison for passing the bad checks!

Byron and Lin Smith, friends from the New Hope Church in Penisquitos, California near San Diego came out in late April to disciple Barnabas and Lydia, using special leadership material developed by Church Dynamics International, an auxiliary of Campus Crusade. One of the concepts Barnabas had trouble accepting was the total forgiveness of God. He said if he knew God forgave all sins, past, present and future there would be no motivation for good works! He was able to put the concept into action as I note in my dairy on April 25, 2001:

> Byron and Lin Smith from Penisquitos near Escondido arrived at 1:00 AM and began teaching Barnabas and Lydia in Discipleship

Training. Barnabas' mind is occupied with the fire. I am having to scramble to find funds to help the believers. The Barnabas Fund gave us $5000, which has helped until now. I am having to hold B and "Paul" back and remind them not to commit us to funds we do not have. B asked me if it was right to take money at interest. He has had to borrow to pay off his debt for a new diesel car. He is under tremendous financial burden since "AA" stuck him with $9000 in bad checks. He basically now does not have money for food. After "AA" went to prison his wife told B that if he pressed charges for his bad checks her husband would be in jail for another year. Instead, B took the family food! His teeth are about to fall out and he will have to have a bridge built soon. If I was not receiving Social Security now we could not stay afloat financially.

The situation got even hotter very soon. On May 4, 2001, we were watching Swan Lake on TV with Moriel and the cell phone rang. It was Lydia telling me Barnabas had been attacked. It seems he went to visit the homes that were burned to take the girls to the hospital. When he got there, two men stopped his car at the entrance of the village. He got out to see what the problem was and they threw a Molotov cocktail that exploded at his feet! His face and left shoulder were burned. Paul showed up with others and put out the fire and took him to the hospital. I was personally angry that he went back there without protection. Paul called later to apologize. He said the men had come to him and asked to meet the man who was helping the villagers after the fire. He called Barnabas but did not mention the men. Later on I repented and took Rose Mary and Moriel over to visit Barnabas and pray for him. He said the fright of the attack was worse than the fire. He was happy that he was found worthy to suffer for Christ. The image of the burned skin pealing from his face is indelible on my memory

We visited Baptist Village congregation the next day. A man from the US Embassy asked me if I was in any danger. He would have the Embassy staff to see that I was protected as a US Citizen. I told him I was all right as long as I stayed out of the Territories.

Barnabas called that afternoon to say that his PA security friend called and said they had arrested the two men who attacked him. He told Barnabas to change his cell phone and sell his car!

You would expect the Christian Arabs would encourage the Muslim believers but that is not always the case. We visited a home meeting in Nazareth and Barnabas gave his testimony. At the end, a Christian Arab, rather than encouraging him, asked him, "Do you believe Jesus is God?" Barnabas refused to answer him since his son and another new believer were with us. For a half hour the group argued about it and the leader lectured Barnabas on theology! I told them it was like making a person swallow a whole bottle of water in one gulp! I also knew the Christian who asked the question had himself married a Muslim and he purposely brought up the matter. Fortunately, the leader of this group has been an encourager to Barnabas throughout the years.

Much happened in the summer of 2001 as noted in our newsletter of August 1, 2001:

Dear Family and Friends,

We are fine. By the time you get this, we would have visited our son Dr. Chuck and his son "James" and daughter Rita in Moscow for our summer vacation. Ray had an unexpected trip to the USA for a week in July for the funeral of his brother-in-law, Dr. Michael U. Kale of Landrum, S.C. who died as a result of an injury sustained in an automobile accident five years ago.

Despite the bad press from our area, the ministry of the IAM people group is expanding rapidly. We now have second-generation leaders who are reaching out to their own people. They have formed their own non-profit organization, "The Society of Light" which will enable them to minister legally after we leave.

Naturally, in the present situation we keep our eyes open, but basically live normally and enjoy our time being close to Cheryl and the grandchildren. She works in the Bible Land Museum in Jerusalem. I am in Jerusalem several times a week for business and continue to enjoy the privilege of living in the Holy Land.

Our plans are to begin packing our household this fall for final stateside assignment next April. We will be training new personnel we hope will arrive at year's end. We hope to find a furlough home in Southern California to encourage the churches in that area to be advocates of ministries in this area, and to be near Rose Mary's mother who lives in a retirement center in Yuma, AZ.

We are continually grateful to those of you who encourage us through your regular support to the Cooperative Program in Southern Baptist Churches. Thanks also to the First Baptist Church, Suffolk, VA and the Great Bridge Baptist Church in Chesapeake, VA who contribute directly to our salary through the International Mission Board in Richmond, VA. A special thanks to the staff at FBC, Suffolk who have sent out this newsletter for many years. Your help is needed now more than ever since the growing number of overseas representatives and the worldwide harvest stretches resources to the limit.

Rose Mary and Ray,
Jerusalem, July 2001

Our family and friends needed assurance for our safety due to the suicide bombings taking place in Israel on a regular basis by fanatical Muslims from the occupied territories of the West Bank and Gaza. Their favorite targets were buses, shopping malls and restaurants. On August 30, 2001, a suicide bomber blew himself up about a block from the Anglican School in Jerusalem where several of our MK's who were friends of our grandson Nathanael attended. Their mothers were having a prayer meeting at the school that day. We lived with the constant awareness that we were in harm's way when we went into town. When our daughter Cheryl lived across from Yad Vashem in Jerusalem, their babysitter missed his bus one day. He took the next bus. **The bus he missed blew up ahead of them!** The resulting ugly wall zigzagging through the outskirts of Jerusalem separating Jerusalem from the territories was a necessary, though repugnant measure of survival. I note in my dairy on August 23, 2001:

> We are finishing the last of food distribution and it does not look like the situation in the West Bank will improve. The Palestinians are killing Israelis every day and the Israelis are retaliating by destroying police stations and the Palestinian infrastructure. They are targeting leading Palestinian commanders for assassination, claiming they were involved in terrorist activity. The cycle of violence is increasing. Despite it all we are having 30-50 baptisms a month. I am concerned about discipling and leadership development and worship and study groups forming.

The swift sword of the Israelis cut both ways. A PA Security guard at a Palestinian prison who helped us numerous times to protect believers lost an eye and a limb in an Israeli retaliation attack. Though the atrocities of the suicide bombers were the result of fanatics aligned with radical Hamas groups, the Israelis retaliated against the more moderate PA infrastructure. Guilt by association is a leading cause of the ongoing conflict.

In the middle of all the turmoil, I had a long daydream about the humanity of Jesus and questions I had asked for years on Saturday, September 8, 2001:

> We have been having a long discussion on the Love the Muslim network about the Virgin Mary. This morning as I was lying in bed thinking about it, the thought struck me that Jesus was a man! The greatest miracle of his life was his humanity. He was born of a virgin by the miraculous work of the Spirit of God. He ate, slept, had pain, and had normal body functions because he was a man. I remembered John Eden's words in the class on the Trinity that, "The man Jesus was never a part of the Christian Trinity." That is the reason Jesus said, "There is none good except God." "Let your works be seen before men so that they may glorify your Father who is in heaven." He was tempted in all ways that we are except without

sinning, as Hebrews states. All that Jesus said and did was to glorify his Father in Heaven. He was the model and living example that a man can be fully submissive to God in all that he does and says. All he did was done in obedience to the Holy Spirit who lived in him. The "none good except God" had bothered me for years. Why should Jesus say such a thing, if he himself were God? The greatest miracle of the incarnation was that Jesus was a man. God raised him from the dead because he was an obedient Son. His obedience began from his birth with his deliberated choice to follow the leadership of God's Spirit. We can make the same choice. This is the reason He told Mary not to touch him, since he had not yet ascended to the Father. He himself would not allow his fleshly body to be an object of worship until after the ascension. God gets all the glory. As the early Christian confession says, "he is fully man and fully God." You cannot have one without the other for the incarnation.

Some Southern Baptist leaders are leading people into the danger of the heresy of patriapassianism (God the Father suffered on the cross) when they teach people "Jesus is God." If they mean the resurrected, glorified Christ, seated at the right hand of God, fine. However, the man Jesus is never called God, even by the disciples until after the resurrection when he took on a glorified body and Thomas said, "My Lord and my God!" They need to use the terms that the New Testament uses, "Son of God," or "Son of man" for Jesus. He was the Son of God through the Holy Spirit. The Jesus is God formula leads into all sorts of misunderstandings for Christians, and the Muslims and Jews they are witnessing to. The full humanity of Jesus must be affirmed to keep things in balance. For the Christian, it means the possibility of living a life of obedience to the Father through the fullness of the Spirit. For the Muslim it means Jesus is the one truly submissive to God. Moreover, for the Jew it means he was the Messiah, the one anointed by the Spirit of God to do good works according to the Law.

While sharing these ideas with Rose Mary after breakfast over our white table with a view of our garden in Ramla I remembered my idea about the capacitor or transformer. God could not reveal his glory and holiness directly to man. Man would be destroyed. Moses face lit up because of his being in the presence of the Lord. *Therefore, Jesus is the divine capacitor or transformer of God.* God limited his glory and power to come in Jesus, as it states in Philippians 2. God is able to limit himself, although man in his prideful theologies wants to dictate to God what he can do! There is a 33-year gap in history where God revealed himself to be in the man Jesus. Jesus was limited in time and space and humanity. He could only influence one person or a crowd at a time. The glorified Christ who is one with the Father on the throne, as the Lamb slain from the foundation of the world can now influence millions through the power of the Spirit. He chooses to do this through our limited human efforts led by his Spirit. He gave us the divine action plan in his humanity. The three, the twelve, the 72 were all human sociological groupings that influence society.

Jesus did not keep all the rules of the scribes and Pharisees because they were human, man-made rules. They only puffed the pride of their humanity. He went back to the original meaning of the Torah or teachings of God.

Rose Mary warned me about sharing these ideas with the wrong people at the wrong time. I can see where I will be branded as a heretic by some, first because I am a "charismatic" and then because of my understanding of the humanity of Jesus. I praise the Father, Son and the Holy Spirit in heaven daily, for they are one God, and I accept the humanity of Jesus as a model for living life on this earth under the guidance of the Holy Spirit, instructed by the written inspired Word of God in the Bible.

I decided not to go to the Jerusalem Church in the Old City on September 9, 2001 because of the security situation. Instead, I took Rose Mary to lunch at the Alladdin Restaurant in Jappa, one of my favorite spots overlooking the Mediterranean. About that time, a suicide bomber blew himself up near the Nahariya train station, killing 4 and wounding 45. I called Paul Treat who lived there. Francine told me he took a train to Haifa to go to the dentist. Later in the afternoon, I called and Paul was home. He missed the blast by two trains! A car bomb went off at Bet Lid and a carload of teachers was shot up in the Jordan Valley. It looks like the Hamas are stepping up the pace of attacks.

On Monday, September 10, 2001, I sent out an IAM Update regarding the local and worldwide plan of fanatical Islam to dominate or liberate the Holy Land and the world. They consider that the Holy Land is Islamic *Waqf* or "holy property" since Umr Ibn al-Khattab "liberated" it after Muhammad died in the late 7th Century. Therefore, the Arabs consider the Jews taking it back in 1948 as a catastrophe or *nak-bah*. For this reason, Yasser Arafat could not agree to take only half of it back for peace. He has to take the whole land for Islam, or the Muslims would kill him. The next afternoon I was upstairs in my office when Rose Mary called from downstairs and said,

"Something is going on in the U.S."

I went down and saw on TV that a plane crashed into one of the World Trade Center Towers in New York City. In a few minutes, another plane crashed into the second tower and I knew it was a terrorist attack! Then we heard that another plane crashed into the Pentagon. Later a plane crashed near Pittsburg. It turned out they were all planes that had been hijacked from Boston and Newark, headed for Los Angeles and full of fuel. **I could not believe that my predictions of only a day before had come true!**

Our Israeli landlord was trying to sell our house since we were planning to move to Baptist Village at the end of the year. He called that day to show the house to some Russians from the Stans. He called while we were watching the terrible news and made a flippant comment about,

"Now the Americans see what it is like!"

I told him that America was suffering for the Jews and the Arabs. I did not like his attitude. I told him I was not going to let them in today and maybe not for a week since I was upset about what was going on and all the Americans losing their lives. I asked him to have a heart! We were upset and it was like a funeral. I was not going to let these people in now.

My cousin Sarah called to ask how we were and asked about my prophecy. I warned her not to give out information over the phone about the location of our President. We stayed in that Sunday since I did not want public exposure in Jerusalem during these tense times. We later attended an insightful lecture in Jerusalem by Moshe Sharon on Fundamentalist Islam and Israel. He told how Muslims cannot make peace with non-Muslims, but only a non-binding truce for up to 10 years. I despaired for American and British politicians who say Islam is a religion of peace. That idea is a deception. There was a terrorist attack on a kibbutz north of Gaza at the same time that killed two young people. During this time, I was proofreading a paper by Avner Bashki on *Jihad*. I realized as I read the paper how much Muhammad was influenced by the murderous corruption of the Byzantine Church. I had been reading a short history of *Byzantium* by Norwich I bought in Russia. It records two or three brutal murders per page. Islam must have been punishment for the bestiality of the church in those days.

Wedding, Hamdi's son, October 2001, Galilee

I traveled back to Galilee on October 4, 2001 to attend the wedding of my friend Hamdi's youngest son. It was a Muslim religious wedding and the local sheik got up and preached a sermon about *Isa* (Jesus) healing the sick, raising the dead and preaching the Gospel. However, the Americans who claim to believe in him are bombing a country with all their might to kill one man (Ben Ladin).

He said, "Islam will win in the end."

All the time he was glancing sideways at David Groseclose and me. Later a sheik who was a friend of mine got up and said, "Yes, everyone knows Islam will win in the end, but will you, Oh Muslim, win in the end if you steal, lie, commit adultery and other sins? You have to ask God's forgiveness every moment of every day, in order to win in the end!"

Later he invited us to visit him in his home.

Unfortunately, it could not save the lives of the believers who were being targeted. Barnabas told me that a Ben Ladin supporter stabbed the leader of the Muslim believer's student movement in a West Bank University on Monday to death during a demonstration on campus. It seems all the Mbbs were hiding in the office on Monday during the riot. The police came and ran them out. The fanatic stabbed "Sammy" as he called him an apostate or *kafir*. Sammy is our first Mbb martyr. His father is a paraplegic who was baptized in a bathtub. I was saddened and reminded that we put these people's lives in danger when we lead them to Christ. To make matters worse the family demanded we pay for his funeral since he was declared a *kafir* and they could not claim blood money for his murder. I was shocked. I forgot that part of the Arab culture.

The rest of the fall was filled with packing, visiting friends and churches from Eilat to Galilee. In an unexpected turn of events, the Israel Ministry of Interior refused to renew all the visas of our Baptist Representatives due to a situation involving a number of Nigerian pilgrims who stayed in the land illegally. The IMB paid for all of us to fly to Antalya, Turkey in order to renew our visas on return. We stayed in a five-star hotel and took trips out to waterfalls, mountain overlooks and the seacoast. The weather was rainy and foggy. The last day we got a guide to take us to the Antalya Museum where we saw Saint Nicholas' knucklebone. Therefore, Santa Claus was a real person! He was the Bishop of the Church in Mira, just a few miles down the coast from Antalya. It was a merry ending to a very tumultuous year!

One of my special good-byes was to Menahem Benhayim, a Messianic Jewish believer. We knew Menachem since 1965 when we visited him in his "Red Door" apartment in Eilat. Menachem and his lively wife Haya were the first Messianic Jews to immigrate to Israel from the USA. He worked in the Port Authority and entertained numerous local and foreign visitors with his infectious smile and heavy New York accent. Later Menachem and Haya moved to Jerusalem. He was a leader of the Messianic Jewish Alliance and friends to Ilan and other Messianic Jews in the land and abroad. Menachem and Haya always had an encouraging word for me in my ministry to the Arabs. They wrote their memoirs from Haya's perspective in 2003, *Bound for the Promised Land*. Menachem passed away in 2004, so it was my privilege to have this time with him in 2001.

Menahem Benhayim and Ray in Jerusalem, October 16, 2001

Chapter 32

BV BEGINNING AND END

Our landlord in Ramie wanted us to stay. He offered to rent or to sell us his house. It was a temptation, since we really enjoyed the location and the beautiful garden, which he personally cultivated. We had a gated garage and could drive to Jappa on the Mediterranean Ocean in 15 minutes and up to Jerusalem in 30. Herzlia was only 20 minutes away. We could zip down the Ayalon Expressway through Tel Aviv and enjoy the tree-lined boulevards, embassy residences and restaurants in the suburb where our children used to attend the American International School. Our daughter Cheryl, with grandchildren Nathanael and Moriel, lived just up the hill on the way to Jerusalem in Meveseret and visited frequently. We could take a 3-hour flight from Tel Aviv to Moscow where Chuck lived with his wife Tanya and our princess Russian granddaughter, Rita. Just our family ties alone were a real incentive to stay.

Years later Rose Mary reminded me of a conversation she overheard between Cheryl and the landlord in Hebrew. His grandfather was a rabbi in Morocco. They discussed the views of the Messiah and the prophecies of his return. A couple of weeks later the landlord knocked on our door about mid-morning. When Rose Mary opened the door the first thing he said was, "When our Jewish Messiah comes and your Messiah Jesus comes again, it is going to be the same person!"

However, reality dictated otherwise. Israel was founded as a country for the Jews. The Orthodox-dominated Ministry of Interior did not grant long-term residency willingly to gentile Baptists! I tried several times to apply for permanent residency but was told to keep the temporary clergy visa, which would be better for us. Barnabas was willing to use whatever influence he had to get us permanent residency but was told the same thing. The sudden refusal of the government to renew all our visas reinforced the reality that it was time to make a departure. Our January 2002 Newsletter laid out our plans for the future:

> We are packing to leave the Land of the Bible after almost 37 years. We certainly hope it is not for good since Cheryl and the grandchildren are still here along with many faithful Christian, Jewish and Muslim friends who became our family, just as the Lord promised. He told us that if we left land and family for him we would receive a hundredfold! He has done even more and for this, we are eternally grateful. In literal terms, we lost land and parents (except for Rose Mary's Mom who is 93!) but He made it up to us in lands and a harvest of Mbbs far beyond our wildest imaginations. He gave us 45 years together in his service, three wonderful MKs who are making their own international impact, and four unbelievably precious grandchildren. He has taken us through the depths of intense sorrow and lifted us with glimpses of Glory. **If there has been any success, it is simply that we have stuck around long enough to see him do it! Also, we had a terrific support system through the IMB-SBC, the Cooperative Program, and the Lottie Moon Christmas Offering. And most important, you saints who have prayed for us faithfully all these years**.
>
> Now, to the future. We plan to leave in April after we orient Sybil W. and Joan C., two valiant ladies who will be joining our team as Master's ISC'ers for ESL in lAM villages. Please remember them along with Pam R. and Cal N. and others who we hope will step into the gap for the harvest among the lAMs. Remember "Barnabas and Lydia" and a host of Mbbs in multiple house groups throughout the Land. They will continue ministry through the Society of Light Charity, which is now a legal non-profit friendly society. We plan to develop IAM Partners as a channel of support stateside for their and other movements throughout the area in partnership with the IMB-SBC and other organizations.

We plan to spend May-June in Marietta, GA at Eastside Baptist Church, July- December in the San Diego area assisting the churches of the San Diego S. Baptist Association.

We plan to "retire" from the IMB-SBC at the end of 39 years of service in June 2003 after this final stateside assignment, Lord willing. For all concerned, this is our choice and seems the Lord's timing. Thank you for continuing with us through this journey.

This newsletter hinted at a tightening of security for our overseas personnel. We stopped giving out names and locations of our colleagues serving in sensitive areas, for their sake and for their families and friends. About this time, we had three attacks on missionaries. One was nearby in Southern Lebanon, where a beautiful missionary nurse answered a knock on the door one morning. They shot her dead! The word got out that local Muslim leadership was disturbed about her telling their children about Jesus and to love their enemies. The other was in Yemen, when a man stepped into the administrative office of the Yemen Baptist Hospital, pulled a machine gun out of his cloak and murdered three of our colleagues. One, Dr. Martha Myers, was one of the sweetest persons we ever knew and always honored us when we met in Cypress. The local villagers around Jibla were so upset at this atrocity they lined the street as they brought her body for burial and sang the hymn she taught them, "This is the Day the Lord Hath Made," in Arabic. She spent 24 years in Yemen and was only 57.

Along about this time a car full of Southern Baptist relief workers was attacked in Mosul, Iraq and four were killed. Our colleague and former journeyman, Carrie Nichole Taylor McDonnall was wounded severely. Her husband drove her to the hospital while she was unconscious. He died before she revived. Carrie shared her experience in *Facing Terror*, (Integrity: 2005). Therefore, in a period of a few months we lost eight precious colleagues whose only crime was serving the Lord in the

Middle East. Unfortunately, this was not the end of the sacrifices of God's children.

A handsome young Arab Muslim man named Ra'fat married Lydia's beautiful niece. Her father was an Israeli police officer in Jerusalem. I lent Ra'fat money to buy a refrigerator for his apartment in Ramie since he was having trouble finding a job. I forgave the debt as a wedding present. He drove for Barnabas to several outreach points around the country. On one trip, the opposition forced them off the road and wrecked the car. The Lord spared his life. As a result, he gave his heart to the Lord.

One day a call came from the West Bank that his parents were in trouble and wanted him to come home immediately. The next thing we heard was that fanatics had murdered him because he had become a believer. The story was that they cut his body in two to make a statement to others. We tried to comfort his pregnant wife who was in a state of shock. To make matters worse, the PA Intelligence put out the story that he was alive and living with his parents. I contacted a pastor friend in Ramallah to check out the story. He said he talked to someone over the phone who claimed to be the man. I asked him to please have him make a picture with him so we could confirm it. The man never appeared.

Later I called Ra'fat's father-in-law, the police officer, and he told me, "Ra'fat was murdered because he became a Christian. I buried him."

Another Muslim friend paid the ultimate price for his faith in Jesus.

Not all was rosy at Baptist Village where we lived the last three months of our life in Israel. We attended the Baptist Village congregation that met on Saturday mornings. The Nigerians and Russians members lined up against the American pastor and tried to kick him out. The Russian treasurer refused to pay the rent of the pastor's apartment. They succeeded in forcing the former pastor to leave. The IMB had previously moved the missionary pastor to Europe and he was involved in long-distance counseling to oppose the current pastor. Things came to a head when the offerings of the church disappeared from the pastor's apartment. He had me bring a detective to determine who could have entered his apartment without his knowledge. Evidence pointed back to a member of the congregation that had a key to the apartment. We were attending worship one Saturday when the pastor got up and started reading emails he intercepted between the congregational leader and the former pastor in Europe. The congregational leader turned around and angrily told me, "You are the cause of all this!"

I had been a member of a Southern Baptist Church for over 50 years and here I was in the middle of my second church feud just in time to top off my missionary career! Fortunately, the Business Manager of the BCI stepped in and straightened out some financial and legal matters and the atmosphere calmed down by the time we left in April.

The good folks up in Nazareth threw a party to celebrate our retirement. A number of friends from all over Galilee gathered at the Baptist School auditorium to say their good byes. Among them were the President of the Islamic College and the Secretary of the Local Council in Turan who made the comment that one Arabic word characterized my ministry, **muthabira, or "persistence!"** He was impressed at how I always came early to the village and visited in the homes to encourage people to come out to the meetings. They awarded us a huge brass plaque with an engraving of Mary's Well. However, a smooth departure from our Galilee wanderings was not to be ours.

We had a final get-together with members of our team who were teaching ESL in the Arab villages of Central Sharon and

Galilee, along with our daughter Cheryl and grandchildren at Baptist Village. Our bags were packed and tickets purchased to fly out the next day. A call came from Lydia. Barnabas received a desperate call the night before that a believer in Eilat was in distress; "Please come immediately." He took off in the middle of the night. It seems he was on the road south when another car came up behind him and ran him off the road. His car turned over and he was in a coma in a hospital in Jerusalem. Rose Mary and I drove up to find him stretched out on the hospital bed on life support, unconscious. We requested that the Israeli doctor brief us on his condition. He asked us, "What happened to him?"

We explained what we knew and told him, "People all over the world are praying for him. Please take care of him!"

He promised he would.

We took off that evening from the Ben Gurion Airport and our Galilee wanderings ended without knowing the fate of our friend.

Barnabas did revive and continued his work through many financial and family trials until he passed away in February 2016. I recapped the end of our Galilee Wanderings in our Newsletter of June 2003:

> We were honored in the Service of Recognition for Emeritus Missionaries on May 4, 2003 at the Missionary Learning Center near Richmond, VA. Thirty other retiring colleagues, along with family and friends joined us to celebrate many years of combined overseas service for the Lord with the International Mission Board of the Southern Baptist Convention. Ray gave one of the four key-note testimonies. We have served 39 years with the IMB. It has been a good journey, best described by Jesus' words in John 4:37-38:
>
> "For in this case the saying is true, "One sows, and another reaps."
>
> "I sent you to reap that for which you have not labored; others have labored, and you have entered into their labor."

We had the privilege of experiencing a 20th Century Holy Spirit renewal and seeing the beginnings of a church planting movement among Muslims in Israel and the Palestinian Territory. We witnessed the development of a strong Messianic Jewish Movement. We worked alongside many brave Christian Arabs and bold Messianic Jews. We heard them praying for and with each other.

As we come to the end of this phase of our service, we have some concerns.

The people called Southern Baptists have always had one main thrust:

Cooperative Program Missions. First, we see the greatest response to the Gospel in history among Muslims in the Arab World. Second, laborers are ready to go overseas in answer to the call of the Lord of the Harvest. Third, Southern Baptists are limiting missionary appointments because of lack of sufficient funding. It is not that we are not giving more. We are simply not giving enough! Fourth, some Southern Baptists have chosen to stop cooperating. They have sacrificed the mission and the harvest for secondary issues.

We are grateful to the vast majority who supported us though prayer and giving during these many years. Especially, we are grateful to First Baptist Church of Suffolk, VA and the Great Bridge Baptist Church in Chesapeake, VA who helped pay our salaries through the IMB

We plan to keep serving the Lord in this new phase of life. We are blessed with good health and a continued vision. Ray will be directing IAM Partners, Inc., a nonprofit charity dedicated to encouraging church planting movements among the Arabs and Muslims worldwide in cooperation with the IMB and other Great Commission Christian churches and organizations.

Thank you for being partners with us on the journey.

I referred to our Galilee Wanderings in my testimony mentioned above at the Service of Recognition at MLC:

Jesus saved the best wine until the last at the wedding feast in Cana of Galilee. He did the same for us.

The Lord had laid a burden for the Muslim people on my heart while I was a student at Southeastern Baptist Theological Seminary. Rose Mary had a calling to work among the Jewish people.

We went to Israel in 1965 to work with Israeli Arabs.

I traveled the hills of Galilee preaching, teaching, and visiting while Rose Mary was busy at home tutoring our three children.

He led a Muslim friend named Hamdi to our house early in our career in Nazareth. Hamdi took me to visit and witness to his many family and friends in villages all over Galilee and the West Bank.

I would spend hours talking, listening, eating and drinking endless cups of Arab coffee and tea. This went on for years with no visible evidence of fruit. Rose Mary would ask, especially when the children were off at college, "Why are we here? We are not seeing any fruit. Maybe we should be at home."

The Lord did bring renewal among the Christian Arabs and Messianic Jews during the 70's, but still no movement among the Muslims.

Rose Mary filled in her time leading the only hand bell choir in the country, volunteering in the library at the Nazareth Hospital and participating in women's work, which included the unique Jewish-Arab Women believers group in Galilee.

Then came the Gulf War of 1991. Things began to change. We had moved north to the village of Josephus where I directed the International Institute of Biblical Studies extension program.

An American friend married to a Jewish Messianic believer living in a settlement in the West Bank began passing our Arabic tracts and Bibles to Muslim building laborers.

When they responded he would meet me at the Jordan River and we would baptize them.

The Church of Samaria started with 12 Muslim background believers. One was interrogated and tortured in the Jericho prison. When he was finally released, he fled to Israel and lived at the Baptist Center until he moved to the town in central Israel where we were then living. He eventually betrayed us and moved back to the West Bank.

Before he did, a friend of his stole my cell phone number off his cell phone and called me for an appointment.

He told me, "I was once married to a Christian woman in Beirut and attended the Orthodox Church with her. I heard the Gospel but did not understand it. I want you to teach me how to be a Christian." He had three wives and smoked three packs of cigarettes each day, one for each wife!

I told him I would do it on one condition; that he would pass on what I taught him to other Muslims.

We met together almost daily to read the Sermon on the Mount, Psalms and Proverbs. His face would light up and he would say, "That happened to me today!"

I taught him the Four Spiritual Laws and he received Christ. I baptized him.

He called me one day and said, "I have a friend who wants to 'hear the Four." I told him, "You give him the Four!"

He called me later and said, "There is a group of young men who accepted the Lord in the Hills and they want to be baptized, but if you do it they will be taken in for interrogation." I told him, "You baptize them!"

His oldest wife was sick and they thought she was going to die, so we prayed for her and she got well! She and her adult children in the West Bank became believers. His second wife, an orthodox Muslim in Gaza divorced him, but her teenage daughter became a believer. His youngest wife held out the longest since her brother was a sheikh near Jericho. He beat her and threw her out of the house when she became a believer, but his two oldest sons became believers! Her sisters, brothers, nephews and nieces became believers and started Bible study groups in their homes.

Through "Barnabas and Lydia," our man and woman of peace, the Lord has started a Muslim background believer movement in Israel and the West Bank that has grown to over 1000 despite persecution which took the form of stabbings, house burnings, accidents, forced divorces and imprisonment.

The Lord saved the best wine until the last for us. If there was any secret to drinking this new wine, it is because we stayed long enough to see Him do it!

Chapter 33

BACK TO JERUSALEM
100TH ANNIVERSARY

In May 2005, I returned to the Land with a team from Calvary Baptist Church in San Diego. We visited Barnabas and Lydia and verified burns she sustained in a firebomb attack on her car after conducting a Bible study in the West Bank. Later we assisted in an English language camp in a Druze town high up the in the mountains of northern Galilee. We also visited Hamdi's family who were like a second home to me during my 37 years in the Land. The only downer was having our rental car broken into in Jappa of Tel Aviv due to the police officers being called out to assist in the evacuation of Jewish settlements in the Gaza strip.

In the summer of 2008, I led a select businessmen's group from Bethel Baptist Church to visit Jordan and Israel. We had an exciting time in Amman, Petra, Jerusalem, Tel Aviv and Nazareth. Many contacts were made with local pastors and leaders, which are still bearing fruit. The improvement in the infrastructure in the Arab sector of the country was notable.

Rose Mary and I returned to Nazareth for the 100th Anniversary of Baptist work in May 12, 2011. We were amazed to stay in the new hotel in Nazareth perched on the Mount of Precipitation over the Valley of Israel. Many of the attendees were adults who used to be young people in Rose Mary's hand bell choir or my ministry in the Galilee Villages and are now pastors and leaders in the Associational work. They were surprised when I gave a brief report on the history of theological education in Arabic. Barnabas attended with a few Muslim friends despite struggles at home. The Association of Baptist Churches gave us a plaque "with gratitude and appreciation for years of faithful and earnest service of the Gospel and in Baptist and Evangelical ministries in Israel." *"God is not unjust. He will not forget your work and the love you have shown Him as you have helped His people and continue to help them."* (Hebrews 6:10) The trip was fulfilling and the capstone of our Galilee Wanderings.

100th Anniversary Celebration Plaque Presentation
Ibrahim Siman, Rose Mary, Ray and Scott Bridger

The words that inspired and challenged my Galilee Wanderings:

"And Jesus went about all the cities and villages, teaching in their synagogues, preaching the gospel of the kingdom, and healing every sickness and every disease among the people.

But when he saw the multitudes, He was moved with compassion for them, because they were weary and scattered, like sheep having no shepherd.

Then He said to His disciples, "The harvest truly is plentiful, but the laborers are few.

Therefore, pray the Lord of the harvest that He will send out laborers into His harvest."

And when He had called His twelve disciples to Him, He gave them power over unclean spirits, to cast them out, and to heal all kinds of sickness and all kinds of disease.

(Matthew 9:35-10:1, The New King James Version)

The Registers in California, 2004
James, Chuck, Ray, Cheryl, Rose Mary

Epilogue
Back to Jerusalem Movement

A friend who works in China came across a copy of **Back to Jerusalem,** Church Planting Movements in the Holy Land and suggested it be translated into Mandarin to encourage the Chinese "Back to Jerusalem" Movement. We are praying for the timing and funding to have **Back to Jerusalem, Dialogue and Interfaith Witness with Muslims,** and **Discipling Middle Eastern Believers** translated and for us to travel to China to train young people and others who are trying to reach out to the approximately 20 million Muslims of China. If you are interested in sharing in this project, please contact us at:

lAM Partners
PO Box 463045,
Escondido, CA 92046-3045
lampartners@cs.com

Bibliography

Abdo, Daud, *A Course in Modern Standard Arabic*, Part I & II, Khayats, 1964.

Accad, Fouad Elias, *Building Bridges*, Navpress, 1997.

Allen, Roland, *Missionary Method: St. Paul or Ours?* Eerdmans, 1927, 1960

The Spontaneous Expansion of the Church, Eerdmans, 1962

Archbold, Norma Parrish, *The Mountains of Israel, The Bible and the West Bank,* 1993

Benhayim, Menachem and Haya, *Bound for the Promised Land,* 2003

Braswell, George, *To Ride a Magic Carpet,* 1977

Bratcher, Bob, *Good News for Modern Man, The New Testament in Today's English Version,* 1966

Bridger, J. Scott, *Christian Exegesis of the Quran*, Pickwick Publications, 2015

Chambers, Oswald, *My Utmost for His Highest*, Oswald Chambers Publications, 1935

Dean, Nadia, *A Demand of Blood, The Cherokee War of 1776*

Dehquani-Tafti, *The Design of My World*, London, 1959

Dorr, Roberta Kells, *David and Bathsheba.* Guideposts, 1980

Fickett, Harold, *The Ralph D. Winter Story*, How One Man Dared to Shake Up World Missions, The Roberta Winter Institute, William Carey Library, 2013

Freyha, Anis, *A Dictionary of Modern Lebanese Proverbs*, Librairie Du Liban, Beirut, 1974

Fuller, Frances, *In Borrowed Houses,* (inborrowedhouseslebanon.com)

Geyer, Sharon, **Daughter of Jerusalem**, An American Woman's Journey of Faith, Faith Walk 2003

Johnson, Johnni, *The Gift of Belonging*, 1975

Harrison, Bill, *A Pedouin Life*, Pedouin.org, 2011

Hoffman, Lisa, *Figtrees and Durbekky's*, unpublished manuscript

Kuunas, Unto, *Kaarlo Syvanto-Pioneer*, Forty years in Israel, c 1990 (translated from Finnish)

Linsey, Robert Lisle, *The Hebrew Translation of the Gospel of Mark*, Israel, 1969

MacDowell, Duncan Black, *Development of Muslim Theology, Jurisprudence and Constitutional Theory*, 1903, 2011

Mahmoody, Betty, *Not Without My Daughter*, St. Martin's Press, 1987

McDonnall, Carrie, *Facing Terror*, Integrity, 2005

McGavran, Donald, *Understanding Church Growth*, Eerdmans, 1970

Michener, James A., *The Source*, Random House Inc., 1965

Pressler, Paul, *A Hill On Which to Die, One Southern Baptist's Journey*, 1999

Muslim World Quarterly, *The Muslim World*, The Duncan Black Macdonald Center at Hartford Seminary, Hartford, CT 06105-2260, USA

Norwich, John Julius, **Byzantium**, The Early Centuries, 1989

Register, Ray, *Dialogue and Interfaith Witness with Muslims*, Moody Books, 1979, Global Ed Advance, 2007

> *(Arabic translation)* **muhadatha beyn al-asdiqa'** (Conversations Between Friends). Beirut, 1984

> **Muslimsing-ga Loinana Nung-gee Thajaba Sakhida Changminnaba Amasung Khanna-Neinaba**, Imphal, Manipur, India, 2007

> *Clothed in White*, The Story of Mavis Pate, ORN" in 1991

> *Back to Jerusalem*, Church Planting Movements in the Holy Land, WinePress, 2000, Global Educational Advance 2015. (Published in Korean by Goodseed Publishing, 2006.)

> *Discipling Middle Eastern Believers*, Global Ed Advance Press, 2009

Rigpen, Nik, *The Insanity of God: a True Story of Faith Resurrected*. B&H Books, 2013

Simson, Wolfgang, *Houses That Change the World*, 2001

Smith, James and Elizabeth, *In Their Midst*, Fields Publishing, 2015

Vander Werff, Lyle, *Christian Mission to Muslims*, William Carey Library, 1977

Wikipedia William Whiting Borden, "**Borden of Yale**," http://en.wikipedia. org/wiki/**Anwar_Sadat**

Rahbar, Daud, *God of Justice*, Brill, 1960

Willis, Avery, *Masterlife*: Discipleship Training for Leaders. 1982

Abbreviations

"AA"   A West Bank Muslim

A-4   Temporary residence visa, given to church workers by the Israeli Interior Minister

ABC   Association of Baptist Churches

AJC   American Jewish Committee

AK-47 Russian Kalashnikov assault rifle

ATS   Academy of Theological Studies

AZ   Arizona

B   Barnabas

BBC   British Broadcasting Corporation

BCI   Baptist Convention in Israel

BCCI   Same as above

BSU   Baptist Student Union

BV   Baptist Village

CBF   Cooperative Baptist Fellowship

CEF   Child Evangelism Fellowship

CP   Church Planting

CPM   Church Planting Movement

CSI   Cooperative Services International

CSTC   Christian Service Training Center

DAWN   Discipling a Whole Nation

DMin   Doctor of Ministry

e3   e3 Partners , equip, evangelize, establish churches.
          Formerly Global Missions Fellowship (GMF)

EMMS Edinburgh Medical Missionary Society

ESL   English as a second language

FMB   Foreign Mission Board

FMF   Familial Mediterranean Fever

GCC   Great Commission Christians

GMF   Global Missions Fellowship (now e3)

IAM   Israeli Arab Muslims

IBM   International Business Machines

IIBS   International Institute of Biblical Studies

IMB   International Mission Board

ISC   International Service Corp

JNF   Jewish National Fund

KPH   Kilometers per hour

Resumé

International Mission Board

Box 6767, Richmond, Virginia 23230

(Revised April 2015)

DR. RAY G. REGISTER JR.

Southern Baptist Representative to

Northern Africa and Middle East

(Appointed May 1964, Retired June 2003)

Born: April 26, 1935, in Columbia, S.C., and considers Charlotte, N.C., his hometown.

Education: Received the Bachelor of Science degree in Commerce from University of Virginia, Charlottesville, VA; the Master of Divinity degree and the Doctor of Ministry degree from Southeastern Baptist Theological Seminary, Wake Forest, N.C.; and the Master of Arts degree in History of Religion—Islamics from Hartford (Conn.) Seminary Foundation. Studied the Arabic language at the Hebrew University in Jerusalem, Israel, on a scholarship. Earned Fraternal Insurance Counselor Fellow (FICF) designation by Kaplan Financial Education in 2009.

Married: Rose Mary Rich (RN) of Peru, Ind.

Children: Three grown children, five grandchildren and three great grandchildren.

Prior experience: Pastor of Whitakers (N.C.) Baptist Church for four years prior to his appointment. U.S. Navy officer 1957-59 with travel to South America, Europe and the Caribbean.

Published (BOOKS):

Dialogue and Interfaith Witness with Muslims, 1979, by Global Educational Advance, 2007 (9th edition)

Clothed in White, The Story of Mavis Pate, ORN, published by Broadman, 1991.

Back to Jerusalem, Church Planting Movements in the Holy Land, published by WinePress, 2000.

Discipling Middle Eastern Believers, published by Global Educational Advance, 2009.

Honors: Eagle Scout. Served as chairman of the United Christian Council in Israel, 1983-87. The council is a fellowship of 20 evangelical Protestant groups working in Israel.

Previous assignment: Worker on a project jointly sponsored by the Home and Foreign Mission Boards of dialogue and inter-faith witness with Muslims in the United States while on furlough in 1975-76. Field evangelist stationed in Nazareth, Israel, since 1966. He directed the building of Rama Baptist Church and directed the printing of an Arabic manual for missionaries. Promoted an Arabic language Bible correspondence course and assisted with its organization. Opened a kindergarten in Rama. Taught English for technical institute in Nazareth in 1978. Served as vice chairman of local committee of Children's Evangelical Fellowship in Nazareth. Served on theological commission of the United Christian Council in Israel and as clerk of the Association of Baptist Churches in Israel. Directed building of evangelistic center and organization of kindergarten in Yaffa of Nazareth. Served as chairman of board of Baptist Bookstore in East Jerusalem. Participated in outreach project into northern Galilee Arab villages, 1992-96. Director, International Institute of Biblical Studies-Israel Branch, 1994. Acting President of Academy of Theological Studies in Jerusalem. Served as strategy leader for ministry team to Middle Eastern people from 1997-2003. Taught Arabic and Middle East studies as visiting professor at Southeastern Baptist Theological Seminary, 1996, 2000. Served as interim Director of the Southern California Campus of Golden Gate Baptist Theological Seminary, Spring 2004. Adjunct professor at Southern California Campus of Golden Gate Baptist Theological Seminary 2004-5.

Current assignment: Emeritus Representative of Northern Africa and Middle East. Director of IAM Partners, Inc., a nonprofit educational charity. Field Representative and Fraternal Insurance Counselor for Omaha Woodmen/Woodmen of the World Life

Insurance Society, 2006-2012. Customer Service Representative for TBI Financial Services in Escondido, CA, 2011. Pre-Planning Advisor for Dignity Memorial, 2011 to 2014. Director for Legal Shield, 2006 to present. Trustee, Bethel Baptist Church, Escondido, CA. Senior Pastor, Arabic Church of Escondido, CA.

Portrait 2015

CPSIA information can be obtained
at www.ICGtesting.com
Printed in the USA
FSOW04n0455261116
27727FS